RIFLE

VICTOR GREGG was born in London in 1919 and joined the army in 1937, serving first with the Rifle Brigade in India and Palestine, before service in the Western Desert. Later, with the Parachute Regiment, he saw action in Italy and at the Battle of Arnhem, where he was taken prisoner. He was released from the Army in 1946. He now lives a peaceful life with his wife in a housing complex owned by his old regiment, the Rifle Brigade, in Winchester. 'They're all lads who have put their heads above the parapet,' he says. 'I trust them, they are Riflemen.'

RICK STROUD is a film and television director. He has received Emmy and BAFTA nominations and teaches at the National Film and Television School. As a writer he is the author of *The Book of the Moon*. He lives with his wife in London.

XB00 000012 5627

RIFLEMAN

*A Front-Line Life from Alamein and Dresden
to the Fall of the Berlin Wall*

Victor Gregg
with
Rick Stroud

BLOOMSBURY

LONDON · BERLIN · NEW YORK · SYDNEY

First published in Great Britain 2011

This paperback edition published 2011

Copyright © Victor Gregg 2011

The right of Victor Gregg to be identified as the author of this work has been
asserted by him in accordance with the Copyright, Designs and Patents Act, 1988

Photographs reproduced in this book are from the author's
own collection except where credited otherwise

No part of this book may be used or reproduced in any manner
whatsoever without written permission from the Publisher except in the
case of brief quotations embodied in critical articles or reviews

Every reasonable effort has been made to trace copyright holders of
material reproduced in this book, but if any have been inadvertently
overlooked the publishers would be glad to hear from them

Bloomsbury Publishing Plc
49–51 Bedford Square
London WC1B 3DP

www.bloomsbury.com

Bloomsbury Publishing, London, Berlin, New York and Sydney

A CIP catalogue record for this book is available from the British Library

ISBN 978 1 4088 2208 1

10 9 8 7 6 5 4 3 2 1

Set in Linotype Garamond Three by Hewer Text UK Ltd, Edinburgh
Printed in Great Britain by Clays Ltd, St Ives plc

MIX
Paper from
responsible sources
FSC
www.fsc.org   FSC® C018072

For my comrades who were left behind.

WOLVERHAMPTON PUBLIC LIBRARIES	
XB000000125627	
Bertrams	27/10/2011
920GRE	£7.99
SV	01382024

CONTENTS

PART THREE

FOREWORD

I met Victor Gregg in December 2009, just after his ninetieth birthday. I was researching the war in the Western Desert and was keen to meet anyone who had been there. We were introduced by Tom Bird who had been his company commander at Alamein. At the end of our first meeting Vic gave me a memoir he had written for his grandchildren. In it he describes the first seventy years of his life. Inevitably, after such a long period, his memory for precise dates is not always 100 per cent accurate, but his recall of events is vivid, honest and gripping.

He tells how he left school at fourteen and spent his teenage years knocking around Soho. Then he joined the Rifle Brigade, signing on for twenty-one years. Nineteen forty found him in the Western Desert seconded to the Long Range Desert Group (LRDG). At Alamein he fought in the Snipe action where the medals won in the action included a VC awarded to the Colonel, Vic Turner. In September 1944 he parachuted into Arnhem, where he was captured. He was sent to a labour camp outside Dresden and managed to sabotage a soap factory. For this he was condemned to death. The night before his execution the Allies bombed the city. Vic's prison received a direct hit and the blast blew him to freedom. He survived the firestorm and spent a week working with the rescue forces. Then he escaped to the east and the Russian army. The bombing of Dresden was a major event in Vic's life; it took him thirty years and a painful divorce to come to terms with it.

After the war, Vic's life continued to be colourful and parts of it read like a cross between *The Italian Job* and *The Spy Who Came in from the Cold*. He became a communist and driver to the chairman of the Moscow Narodny Bank. The Russian embassy sent him on mysterious errands and he was recruited by shadowy men from the British security services. His passion for motorbikes led him to travel extensively to bike rallies behind the Iron Curtain, where he became involved in dissident politics. By one of life's more far-fetched coincidences he was reunited with Major Albert Jünger, the German officer who had sent him off as a POW from Arnhem. Through Jünger, Vic became involved with Wehrmacht veterans in East Germany and served as a link between them and the Hungarian People's Democratic Forum. In August 1989 the seventy-year-old Vic was invited by the Democratic Forum to be one of the guests of honour at a rally in Sopron, near the border with Austria. Vic was asked to be one of a small party that was to make the first cut in the wire that divided East from West, and a few weeks later the Berlin Wall itself was breached. Vic had played a small part in its downfall.

Vic is still a player and old habits die hard. When I first met him he said he would pick me up from Winchester station. I arrived and waited: no sign of Vic. Eventually I realised that some-one was watching me from a car parked about a hundred yards away. It was Vic checking me out, making sure I wasn't trouble before making contact. He drove me to a pub where we talked about the war in the desert. Vic was still checking me out. I must have passed the test because he invited me to his home to meet his wife, Betty. It was after this that he gave me his manuscript. I didn't realise it at the time but he was giving me the thumbs-up and we were off on what was to be another of his adventures.

More than seventy years separate Rifleman Vic Gregg from the British soldiers who are fighting today in Afghanistan, but the lessons are the same. The fight does not end when a man walks off the battlefield – the consequences of war reverberate right through a soldier's life. Vic has always been on the emotional as well as the physical front line.

Rifleman was not written lightly or easily. Mixed with the excitement and the action are some very painful memories. Vic does not flinch from criticising some of the people he has met along the way but there is no one he is more critical of than himself. The better I have got to know him the more I have come to respect and admire him and hope I can now count him as a friend.

Vic's Certificate of Service, issued in 1946, when he left the army, contains a paragraph which was meant to sum up his military record, but in a way it sums up his whole life:

> *During an exceedingly colourful career, this rifleman has served long and continuous periods in active operations with front line units.*
>
> *He is an individual of great courage, capable of applying himself best to a task when the need is greatest.*

This statement accurately describes the ninety-year-old Vic I met on that cold December day in 2009. If I have been of any use to him in getting his book ready for press, the pleasure has been all mine.

Rick Stroud
London, November 2010

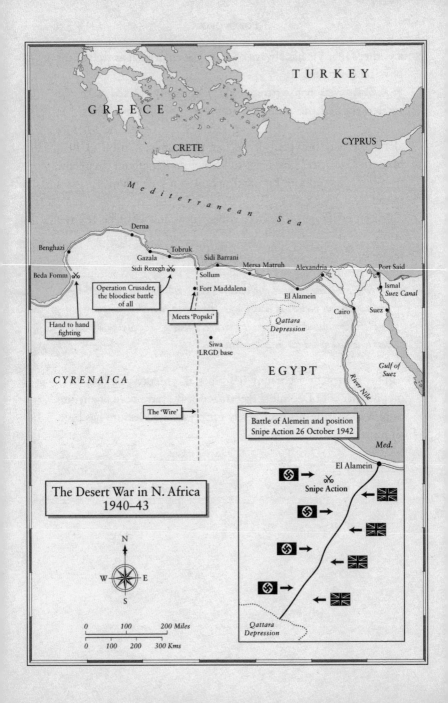

TURKEY

GREECE

CRETE

CYPRUS

Mediterranean Sea

Derna

Tobruk

Benghazi

Gazala   Sidi Barrani

Sidi Rezegh ✂ Mersa Matruh   Alexandria   Port Said

Beda Fomm ✂ Sollum

Ismal
Suez Canal

Operation Crusader,
the bloodiest battle
of all

Fort Maddalena

El Alamein

Cairo   Suez

*Qattara
Depression*

Meets 'Popski'

Hand to hand
fighting

Siwa
LRGD base

Gulf of
Suez

CYRENAICA

EGYPT

River Nile

The 'Wire'

Battle of Alemein and position
Snipe Action 26 October 1942

Med.

El Alamein

卐 →

✂
Snipe Action

卐 →

卐 →

卐 →

*Qattara
Depression*

The Desert War in N. Africa
1940–43

N

W   E

S

0   100   200 Miles

0   100   200   300 Kms

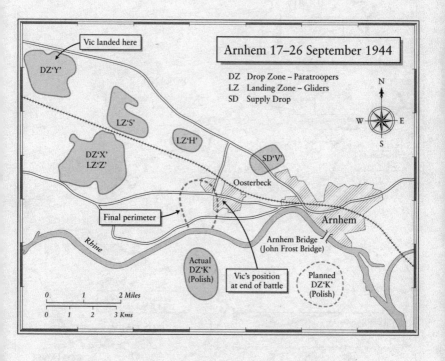

Arnhem 17–26 September 1944

Vic landed here

DZ'Y'

LZ'S'

LZ'H'

DZ'X'
LZ'Z'

SD'V'

Oosterbeck

Final perimeter

Rhine

Arnhem

Arnhem Bridge
(John Frost Bridge)

Actual
DZ'K'
(Polish)

Vic's position
at end of battle

Planned
DZ'K'
(Polish)

DZ   Drop Zone – Paratroopers
LZ   Landing Zone – Gliders
SD   Supply Drop

N
W   E
S

0   1   2 Miles

0   1   2   3 Kms

Trips behind the Iron Curtain
1972–89

━━ Iron Curtain

N
W — E
S

EAST
GERMANY
(DDR)

POLAND

First meeting
with Marcus

*Hartz
forest*

Main pick-up
area

Efurt •   ○ Leipzig
        Chemnitz   ○ Dresden
        (Karl Marx Stadt)
        ○
    • Hof

Nuremberg
○   Prague ◉

CZECH REPUBLIC

WEST
GERMANY   SLOVAKIA

                    Vienna ◉

            AUSTRIA   Sopron
                        ◉ Budapest

                    Where the wire was cut,
                    19 July 1989

SWITZERLAND   HUNGARY

                                        ROMANIA

            Adriatic Sea   YUGOSLAVIA

ITALY   Belgrade ◉

            0   50   100 Miles
            0   50   100   150 Kms

PART ONE

I

The Early Years

When I was born the Great War had been over for almost a year. Of my father I remember little; my brother, John, came along the following year, my sister, Ellen, six years later. That was when Father decided to exit our life for ever, never to be seen again. We heard that he had gone to Australia, but we never found out for sure.

We all lived on the second floor of a house in Compton Street, near King's Cross, London, a right hovel of a place. Like every other building in the neighbourhood, its lath and plaster walls were a breeding ground for vermin. Every weekend Mother would go through the ritual of delousing us. It was a futile task but she did her best using copious measures of carbolic with water and a fine-tooth comb. It would be many years before I appreciated what she had to endure to keep us fed and halfway clean and presentable.

At the age of five I was packed off to the local infants' school; at the age of seven we would be transferred to the junior boys' school. There we were taught simple arithmetic, reading, writing, and how to behave ourselves. The next step up would be the boys' school, where the discipline was harsh, especially considering how young we were. The slightest deviation from the straight and narrow was severely punished. A boy would be caned hard for the slightest misdemeanour. But neither the boys nor their parents thought it necessary to challenge the authority of the school. It was accepted: the boy had done wrong, and he had to take his medicine.

Yelling while the cane or strap was doing its worst was allowed. Crying wasn't. If you were silly enough to complain to your father, or in my case my mother, they would give you another whack for good measure. 'Spare the rod and spoil the child' was a maxim that was fully endorsed by every God-fearing parent of the day.

Outside school there was the discipline of the gangs. Every boy belonged to a gang, usually related to the street where he lived. Streets were sacrosanct to the people who lived in them. If three or more strange boys entered a street they were treated with suspicion and usually challenged. Singly or in pairs you were no threat; mob-handed meant only one thing, and then out came the knuckle-dusters, the coshes, and any other weapon which might come to hand. If by chance the injuries to the interlopers were considered to be excessive war would be declared. The fighting would go on until such time that a peace conference would be arranged, or until the police intervened in the proceedings. These wars happened all the time and were a sort of apprenticeship for life.

Mother's wages for her weekly work weren't enough to feed us properly, so at the weekends my brother and I would be turfed out of the house and sent off to Covent Garden or Smithfield or even the fish market at Billingsgate to see what we could scrounge. With a couple of jam sandwiches and twopence to buy a bottle of 'R White's Lemonade' (there was a ha'penny deposit on the bottle), we would be sent on our way.

'Wotdya want us to bring back, Mum?'

'Go down to the Garden and bring back some pot herbs and don't forget to get some wood for the fire.'

Off we would scuttle, out of Compton Street, into Tavistock Place and through Marchmont Street, into Russell Square. Here we would consider trying to annoy the major-domo standing at the entrance of the Imperial Hotel. Then down Southampton Row to the junction with Kingsway.

This was an area which we considered to be very posh. One of our favourite ploys was to stand outside a pastry shop trying our best to look like the Bisto Kids – hungry, forlorn and unwanted. Then we would summon up the courage to go inside and ask: 'Got any stale cakes, missus?' If we were lucky a bag of broken cakes would be thrust at us. It was not often that we tasted the luxury of cream cakes, even if they were stale. We might have looked like waifs but we weren't; we were just two kids trying to make the best of the life we were part of.

So on we would travel, through the backstreets to Drury Lane and then into Covent Garden Market itself. The first objective would be to get some string or rope and a couple of wooden boxes. This was easy: the whole area would be littered with the debris of the early morning trading. Then we would start scrounging.

From the pavements of the Garden we could easily pick up enough potatoes and greens to fill a sack. At Smithfield we would scrounge the bits of meat that were normally left for the sweepers. Having crammed everything into the fruit boxes, we would then have to drag our loot back home. The string would constantly break under the strain, either that or the boxes would collapse leaving a trail of vegetables in our wake. The other problem was the danger that a larger force of boys would descend and demand their share of the booty. If you were outnumbered all you could do was be philosophical and give in to the inevitable, hand over the goods and start all over again.

Getting to Billingsgate meant a trip through the very hostile territory of Hackney, or, worse still, Shoreditch. To get home we would make a detour along Fleet Street, through High Holborn, and down into Gray's Inn Road. A longer but much safer route.

When we finally made it back, Mother would give her opinion as to the worth of the spoils. She would always give some to the old lady who lived above us and that night we would go to bed with a good vegetable stew in our bellies.

2

The Concrete Playground

In our neighbourhood, most families lived in two rooms. One room would have a gas cooker and a bed, the other would also serve as a bedroom for the rest of the family, and would often be divided by a curtain. Not surprisingly, Mother would chuck us out on to the street as often as possible and it was there that we found our amusements.

There were three gangs in the area. By far the most dreaded of these was the Harrison Street Gang. They could muster a force of about twenty. Then there was the Sidmouth Street Gang, no less vicious, mustering about fourteen. Finally, the lot my brother and I mixed with, the Wakefield Street Gang, with a full force of about nine. You had to gain the respect of the other gangs; giving in to force was never a good idea. Any adventure by our gang into foreign streets meant considering the strength of the opposition. Luckily we had plenty of places to go where there were no other gangs.

For a start there were the three main line railway stations, Euston, St Pancras and King's Cross. We loved to watch the steam engines, huge monsters belching smoke, as they pulled into the station. The noise and bustle was very exciting. If we were lucky, we would get to carry a passenger's luggage to the nearest hotel. This didn't happen very often. Any attempt to do the porters out of earning a bob or two would get us a cuff round the ear, and we would be chased out of the station.

Behind King's Cross and St Pancras was the 'coal base', the area where mountains of coal were stored to supply the never-ending hunger of the engines. This was one of our major sources of free fuel. A raid down the coal base would involve a certain amount of advance planning. A couple of boys would be sent down to determine the strength of the railway police, then, as soon as night fell, we would bunk over the wall and throw huge lumps of coal to our waiting mates. If you were caught it meant an appearance in the local police court charged with theft. This led to real trouble as your parents would have to pay up. The winter had to be really cold for us boys to do the coal base.

To the rear of the stations were the stables. This was another area where we could earn a little cash. 'Clean yer 'orse darn, mister?' For sixpence we would have to wash and brush the horse (or horses) and clean out the stables.

The greatest fun of all would come from a foray 'up the other end' into the West End. There we would spend our time doing our best to annoy the toffs, or, failing that, the doormen who worked outside the big hotels. These doormen would reign in great splendour dressed in black coat and tails, shiny top hat and campaign medals polished until they dazzled the eyes. Their job was to control the endless comings and goings of guests and luggage, call cabs and, of course, pocket the tips that the guests seemed obliged to hand over.

We would go up to one and out would come the phrase: 'Gisusasprazeemister.'

Back would come the reply: 'Bugger off, yer little turds, or I'll get the rozzers.'

This would constitute an outright declaration of war, which would last five minutes at the most. In the end he would dip into his pocket and out would come a coin, but he knew full well it had to be silver. Copper would be an invitation to more abuse. This type of operation would be, at the most, a once-a-week job. The law at Savile Row had a very nasty reputation.

Another source of entertainment would be bunking in at the London Zoo in Regent's Park. The keepers could tell at a glance that none of us had resources to fund the sixpence entry fee, and would chase us all around the zoo.

Regent's Park had quite a large lake where brother John and I would go to fish. Mother would make nets out of some old stockings fixed with a piece of wire to a couple of canes. Then off we would set to spend the day fishing for tiddlers, complete with jam jars, the obligatory sandwich and a penny each to spend. Mother's usual parting shot would be: 'And don't come back here soaking wet.'

The day would end when it was impossible to cram another tiddler into the jam jars. When we got back home to proudly display our catch the poor fish would most likely all be dead.

Another favourite activity was to walk to the Tower of London. At low tide it was possible to swim in the Thames. On one occasion, as we were larking about on the steps of Cleopatra's Needle, my brother John slipped into the river and I had to pull him in from a watery grave. We both got a walloping for coming home soaked.

There were three cinemas in the area: the Euston Cinema near the corner of Judd Street and the Euston Road, the Tolma up the other end of the Euston Road in Tolma Square, and the Cobo, so named because it was in Copenhagen Street up the Caledonian Road (the Caley). All three of them were out and out fleapits. On Saturday mornings, for threepence (or twopence in the case of the Cobo), we'd witness the exploits of Tom Mix, Bronco Bill and other favourites. These were all silent films but there was nothing silent about the audience: loud boos if the baddies seemed to be getting the upper hand, the boos soon turning to cheers as the villains got their comeuppance.

Then there was the Tonbridge Club on the corner of Cromer Street and Judd Street, named after the sponsors, the public school based in Tonbridge, Kent. The school was part of a growing movement in the better parts of British society which saw the need to alleviate the poverty and deprivation that blighted the lives of the so called 'working classes'. Tonbridge School raised considerable sums of money to erect and run a club where we could learn the finer aspects of traditional British sport.

The senior boys of the school would come to London to teach us the rules of cricket and football. The sports master would occasionally put in an appearance, too. Boxing was his speciality, and we had a proper ring, with proper boxing gloves. We also had our own ideas as to what was fair and what wasn't. The well-meaning master would attempt to teach us the rudiments of the Queensberry Rules. The contestants usually came from different gangs and no quarter was given. Seventy years later the Tonbridge Club is still there, or at least the building is.

Other amusements would be to go to the Round Pond in Kensington Gardens to watch the posh people sailing their model boats. Sometimes Mother would be able to give us sixpence each to get a return ticket to Edgware on the Underground from Russell Square. Edgware was out in the country in those days and it would be very exciting for us. If by chance we lost our return tickets (as we often did), a pair of doleful eyes would get us past the ticket collector. Even looking into the shop windows of the West End transported us into another world, a world, funnily enough, against which we held no grudge. We were poor, they were rich: that was the way it was to our young minds.

We also played cricket and football in the streets. The goalposts were bits of clothing with the ball made up of rolled-up newspaper and tied together with string, and that would be it. Sometimes a game would be arranged with the kids in an adjoining street. Getting the ball past the opposing goalposts by any means possible was the name of the game. Kicking, punching, shoving and push-ing were all allowed. One thing that was completely out of order was kicking anybody when they were down on the ground. This would be considered a foul, and at this point the game would end and a 'bundle' would start. A 'bundle' was our word for a fight. It would go on until one side gave up or the police came, in which case a general truce would be called and both sides would 'scarper'.

Cricket was riskier than football. A wicket would be chalked up on a lamp post or wall. A bat would be made out of a piece of wood and the ball would be solid rubber. Sooner or later (generally sooner) the ball ended up through somebody's window and that would be that.

At the age of eleven I was despatched to the senior school in

Cromer Street. This was a very good school run by a highly intel-
ligent and dedicated headmaster, Mr Thornton, who wanted us to
have more than the basic education that was the norm for deprived
areas of London. As well as the usual curriculum we were taught
the rudiments of music, poetry and painting, the latter mostly
watercolour because oils were too expensive.

3

Out of the Rough

My grandparents were like characters out of *The Pickwick Papers*. Grandfather was of a short, rotund stature, with red cheeks and a huge curly moustache, and a black Homburg hat, all topped off by his Gladstone bag and a larger than life gold watch chain strung across his chest. Off he would set every morning with his rolling gait on the walk to Hatton Garden where he worked. The world will not see his like again.

Grandmother was the opposite, tall and angular, her black hair swept up into a tight bun, eyes that looked right through you. I remember her wearing a long black dress which encased her from her high, ruffled neckline to her ankles. She wore a chain around her waist from which dangled various keys, none of which seemed to be used, apart from the front door key.

This doughty pair resided in the lower part of the house in Kenton Street. The kitchen was in the basement where nearly all the waking hours were spent. Behind the kitchen was the scullery, complete with a huge open boiler in which the weekly wash was done (and the Christmas puddings were cooked). The bedroom was on the ground floor at the back, while the front room, or parlour, was reserved for special occasions like Christmas and birthdays. The centrepiece of the parlour was a large aspidistra that my gran would religiously polish once a week. In the summer months she would take her place at the window and look out on the street, commenting on the qualities, good and bad, of the neighbours.

My grandparents referred to my vanished father as 'that scan-
dalous plumber from Kentish Town. You never could trust them
as comes from that neighbourhood.' They were very concerned
about the squalor their daughter was living in and were worried
that my mother was having to work too hard to support us. They
finally decided that Mother was in an impossible situation and so
we were removed from the sordid surroundings of our early years
and went to live in the rooms on the first floor of their house.

Their house was much cleaner than the dump at Compton
Street, though we still lived in two rooms: a kitchen with one bed,
and the front room, and that was it. The toilet was on the landing,
shared with the people upstairs. The rent was ten shillings a week.

My grandparents were solidly Victorian in their outlook. There
was never any messing about. At the meal table you were served
according to your station in the household, small boys being last,
and not only that, seen and not heard: 'Don't talk with your mouth
full!', 'Eat what's given you!', 'Ask permission if you wish to leave
the table!', and to be certain that discipline was maintained there
was a convenient shelf under the edge of the table where rested
The Cane! My grandmother was an expert at wielding this formidable instrument. Grandfather just sat and ate, occasionally giving
advice as to where the next stroke should fall.

As soon as we were installed in our new home Grandmother
announced that, come Saturday, we were going to the 'Crusade of
Rescue'. This emporium had its premises in Tavistock Place, just
at the end of Kenton Street. The 'Crusade' was the Oxfam of the
day; a shop with a huge open front, filled to bursting with second-
hand clothing, all donated by charitable organisations.

Mother and Grandmother took us there to buy new clothes, or
new to us at least. John and I stood like a couple of clowns while
Mother and Grandmother debated the suitability of various
garments. After the suits they bought boots, and once these were
selected they were taken up to the mender to have as many studs
put in the soles and heels as possible. By the time we came to

wearing the boots, the soles and heels were almost solid steel, 'and don't let me catch you sliding about on them'.

The move to Kenton Street brought us into contact with all the aunts and uncles (those who had managed to escape the Grim Reaper during the Great War) from Mother's side of the family, the Hamblins. Uncle Will lived quite near, just off Gray's Inn Road, Uncle Tom lived out in the wilds of Epsom, while Uncle Sam came from Kentish Town. Another uncle, Bob by name, lived in the council flats in Rosebery Avenue. Once a month these relatives would visit to 'pay the Club', the club in question being the Sir John Peel Working Men's Mutual Society, of which Grandfather was one of the trustees. He would take me along to the monthly meetings up in Marylebone Lane. After handing over the dues he had collected he would then, with much puffing and blowing, assume his place at the committee table along with the rest of the hierarchy. The walk home would often be in the company of one or two of the dignitaries of the club. A halt would be made at some drinking establishment. I, of course, would be ordered to remain outside, 'small boys not allowed in here'.

If the refreshments had flowed too freely I made myself scarce until the ensuing battle between my gran and her somewhat tipsy husband died down. I never knew my grandfather to get really drunk and, in any case, my gran wasn't going to give him the chance.

Being a slightly better-off area, the streets would be targeted by all the various costermongers of the day, especially on a Sunday afternoon. The Muffin Man, walking along in the centre of the road, ringing his huge brass bell, the Shellfish Man, also known as the Winkle Man, trundling his barrow, announcing his presence with a large motor horn. Not forgetting the Cats'-Meat Man, the Fruit and Veg Man, and last but not least, Tony the Ice-Cream Man. There used to be a song the kids would sing, and it went something like this:

I come all the way from Italia,
And I find my way down Saffron Hill, how do you feel?
In winter I sell chesanuts a hotta,
In summer I sell iceadacream bigger da top, no taster,
Hurrah, hurrah, hurrah for the Italian Man.

I almost forgot the organ grinders, mostly ex-servicemen with one or more limbs missing, reduced to begging as their only means of support.

Bloomsbury, as the area we were now living in was called, was almost a village in those days, but people were not born there, they moved in. A person would proudly say that he came from Bermondsey, or Poplar, but you never heard anyone say they 'came from' Bloomsbury. They might well live there or otherwise 'I am at present in rooms in Bloomsbury'.

The area was bounded by Russell and Gordon Squares, Gower Street, Museum Street and, of course, Bloomsbury Square itself. All sorts lived there. The arty-crafties, the weirdy-beardies, the folksy-wolksies and every political creed under the sun. The Reds as we called them would parade around with their red ties, the Anarchists wearing something green, all earnestly discussing ways and means of putting the world to rights. This and the area on the other side of the Tottenham Court Road, known as Fitzrovia, was where I learnt the art of growing up.

I also learnt about the seamier side of life. The area was a happy hunting ground for the street girls and their pimps, and the gangs from Soho who controlled them.

For the princely sum of sixpence a week it was our job to keep them informed of the imminent approach of the rozzers. We would give the signal and they would dash off to the nearest café or fish and chip shop. Business would be suspended until we signalled that the coast was clear. If the girls lasted a month without going before the local beak then likely as not we would be rewarded with a bonus of a shilling from the ponce who looked after their welfare. Not that there was much welfare in evidence, more likely a beating up if they failed to meet a given target. But all in all they were a carefree and happy enough group who took the rough life they led with a shrug, knowing full well that their position lasted as long as their looks held out. When they started to lose them it was downhill all the way, starting outside the railway stations of Paddington and King's Cross.

Another landmark was the swimming pool in Endell Street on the south side of New Oxford Street. One of the pleasures in our lives as kids was that swimming pool; for just twopence you could spend the whole of Saturday morning in the baths. It was in Endell Street that I first became aware that there were men who gained much pleasure from association with small boys and good-looking youths. Week after week the same men used to be in attendance at the baths. Quick-witted as we were, it didn't take long to suss these individuals out for what they were really after. I remember there used to be a clique of about four of them, always handing out bags of sweets which, naturally, we accepted – 'Fanks, mister' (London kids never sounded the 'th'). It was through these gentlemen, as we grew older and into our teens, that we were able to get night-time employment as washers-up in the clubs and cafés of Soho.

The work would start any time after seven in the evening and there we would be, washing the crockery and cleaning the glasses until ten at night. For this we would be paid the exorbitant sum of ten shillings a night, as much as we would earn for a week's work when it came time to leave school.

Soho then was not much different from today, except for the fact that in those years everything wasn't quite so blatant. The whole area was alive with queenies, prostitutes, pimps, pickpockets and pansies, along with the other ragbag elements of society. It was a melting pot of every evil that my mother and grandparents strove in vain to keep my brother and myself away from, but if there was money to be earned then we would offer our talents to earn it.

What saved us from turning to a life of crime was the fact that there was always a surplus of volunteers and so it never became a regular part of our life, and there were other ways one could earn a coin or two.

When I was about twelve years old, Grandfather dragged John and me round to the church in Woburn Square. He had heard that they were short of choirboys. 'Put the two of you on the straight and narrow,' he said.

Unfortunately I had acquired a certain reputation in the area: 'bit of a scruff that one'. The vicar was not at all keen; he said he could take one of us, but what he really needed was a boy who could sight-read a music score. He must have thought that the extra qualification needed would see me off. He shoved a score under my nose, and without hesitation I gave a true rendering. This must have shaken him to his foundations. Though I wasn't keen on being a sissy choirboy, whatever my mother and grand-parents thought it would do for me. But to please Mother I stuck with it for nearly nine months.

My voice was hopeless, but I used to help the organist out with the score arrangements for the different church activities. When I told him I was leaving he promised me the earth if I would stay on: 'Be a good lad and think of your future.' He even made contact with the headmaster at Cromer Street School, who also gave me a lecture. I suppose that they were both trying their best to help me, after all it was obvious that I did have some talent. I enjoyed being involved with the choir, and I liked music. We had a school band, which used to play every morning at prayers, and it was there I learnt the violin. In my last year I passed a scholarship to be considered for entry into the London School of Music. We were far too poor for me to take up this chance. At fourteen all us boys had to go out into the world to earn money. I will never know whether I missed my vocation there or not.

4

Growing up in Bloomsbury

My years at Cromer Street School ended at the age of fourteen, when I presented myself to the local Labour Exchange in Penton Street. The next week I was working for an optical firm just off Rosebery Avenue. The work was not in any way seen as the start of a career, just a means of making a wage in order to have money in your pocket. I earned a princely ten shillings a week, about the norm for a youngster at the time, half of which I gave to my mum. The other five shillings was all mine to spend on clothes (mostly second-hand), and anything else that took my fancy. I would be broke by Monday at the latest.

I was given the job of operating a machine milling out plastic frames. The milling machine had a cutting wheel which whizzed around at thousands of revs per minute, just a bare cutter protruding from a hole in the bench with no protection of any kind. Consequently a lot of fingers were cut off. The Royal Free Hospital in Gray's Inn Road knew the firm quite well.

Work would start at eight o'clock with a break at 10.30 for ten minutes. Then would follow half an hour for dinner when we ate whatever our mums had provided in the way of sandwiches and the firm provided the tea. Then it was the final slog until the whistle blew at 5.30. When a mishap occurred, such as a finger being cut off, the cry would go out, 'BLOOD UP'. While the unfortunate was whisked away to the Royal Free, one of us boys would be detailed to wash the blood off the wall. This would be followed by liberal doses of distemper, painted over to hide the stain.

It was during a slack period that the boss of the firm asked me
to take a bucket and some polishing kit and go down to the local
garage to wash his car, a big American Buick. The garage was the
home of the Mount Pleasant Taxi Company, run by the son of old
man Levy who owned Levy's of King's Cross. It was the major taxi
firm of the day. I used to polish this Buick and then polish it
again. Unbeknown to the boss, I also learnt to drive it around the
garage, much to the amusement of the fitters and cleaners who
worked there.

One fine day old man Levy's son Tom came up and asked me,
could I find the time to wash down a couple of his cars? 'Not 'arf,'
says I, thinking about the extra money. Tom had a couple of small
MGs which he competed with at Brooklands and sometimes
Donnington. It was these cars that he wanted me to keep 'nice and
shiny', as he put it.

Tom Levy started taking me along to Brooklands and life got
more interesting. I met all the famous racing drivers of the day.
Men like Freddie Dixon, who used to drive for Riley, Tom Birkett
was another character, and last but not least, Earl Howe. Howe's
most famous car was a huge Napier-Railton. It was an unforget-
table sight to watch this giant of a car lapping the bumpy surface
of the Brooklands oval at speeds of over a hundred miles an hour.

I became a sort of errand boy and general dogsbody at these
meetings. 'Hey, Levy, where's that kid of yours?' and I would be
called over to give a hand and get smothered in oil and grease. I
loved it. I never seemed to get any money thrust into my hand but
I would be given rides around the track in some of the bigger cars
during practice. I would be told to pump the oil whenever the
pressure needle dropped. Safety precautions were non-existent, no
such things as safety belts and the like. I used to wear a pair of
greasy overalls, supplied by the boss, and one of the drivers gave
me a black beret. That was my uniform; it smelt of castor oil and
was covered in grease and dirt. It was all very exciting, a young
boy's dream.

Nearly all the drivers had some form of independent means. It wasn't unusual for the whole family of an aspiring driver to be sitting at tables in the pits, while a butler served dainty sandwiches. The champagne would flow, especially after a win.

I once witnessed a tragedy which gave me an insight into the way these elite people hid their emotions. It was at an Easter meeting at Brooklands, the opening meet of the year. A young scion was trying to overtake on the Byfleet banking. He came adrift and shot over the edge of the track. The result was flames, smoke and a very dead driver. A couple of labourers were despatched to bring the remains of the lad back to the pits. The family were still supping up the champagne! Very little sign of grief.

On the way home the crew were talking about the crash. Tom Levy said, 'That's what they're like, some of them have no apparent emotions, not like us.' Tom Levy was never really 'one of them'. First of all, he worked for a living, and more importantly I suspect, he was Jewish.

The traits that were to follow me all my life were now beginning to show. I got accustomed to the job and, having done that, lost interest, packed it up and went looking for fresh pastures and more money. I was earning fifteen shillings a week, not enough.

Girls came into my life at the tender age of sixteen when I became the focus of a girl who lived opposite the Tonbridge Club. We used to take long walks together during the evenings. Gladys, as her name was, had feelings stirring within her breast that I knew nothing about. She dropped me after a few months for a tall ginger-haired chap who promptly put her up the spout and then had to marry her. Neither of them were yet seventeen. That was a close shave if ever there was one.

My next step into the world of work was as a pastry cook's assistant, at a small bread shop in Tavistock Place, almost next door to home. The job lasted until one day I was talking to the under chef. I don't remember how it came up, but in the heat of the moment I called him a 'Scotch bastard'. He let fly at me with the big wooden shovel that was used to draw the cakes out of the oven. After he had cooled down he said that he was quite sorry it had happened. It taught me never to call anyone a bastard unless I was prepared to declare war. So that was it, another job down the drain.

From there I drifted into a cloth warehouse in New Oxford Street. I soon got browned off with that and took work as a delivery boy for a grocer in Marchmont Street. It was there I had my first brush with the law. I got done for dangerous driving while demonstrating to all and sundry how easy it was to drive a three-wheeled tricycle, not on three wheels but two. That cost me five bob at Clerkenwell Magistrates' Court.

An interesting thing about this was that more than twenty-five years later I applied for a job with London Transport as a bus driver and having passed the training had to go to the carriage office to get my PSV licence. One of the questions was about past convictions. Naturally I had long forgotten the five bob fine, but the police hadn't. My application was returned as inaccurate. I was completely at a loss. They told me to think back, but for the life of me there was no way I could bring this misdemeanour to mind. Finally they told me. It goes to show, they've got you down from the cradle to the grave.

Although only a bare ten minutes' walk from the wretchedness of Sidmouth Street and Harrison Street, life in Holborn was like being transported to another planet. The streets where we had played and grown up were still solid working-class areas, people still worked for a pittance, the pubs carried on a roaring trade, and in general it was just as much a struggle to survive as anywhere else, but mixed in with all this, floating right on the surface, in the middle and round the edges, there was the potent mix that was Bloomsbury society.

The poets, the writers, the politicals of all creeds and, of course, the girls, who as darkness fell would take up their stations under their favourite lamp post or in a shop doorway ready to pounce on any male passer-by who happened to enter their domain. The girls were constantly on the lookout for the cops.

As well as paying their attentions to the girls, the police would occasionally come unannounced into the cafés that catered for the more unconventional political groups. All of these had their own sacred venues, probably the most famous of these being the Red Book Club in what was then Parton Street, just by Red Lion Square, right next to the London School of Economics. The RBC was the home of the local communists and fellow travellers. The anarchists had a den in Red Lion Street, where their national paper was printed, while the Trots met up in a café in Museum Street. What a mix to grow up in! On top of all this, we had the show-girls and the dancing boys (the pretty boys), all living in the boarding houses that filled the streets from end to end.

I was working as a delivery boy at Hales the Grocers in Marchmont Street. Charles Laughton, the celebrated actor, who had a flat in Gordon Square, was one of the customers. One day I came face to face with the famous man. Would I care to earn some extra money?

'Not 'arf,' says I.

'Be here at seven sharp.'

It turned out he was holding a reception for some visitors from America. My job was to wash the glasses and make myself useful to the cook. I earned myself a fiver that night. Laughton must have put it around to some of his cronies, as I was called upon to carry out similar work quite a few times. As I could only be contacted through Hales I was also in the manager's good books for bringing in new custom.

Then there was the more dubious work of keeping an eye out for some of the villains of the area. These characters were known as 'screwsmen'; professional thieves, they were mostly based in the nightclubs around Greek Street and the darker areas of Cambridge Circus. They operated in the classier areas of London – Mayfair, Knightsbridge, Belgravia and such like.

Our job was to keep a watch out for the law. Much later in life I learnt that this was termed 'aiding and abetting'. To us boys, it was all a bit of a lark and a way of earning a few bob on the side.

I learnt a lot at that time. I came across different political groups and listened to them arguing. Each political sect hated the guts of all the others. Although I wasn't aware of it at the time, what I was listening to was a hundred differing answers to the problems of the era: the growing strength of fascism in Europe, communism as the ultimate Garden of Eden, the Trots blasting away at anything that emanated from the soul of Stalin, the poets and the writers trying to find common ground and come up with a solution.

These were the days when opinions were formed by reading newspapers, listening to the wireless and taking part in discussions. The different papers all had their own specific points of view. The worst was the *Daily Mail* with its rabid support of the Hitler regime in Germany and its backing of the British Union of Fascists led by Oswald Mosley and his Blackshirts.

Blackshirt gangs used to go round the streets causing mayhem, breaking the windows of Jewish shopkeepers and doing their best to put the fear of God into anyone who opposed them. The worst thing about all of this was the protection they had from the police. If the Blackshirts were involved in violence it wasn't them who ended up in court the next morning.

All these fun and games lasted until my eighteenth birthday when my life took a completely new direction. I took the king's shilling and became a soldier boy.

5

The King's Shilling

It was 15 October 1937, my birthday, and I was out of work again after having had an altercation with yet another boss. It was cold and I had strolled down to Whitehall, to watch the Horse Guards perform their four-hourly ritual. A uniformed character with a big red band over his shoulders and more stripes on his uniform than a zebra spoke to me.

'Feeling a bit cold, son? What about coming over and 'aving a nice cup of tea and a bun, all on the 'ouse?'

Having nothing better to do, and more to the point being broke, I readily agreed – too readily as it turned out. Across Whitehall and into a room in a big redbrick building in Scotland Yard.

'Name, address, date of birth?'

Into another room, where two men in white coats were standing.

'Had any illnesses, son?'

'No.'

'Good, strip off, bend over, cough, you're all right, son. Send in the next one.'

That was the medical. Inside half an hour I stood with the king's shilling clutched in my sweaty hand, a railway warrant and instructions to make my way to Winchester as early as possible on the following day. I had joined the Rifle Brigade. As far as I recall I never did get that cup of tea.

I was halfway up Drury Lane and on my way home before the

enormity of what I had done began to sink in. By the time I reached home I was shivering in my shoes. I didn't tell a soul what had happened. I managed to slip out early the next morning. I left a note on my bed saying I would write home as soon as I had settled in. I got to the barracks at Winchester that afternoon.

The following morning, me and the other unfortunates who had fallen for the nice-cup-of-tea routine were kitted out and given a lecture by the officer commanding the depot. Then we were screamed at by a sergeant who looked as old as the hills, introduced into the mysteries of making up an army cot and told that reveille would be at 6 a.m. sharp. Next, on to the parade ground in vest, shorts and plimsolls, freezing cold and cursing along. The draft included a small-time bookmaker who had come unstuck when the favourite had, against all the odds, come home first, men running away from their matrimonial entanglements, thieves, con-men, all the riffraff of society. The British Army opened up its protective arms and took them all.

There was also a contingent who had been given the opportunity to serve their country by the local magistrate. 'You can repent and do something useful for society by signing on, or go down for two years.'

So there we were, lined up on this parade ground way out in the sticks with a madman standing in front of us shouting and yelling and explaining to us how he wished he had committed suicide before he met such a miserable lot as now stood in front of him. But him and his mates were going to change all this, and this change was to start now. That first day of hell at an end, we were told that the next day, as a special concession, we would all be given a week's pay of ten shillings. I found out much later that it came from a levy placed upon the officers of the Regiment. This was not a practice common in the British Army of the day, but the Rifle Brigade considered itself a very special regiment, and so it turned out to be.

We spent six months at Winchester learning the skills that

made the Regiment famous. At 6.30 we were out on the parade ground in shorts and vests, half an hour of physical exercises, and then we got changed into what was called fatigue dress, breakfast in the canteen, and the day started properly at 9 a.m.

At least an hour and a half every day was given over to the handling of firearms, and once a week we were off to the rifle butts. A Rifleman was expected to hit at least five bulls and four inners out of ten at five hundred yards, and to fire at ten rounds a minute. Failure meant encouragement to apply for transfer to another unit.

The day ended at about 5 p.m. After the evening meal groups of us would walk down to the town centre, resplendent in our nice new uniforms and attempt to chat up the local talent. These expeditions never came to anything. Winchester had been a garrison town for centuries and the local talent shied away from the likes of us. Sunday evening would see most of us stony broke, then it would be down to the canteen for the never-ending card games.

An army training depot in those years was not a good place for the weak-willed. It took about two weeks for the training squad to get up to strength, anything between twenty and twenty-five men. By the time the training started the squad would have sorted out who was who and who were going to be the top dogs. Life was the same as in the streets. If you didn't stand up to the pushing and shoving your life wasn't worth a candle. It was life as I had learnt to accept it. It wasn't always the case that those with the best fists turned out to be the best leaders. Men who used their strength to bully others rarely showed the courage to stand up to the hard reality of mortal combat. But in the army you have to be able to stand up for yourself – if you can't you are in the wrong business. After six months, when the basic training ended, we were all sent to Tidworth, a remote and hostile military outpost on the edge of Salisbury Plain.

The 1st Battalion Rifle Brigade was the first British infantry unit to be fully mechanised. We spent the whole time driving the length and breadth of Salisbury Plain. My section corporal was a typical devil-may-care Cockney, with about five years' service under his belt.

'Come on, lads, get yer finger out, I could kill yer quicker than you can blink.'

His name was Cross, Corporal Cross. He was killed in 1940, defending Calais.

Come November, there was yours truly posted up on the detail board, listed on the next draft to India for posting to the 2nd Battalion at Meerut. The next stage of my young life was about to begin.

6

Goodbye England

On an icy cold wintry day, 24 December 1938 to be exact, 680 other ranks and twenty officers boarded HMS *Hampshire* at Southampton. Some would disembark at Gibraltar, others at Malta, some at Alexandria, some at Aden, and the rest would complete the voyage to Karachi.

It would be the last many of those men would see of their motherland for at least seven years. Before the Second World War it was the practice for a man to sign on for a minimum of seven years with the colours, plus five further years on the reserve. In reality it worked out that you finished up doing eight years with the colours. We called it 'seven years for the Army and one for the King'. A soldier would often then sign on for the rest of the full service, coming out, time expired, after twenty-one years, completely institutionalised and fit for nothing but a doorman's job at some posh hotel or standing guard outside the local cinema or theatre. The men who sailed away that cold December day formed the last peacetime draft to leave the shores of England before the war began.

I'd had two weeks' embarkation leave to say goodbye to my nearest and dearest. My mother and grandparents had accepted the fact that they wouldn't be seeing me for at least another six or seven years and after the tears, hugs and kisses I was given a small parcel of goodies, including knitted gloves and socks which I wasn't allowed to wear: 'Not regulation kit, sonny boy.' I also received a last reminder of civilised life, a nice cake. As the ship pulled out of Southampton Water the snow came down like a huge white blanket. The whole draft sat up on the port side watching the shores of their homeland receding into the mist. We were wrapped up to the eyeballs in greatcoats and scarves to keep out the icy blast. Four days later the ship docked at Gibraltar, and there we were, all sweltering in what seemed to us to be tropical sunshine. It got hotter every day.

It's enough to say that the voyage was hell. The 'other ranks' were each issued with a hammock and two blankets, crammed into the bowels of the ship, and told to get on with it. It was a different story for the officers: two subalterns to a cabin, captains and above had cabins to themselves. We were all let up on a restricted part of the deck during the day, going below for meals and sleep. Below decks the temperature could reach 120°F, sometimes even higher. Seasickness was commonplace. These particular types of troop carriers were flat-bottomed, a design feature which enabled them to navigate into the ports of thousands of small outposts of the Empire.

When a contingent was to disembark, the ship would slowly enter port, native kids swimming round it, inviting us to throw coins to them. They would dive down through water so clear that you could easily see them scrounging about on the seabed. To us rookies – we were mostly under twenty – this was a new world, completely outside our experience. We brushed aside the warnings of the old salts: this was the life, never going to get browned off with this! So the ship wallowed its way across the Mediterranean, along the Suez Canal and on into the Indian Ocean, finally berthing in the great port of Karachi.

We disembarked and entrained at the railway station, a huge Victorian edifice. The carriages were filled with massive blocks of ice, the nearest thing in those days to air conditioning. The next stage of the journey took about three days. We crossed the Hindu Kush and travelled on to Delhi, the capital, arriving at the small city of Meerut around midnight. Meerut, by the way, is famous as the starting place of the Indian Mutiny, and I was heading for the very place where it all kicked off, the Meerut Cantonment, Indian station of the 2nd Battalion The Rifle Brigade.

When we finally got off the train, we had our first true introduction to the Indian subcontinent, the place that so many English men and women, having tasted its divine magic, feel the urge to return to. Years later, I can still remember the sense of excitement I felt that first evening, as if the whole vast continent was waiting out in the dark, the sweet smell of jasmine, its peaceful aroma pervading the still, hot night air. I had never experienced anything like it. We marched off, a bunch of raw rookies about to be introduced to the real meaning of serving His Majesty the King. Blow the bugles, roll the drums, and never disgrace the Regiment. The next day I met some of the men who were going to be my comrades for the next seven years.

7

India

The evil intent of a certain Austrian ex-corporal limited my stay in India to a mere nine months, but those nine months left a lasting impression. The strange contrast of frenzied Indian street activity and the calm politeness which seemed to be a way of life among the individuals who made up the population was an eye-opener for us young soldiers. The Caledonian Road, Covent Garden, all the places we had left behind in London had nothing to match it and hadn't prepared us for it.

But in those days a soldier didn't mix with the natives; he had nothing other than his regiment, it was his whole world. Life centred around the barracks, otherwise known as the cantonment. All the entertainment was supplied by the Regiment – the weekly tombolas, card schools, competitions of various sorts and sports meetings with other regiments. Because of the heat all activity took place before ten in the morning, or after five in the evening. It was an offence to be caught outside any building bare-headed. Heatstroke was a self-inflicted wound, punishable by twenty-eight days in the glasshouse, a dire experience. It was so hot in the middle of the day that even the flies took shelter. It was said that any insect foolish enough to move in the midday sun would drown in its own sweat. Insect, animal, man – nothing moved. So the days would be spent in the cool shelter of the bungalow, with the punkah wallah pulling on the rope which kept the huge fans swishing slowly to and fro.

Sitting outside on the veranda would be the char wallah, the dude (milk) wallah, the bhisti (water) wallah, and all the other odds and sods who made their living from the cantonment. Each wallah kept a book, totting up what his customers spent, so many annas for a piala of char, the pastries or other goodies he had on offer. It was considered a major disgrace to the Regiment if you failed to pay your way with the wallahs. If you were marched before the Commanding Officer charged with non-payment of dues you would end up with seven days' defaulters and a heavy fine, so everybody paid. Full stop.

Once a week, at night, we went on a twenty-mile route march. We were accompanied by the regimental mascot, a mangy dog of no known breed which answered to the name of Rufus. I had been with the Regiment for almost five months when a truck driver ran over and killed the beast. The Regiment went into mourning and Rufus was given a full military burial, complete with wreaths from all the companies and platoons. All this for a flea-bitten mongrel, *but it kept the men occupied*!

The bungalows were huge buildings, high and wide enough to allow maximum airflow within the walls. Each held a company of men. The beds were spaced about seven feet apart. The rifles and all other arms were chained to a central-locking area down the centre of the building. Loss of a rifle or side arm, along with insubordination, could mean a full year in a military prison. It didn't often happen.

Once a month we had guard duty. The job itself was simple enough, a twenty-four-hour duty, four hours on and four off, split up between the guard room and the magazine (where all the ammo was kept). It was the preparation for the inspection of the new guard that was the problem. This took the whole month between duties. The slightest blemish or shadow of a smear on one's highly polished belt, boots or scabbard meant an appearance before the Guv'nor himself, the CO. 'Disgrace to the Regiment. Seven days. March the man out.' A man who thought he might have a chance of being picked as 'stick man' (having the smartest turnout) would get his mates to carry him to the parade ground on a table. This was to stop the heavily starched KD (khaki drill) from creasing. Being stick man was considered an honour to the section; the recipient was excused the drudgery of mounting guard, and he would be the battalion runner for the day. Alas, the good soldier Gregg never came anywhere near to achieving that exalted position.

All over India the British Army was used to quell the increasing number of civil disturbances. These periods of unrest could involve crowds of five to ten thousand screaming natives. The joke was that we never took any ammunition with us, only empty rifles and fixed swords (which is what the Rifle Brigade calls bayonets). Had the mobs decided to attack there was no way we could have survived. But there it was: a show of force nearly always wins the day.

My first indication of what was expected of Riflemen as opposed to the ordinary brass-button Guards mobs was when I reported sick with toothache. The Medical Officer said that I would have to travel to Kalahna to have the offending molar removed. Kalahna was a hill station used by the Regiment during the hot summer months and was five hundred miles away up in the foothills of the Himalayas.

'Report to the battalion office and get the necessary passes, draw some pay and don't get lost.' That was the sum total of my instructions. Not having a clue as to the language or the geography of the country, I ventured to explain to the officer, a decent chap by the name of Sinclair, that I might have some difficulty finding the place.

'Rifleman Gregg,' says he, 'you are a member of the Rifle Brigade, not some half-arsed county mob. If you can't find your way to overcome a little difficulty like this then you're no use at all to your regiment. Report back within the next eight days. Dismissed.'

The next morning saw me being delivered to the railway

station. From there I went miles up north to a place named Derha Dun, off the train, and then, with much question and answer, I managed to find my way to the nearest British Army post where I was put on an Indian Army convoy that was going to Kalahna and all points north. For the first time in my young life I was transported above the tree line, up above the cloud base, up and up until finally we reached the destination. I had the tooth removed and a couple filled. I was given two days to recover and then put on another Indian Army truck, for the trip back down to Derha Dun.

The trip up into the hills had been an experience; the trip down nearly killed me. These Indian drivers knew all about earning a few bob on the side. I cannot remember the engine ever being started up during the hundred-mile descent, a huge rock face on one side of the road, a sheer drop through the clouds and into oblivion on the other. The driver pocketed the money that should have been spent on petrol. It was one of the most hair-raising experiences of my life. I got back and reported to Captain Sinclair. 'Good show, Rifleman Gregg, keep up the good work.' After that trip I scrubbed my teeth with furious energy every day.

While we were preparing to leave for parts unknown, I was confined to barracks for a week – my first experience of the punishment known as 'seven days' defaulters', or 'jankers'. White lines in the shape of rectangles had been painted on the parade ground. At five o'clock one warm morning the battalion was ordered out in full marching kit (everything we owned) to practise disembarking from the train and getting ready to board the troopship that was going to take us to Palestine. We were not drawn up in the normal fashion; instead we were split into groups of eight men and each group was installed in one of the rectangles of whitewash, each of which represented a railway carriage.

Five o'clock, six o'clock, six thirty came and went, I just couldn't hold it any longer, so not seeing any non-coms or officers in the near vicinity I unbuttons and has a slash. Halfway through the act a shadow crossed our imitation carriage. Sitting high up in the saddle, astride his horse, was none other than 'Wingy' Renton, the Colonel himself. The Colonel was known to the ranks as 'Wingy' because he only had one arm. 'Wingy' referred to his empty sleeve which had a habit of fluttering in the breeze.

'WHAT'S THIS MAN DOING?'

'I'm relieving meself out of the window, Guv.'

'FALL IN TWO MEN!' shouts 'Wingy', almost falling off his charger. 'Off to the guardroom with this man.'

I spent the next seven days in the guardroom scrubbing my way around the veranda, and that's how I got my first dose of the horrible bumpy rash known as prickly heat. Almost every soldier in the Middle East got it at some time or another.

Three weeks later, after only nine months in India, we embarked on the good ship *Dunera*, bound for Haifa and active service. Goodbye India, hello again Suez Canal, good morning Palestine.

8

Palestine

The Med was as calm as a millpond as our old trooper docked in the port of Haifa. The whole battalion was paraded on the foredeck and ordered to take a good look at our new posting. Before we disembarked we were all issued with fifty rounds of .303 ammunition.

'Put seven rounds in the magazine with one in readiness up the spout, and don't forget to put your safety catch on, we don't want no accidents.' Nobody knew just what to expect. As it turned out disembarkation went ahead smoothly. Nothing happened, and we were bundled into a train and in a matter of three hours we had arrived in Nablus, a fairly large town with a predominately Arab population. Nablus was to be our base for the next six or seven months.

The contrast between the country we had just left and Palestine, as the country we now know as Israel was then called, could hardly have been sharper and more defined. The lazy atmosphere and politeness of life in India disappeared for ever. What we had now was violence set against a harsh environment of rock and scrub, sometimes broken by green meadows hidden behind clumps of cypress trees.

The coastal areas around Haifa and Tel Aviv were occupied by the more prosperous Jewish communities. The newer Jewish immigrants were generally moved on to the more dispersed communes. These were true socialist communities. Private ownership was almost non-existent. All the work, the finished products, the food growing and cooking, was carried out for the benefit of the whole. Known as the kibbutz system, it was a highly organised and deeply religious way of life. There was never any trouble with the inhabitants of these societies, and to be invited to spend a day in a kibbutz meant a day of hospitality and good eating.

Our prime task was to uphold the rule of British law, a duty that was resisted by every red-blooded son of the Jewish and Palestinian communities.

The Palestinians worked in groups of two or three men, laying mines on the railways and roads, and sniping at us at night. The Jewish Zionist Haganah movement, along with the far more violent Stern Gang, carried out campaigns of murder and terrorism. Nothing that the Palestinian movement could come up with approached anything near the ferocity of those two Zionist organisations. The Stern Gang was dedicated to murdering as many British soldiers and officials as possible.

It was the battalion's job to maintain the peace and, if possible, run down and neutralise those factions that took it upon themselves to cause mayhem and destruction. The battalion, about eight hundred men, would work in companies, strung out over the hills and valleys that ran down the centre of the country. When the culprits were finally cornered it nearly always ended with a shootout, and, as we were marksmen, our aim was lethal.

One day I was ordered to appear before the dreaded 'Wingy' for some minor infringement of the rules. After listening to my feeble excuses he said that, as it was not possible to give me a session of 'jankers', my punishment would be to become his runner when the battalion was out on patrol. I couldn't believe my luck; after all, if I stuck close to the Colonel I would most likely be out of any real danger.

The battalion was sent out to capture some very nasty individuals who had been blowing up railway lines. To assist us we had two RAF Gladiators flying around. I had to hold up a huge multicoloured umbrella to show the pilots the position of Battalion HQ. The planes pinpointed a small group of hostiles and flew over our heads to give them a few bursts to try and make them break cover. The aim of the two pilots left a lot to be desired as the brolly suddenly took on the appearance of a vegetable colander.

'Throw that bloody thing into the nullah,' shouts 'Wingy' (a nullah was a dried-up riverbed), 'that's the last time I trust those bastards again. Follow me, Gregg.'

Down into the nullah scrambles 'Wingy' with me in the rear, sans brolly. By the time we reached the riverbed the unlucky Palestinians were dead, stretched out in the noon-day sun, proof of the deadly accuracy of Rifleman shooting.

If we suspected a group was hiding in a village, then that village would be surrounded and the headman called for. Unless the culprits were handed over the leaders of the village would be arrested and hauled before the local British magistrate.

We Riflemen were barely twenty years of age; the glory of the British Empire had been drummed into us since we were tiny. Bang the drum, blow the bugle and finish up with a rousing chorus of 'Land of Hope and Glory'. I didn't question what I was doing until much later in life.

In June 1939 I was packed off with about twenty other men to Sarafand, the British Army's motor training base. A full month away from all the bullshit, a month spent tearing apart engines of all types and then putting them back together again.

We were taught to drive every sort of vehicle the army possessed, over every type of terrain imaginable. Within a month the 2nd Battalion was fully mechanised, the first fully mechanised unit in the British Army overseas.

Then, on 3 September 1939, while we were out on patrol, the news came through: 'War with Germany'. We were about to earn our keep. Our spell in Palestine had served a purpose: we had been blooded, we were no longer strangers to incoming fire. This apprenticeship was to save us valuable lives in the months to come.

*   *   *

It is time to backtrack a couple of years, to the weeks before my posting to India. I had discovered a girl called Freda. As far as I remember we only had about seven or eight days in each other's company. At first I was struck dumb, unable to say a word. Freda used to do all the chattering. We never got beyond an embarrassed kiss. She must have thought that she had picked a right drip. As it turned out she picked a right sod.

The night before I was due to sail, my last night in London, we were supposed to meet. Instead I met up with a chap who had joined up on the same day as myself and was on the same draft. Frankie Batt his name was and he was killed at Alamein. We went and got blotto and Freda got stood up.

There are times when I look back over the years and I realise that this was the first hurt I inflicted on Freda. Many more were to follow. To my amazement she continued to write to me. Much later I learnt that my mother had implored her to carry on writing. Which was just as well, because if she hadn't we wouldn't have had our children, Judith, Alan and David, and all the wonderful grandchildren. When I stood her up that night, I had no inkling of just how much she was going to mean to me in later life.

Getting back to the story, I was on the start line of a world catastrophe, and to see me through I was getting Freda's wonderful letters from home. None of us doubted that we would reach the end, wherever and whenever that might be.

PART TWO

9

Eggwhite

Eggwhite, the code name which signalled our move to Egypt, came over the wire on a bitterly cold day towards the end of the year. We were to entrain for Cairo within three days. Things were happening with lightning speed. Every sort of rumour that could be invented was invented.

By January 1940 we were installed in the Citadel in the centre of Cairo. The Citadel was the dirtiest, smelliest and most soul-destroying billet we had yet experienced. It stood on a slight rise above the centre of the old town; its great dome could be seen for miles around, a huge decaying building, a sometime fort and holy place. It had been taken over by the British authorities to use as a transit camp for troops as they began to pass through Cairo en route for other places. When we arrived, the first job was the removal of the dead carcasses of animals. It took us a week to clean it up.

One morning we were summoned to a General Parade. Standing on a table in the centre of what passed as a parade ground stood our good Colonel, his empty sleeve flapping about as usual in the breeze. We were told that our stay in 'the Hole', as we called it, would be short, so, until we had further orders, we would be allowed to roam the city at will. He warned us not to disgrace the name of the Regiment and to 'have a good time, as it may well be your last'. On that happy note we were dismissed.

Cairo was like a frontier town. Gambling saloons, although forbidden, thrived. Nightclubs, in reality drinking dens, lined the three main streets in the centre of the town. Down in the Berka, right under the shadow of the famous Shepheard's Hotel, were the brothels. It was said that you could get a dose of clap just by smelling the place. The Shari el-Berka, to give this street of ill repute its full name, was finally placed out of bounds sometime in the middle of '41 when it finally dawned on the high-ups that more men were going into hospital with VD than were being wounded by the enemy.

This period came to an end when, after having been issued with new trucks and Bren-gun carriers, we were packed off to Mersa Matruh, the forward military base of the British Army in Egypt.

Mersa was the beginning of the Western Desert which was to be our home for the next three years. We called the desert 'the Blue'. It was at Mersa that, for the first and last time, we slept under canvas, proper tents, with proper latrine lines, a camp shop and an open-air cinema. There must have been around ten to twelve thousand troops at Mersa, all waiting for something to happen.

The flies were everywhere. An infestation of enormous beasts that would come down and pinch the food off your plate unless you continuously waved your hands about, and this is what men learnt to do. It was said that for nine months of the year you were waving your hands in front of your face, then you took the next three months to get out of the habit. There was no escape; however far you went into the desert the flies followed. You just got used to it.

Things started to get tense around the middle of May. Our sister regiment, the King's Royal Rifle Corps, was moved to Sidi Barrani, halfway between Mersa and the border with Italian-ruled Libya. On 10 June, Mussolini rolled the dice and Italy entered the war.

That same day the battalion had its first casualty. One of the lads committed suicide. Later it became regimental practice to send men back to base if they showed signs of instability. This happened on quite a few occasions. It was this type of enlightened attitude that earned Rifle Brigade officers the respect of the men under their command.

The King's Royal Rifle Corps was moved to the Libyan border, which was called 'the Wire', and we took over their positions at Sidi Barrani. The move up to Barrani was carried out overnight. This was because the British only had two operational squadrons of old Gladiator biplanes, while the Italians had at least ten squadrons of modern attacking aircraft and a large bomber fleet. It was too dangerous for us to move in the day so we used the dark as cover.

We had two signals, a blue flag, which meant 'proceed in a forward direction', and a red flag, which meant 'stop'. There was no signal for going back. So, equipped with this high-tech signalling equipment, off we went into the darkness, bumping over the desert scrub, with scarves over our faces to protect us from the clouds of dust and sand. Swearing and cursing, we drove into the unknown. At last the waiting was over; now it was shit or bust.

The move was made without incident and by the first rays of dawn we were taking up our new positions. The order went round: 'Forget about breakfast, start digging in'. What a joke! How can you dig in to solid rock? Nevertheless, defensive positions were established.

The Italian planes attacked just as we finished our first meal of the day. They came in at ground level like a hoard of angry bees. It was all over inside a quarter of an hour: no damage to us but we had the satisfaction of seeing three of their planes hit the deck. We were attacked a further three times during the course of that day, and we witnessed the death of one of our own bombers, a Blenheim. It came down right in the centre of our position. It had been on a raid, had been hit and just didn't make it back.

The Colonel did the rounds that evening and congratulated us all on the way we had behaved and said that he asked nothing more than we carry on the way we had started. For us it proved that we could hit back, and everybody felt that maybe it wasn't going to be so bad after all.

After a week we moved up to the Libyan 'Wire' to relieve the King's Royal Rifle Corps. From now on we would patrol night and day, harassing the Italians. Sometimes we would run out of water, which meant going into the Italian defensive positions, the only place where water was on hand. Under cover of darkness we would empty the enemy radiators; the water was filthy, but without it we couldn't survive.

The Italians we captured were a disillusioned lot, who didn't seem to want to fight for this stretch of inhospitable and useless desert. They used to let off a load of ammunition at us, but often couldn't see what they were firing at!

Nearly all of us facing the Italians were Londoners, and in our letters from home we were beginning to read about the plight of our families and the terrible bombing they were enduring. Many a poor, hapless Eyetie felt the agony of a bayonet going in, wielded by an enraged Rifleman who had just got a letter from home bearing bad news. Normally we just rounded up any prisoners we took, but there were those times when a man would go berserk and kill them. It didn't seem to worry 'Wingy' Renton. 'Get at them and give them stick' was one of his favourite sayings, and on the whole we agreed with those sentiments.

As the weeks went by we learnt more and more about the trade of war, when to show yourself and when to apply caution, and how to keep our casualties down. We also learnt the most valuable of all lessons: never underestimate the enemy. In the same way as you can never know a person until you live with them, so you can never judge the calibre of the enemy soldier coming towards you until he is close enough for you to see into his eyes. That's the moment when you know whether he's got it in him to kill you. Inside two months our casualty rate dropped almost to zero. We were learning fast.

Our force was made up of our own battalion, the King's Royal

Rifle Corps, a detachment of the Royal Horse Artillery with twenty-five-pounders, and a squadron of tanks, the armoured cars of the 7th and 11th Hussars plus a few other odds and sods. This was known as a 'Jock Column'. About the beginning of September we started to notice increased activity on the part of the Italians facing us. Large quantities of enemy armour were being brought right up to the border wire. Our small force was now under almost constant shell-fire. It was clear to all of us that something unpleasant was afoot.

Then almost the whole lot of us were ordered up to the Wire. The patrols of the previous night had reported non-stop activity by the Italians, and, sure enough, through the growing light of the coming day we could see a huge black mass of vehicles, tanks, armoured cars and the like, and behind them another mass of the huge lorries that the Eyeties used as troop carriers. They were about a thousand yards away. For some reason they had shut off their engines and seemed content just to sit on their haunches and threaten our puny force.

Peddler Palmer, our Company Commander, drove up in a cloud of dust and gave our platoon the order to cross the Wire and attempt to get some reaction from the mob who were sitting there. We had a new young officer with us at the time by the name of Mr Vernon. He didn't seem too happy about things.

'OK, Gregg,' says he (me being the driver of the truck), 'off we go, and don't get too close to them.'

Blue flag up and off we trundles, through one of the many breaks in the Wire, closer and closer to the huge black hazy cloud. Without warning we break through the haze, and there we are, two carriers and two trucks, about three hundred yards away from a huge mass of silent armour. We were sitting ducks.

Our two trucks, each with a section of six men perched in the back, were about a hundred yards apart. The two carriers drove one on each flank, keeping close to protect the trucks. Vernon was sitting next to me. He says that we should get a bit closer as he had been ordered to get a reaction. By this time the whole platoon were thinking that maybe the war was going to end for us in about two minutes flat. We were that close to the enemy that we could hear them shouting at us. Then, without warning, we got the required reaction, with a vengeance.

'Put your foot down and let's get out of here.' No second order was necessary. Off we went, as if there was no tomorrow.

By now the Eyeties had our range and all sorts of muck was being thrown at us. It's a wonder that the Morris engine didn't blow itself right off its mountings, such was the speed of our exit. The platoon finally made it back to the gap, to loud cheers from all present. When we inspected the truck the whole of the rear tailboard and one side of the vehicle was a mass of holes. How did we get away with it? None of us had so much as a scratch. Pure luck.

The next morning we were given a lecture by 'Wingy'. When the enemy advanced our job would be to keep in contact at all times, to watch what they were doing and report it back, but on no account were we to mix it with them.

10

Under Pressure

On 13 September, without any warning, the Italian army started moving forward. The roaring and rumbling of a thousand or more heavy diesel engines filled the air and clouds of thick black smoke darkened the sky. We didn't fire a shot until they were a thousand yards from our front. Then all hell broke loose. The twenty-five-pounders to the rear of us opened up, and they were only five hundred yards from us when we were ordered to withdraw.

The whole battalion slewed round to the south of their columns, letting them pass while we kept up a relentless barrage of small arms into the side of their advance. It was a bit like shooting into a herd of cattle. There we were darting about, firing for all we were worth, then beating a hasty retreat when they got our range. It was all clever stuff and not a man or a vehicle was lost in the process.

So began our withdrawal all the way back to Sidi Barrani. We quickly established a routine whereby in the evening both sides would leaguer up for the night. On our side each company, about eighty men, would use their vehicles to form a square with Company HQ in the centre. Out would come whatever rations we might have on board, mainly bully beef and hard-tack biscuits. These would be emptied into a disused petrol tin with the top cut out and this would be placed over another petrol tin half filled with sand with some petrol and oil mixed into it. The petrol was set alight and that was our way of cooking in the desert. The subsequent glutinous mess would be eaten with some relish and followed with liberal helpings of tea. The water was very brackish and always a bit on the salty side. The powdered milk that was added to the brew gave the tea the appearance of curdled Devon cream. When we were lucky enough to be in an area where the water supply was fairly fresh we could escape from this horrible concoction, but that wasn't very often. The Italians pushed our meagre force back to Sidi Barrani and there, for reasons known only to themselves, they stopped. After a week had passed it seemed that the Eyeties were not going to move and we were pulled out of the line for a refit

For the last five or six months we had been living like Bedouins and the battalion had taken on the appearance of a band of Afghan tribesmen. Our daily water ration was about half a gallon per man for everything; we pooled it to wash in. It was common to toss up or take it in turns as to who had the privilege of washing first in the morning. The last man in the section usually gave his wash a miss for the day. We hadn't had a proper wash in months. Our uniforms were in rags, we were lousy and covered in desert sores.

At the end of each day one of the section would go to the company radio truck to get the latest news. If conditions were right the operator could pick up the BBC World Service. After the evening meal we would settle down to a game of cards. As it got dark we'd get out the sleeping gear. We each had the regulation army issue of two blankets which we supplemented with stuff we managed to salvage from captured enemy vehicles, some of which was very elaborate and went a long way towards giving us the comforts of home. Then we would kip down by the side of the truck or carrier and give ourselves up to dreams, lying there until we were rudely awakened by the first rays of another day and the ever-present army of flies, bullets and bombs. As well as the trade of war, we were learning the lessons of survival and the black art of scrounging – rations, equipment, clothing, you name it and one way or another we could beg, borrow or steal it.

We were now back at Mersa Matruh and were part of the 7th Armoured Division's Fourth Armoured Brigade Support Group. Which mouthful meant that any action fought by the brigade would have us and the King's Royal Rifle Corps at the sharp end.

In the first week of December we were all given a pep talk by the Brigadier, an imposing figure by the name of Caunter. We were told that the honeymoon was over. From now on our job would be to kill the enemy whenever and wherever he showed his face.

On 8 December we were told that the British Middle East Army was to move against the Italians at Sidi Barrani. We were outnumbered ten to one. Our objective was to capture as many prisoners as possible.

While we were at Mersa a fresh contingent of recruits joined us, the best known among these being the actor David Niven and a young officer called Quintin Hogg, later to become Lord Hailsham. I was the humble Rifleman detailed to drive Hogg around. After a brief stay, both of these worthies were called back to Britain.

Around this time a Lieutenant Tom Bird joined the battalion as part of a new draft. We immediately christened him 'Dickie'. Dickie Bird, or Birdie as he fondly became known, will always be remembered by those who served under him as a man of exceptional courage. When all seemed to be lost, there would be Dickie boy, calm and seemingly aloof from the dangers around us, while we, to put it bluntly, were shitting ourselves. If Birdie said, 'Come on, lads, let's go forward', you went with him all the way. Good on you, Dickie. I hope you're still with us, on terra firma. I single out Tom Bird for the simple reason that I served under him on many an occasion, but it is also true to say that he was typical of the type of enlightened officer that the Rifles were lucky to have.

The next battle was code-named Compass. It was one of those rare battles that went according to plan. Our job in Support Group was a bit sticky. We were to make our way around to the rear of the enemy to stop his reinforcements coming up. We would be out of contact with the main army which would be attacking the enemy's front and flanks. In other words, if we got into trouble, we couldn't expect any help – we would have to fight our way out under our own steam.

Even so, many of the older hands, including yours truly, thought that we had the best of the bargain. After all, we weren't going in with fixed bayonets like some of the other troops.

The Italians had a tough time. They faced the Fourth Indian Division, they were constantly bombarded from the sea by the navy with sixteen-inch guns, and they found that our new Matilda tanks were impervious to everything they threw at them. Those who avoided capture promptly got into their remaining tanks and other vehicles and started to withdraw to the west, right on to our guns and infantry. There were ten thousand of them against our paltry fifteen hundred or so. They went right through us leaving their dead and wounded lying in the sand. We collected the wounded of both sides, reorganised and gave chase. Our spirits were sky-high; we were certain that, in spite of the immense superiority in numbers enjoyed by the Italians, we had little to fear.

The battalion inflicted serious casualties on the luckless enemy and our section did its bit. Normally each carrier was armed with our rifles, one Bren gun and a useless Boys anti-tank rifle. We had supplemented these with two Browning machine guns rescued from a crashed Hurricane.

This is how we acquired them. We were out on patrol, four carriers, and we saw a huge plume of smoke in the distance which turned out to be a Hurricane, with the pilot, an Aussie, trapped inside it. We got him out OK but could see he was not going to last long. He was shot to pieces. So we put the brew on to make a cup of tea. He's sinking fast, all he wants to know is who won the Melbourne Cup. By a chance in a million, a lad called Andy had heard this vital piece of information the night before on the company radio and was able to give him the answer. The stricken Aussie died a happy man, before the tea was made. We stripped the plane of its eight machine guns, trebling the firepower of our carriers. And that's how we were able to inflict such grievous bodily harm on three hundred of the poor Italians who were hurtling through our lines as if there was no tomorrow – which for them there wasn't. Next stop Derna, where they again halted their headlong flight.

11

Beda Fomm:

A Different Form of Killing

After the showdown at Barrani, our CO, 'Wingy' Renton, gave strict orders that no matter what happened we were to stand firm. So that's what we did. There's me, my mate Reggie and the driver Andy, sitting in a Bren-gun carrier all guns blazing and not knowing whether or not we hit anything. By 24 January it was over. Tobruk had come and gone and we were on our way to an Italian position some distance south from the main road, where it was known that a force containing several enemy tanks was positioned. We were to stop the enemy infantry from escaping. We succeeded in doing this with no loss to ourselves. The Italian tanks were destroyed and the whole force captured. Events moved slowly for the next few days. Fresh food and supplies were brought up, and, more importantly, a huge stack of mail. My share was a bundle of at least ten letters. We hardly had time to enjoy these precious moments before the order came to prepare to move. The Italian army, 250,000 men, was on the march. Our small brigade was ordered to force-march over an inland area of the desert. Before we knew where we were the blue flag was fluttering in the breeze: 'move forward'. The column was on the move, and it was chaos. Some of the lads were still throwing bedding rolls and the other stuff that we carried into the back of the trucks and carriers, while others, men who were in the middle of eating the evening meal, swallowed what they could and ran to their vehicles. We set off

towards the setting sun, then, as darkness fell, the column swung
south into uncharted terrain. It was unmapped, with no tracks,
and even the local tribesmen rarely set foot there. We relied
entirely on compass bearings. The route ran south of the Jebal
Aktar, and with every hour the going got rougher and in those
days we didn't have four-wheel drive. We were led by the 11th
Hussars who, to save time, had just drawn a straight line across
the map, a line we had to follow without deviating. We were
heading towards a place called Beda Fomm, a small rocky outcrop
astride the main road between Benghazi and Tripoli. This type of
terrain was new to us, partly mountainous, strewn with rocky
outcrops and deep, sandy wadis. It was soon obvious that the tanks
were going to be left miles behind. We left a trail of broken vehicles behind us, but, even so, a good proportion of the force survived
the journey. At dawn, the survivors of this epic manoeuvre arrived
at the rendezvous.

The immediate order was: 'Don't worry about food or sleep, dig
in for all you're worth', which, with the usual cursing and swearing, we proceeded to do. The battalion was strung across the road,
the main artery between Benghazi and Tripoli. Our trusty
Bren-gun carrier had given up the ghost and I was back with the
lads in A Company. Digging through the rock was impossible, so
we built small walls of rock and stones. B and C Companies were
either side of the road, the Hussars were in our rear, with the artillery behind them. After we were dug in, permission came to brew
up and eat whatever food we could. We had tried to position the
trucks safely to the rear, out of harm's way.

The next day dawned wet, cold and miserable. We could hear
the sound of shelling in the far distance. This in itself didn't
bother us too much; we had heard it all before. What livened us
up was the urgent shouting from the piquets to stand to. We
could hear an incessant rumbling, and, worse, the unmistakable
clanking of tracked vehicles: tanks. Soon enough, we saw them,
the leading elements of the vast army, emerging out of the early

morning mist, a thousand yards to our front, like a huge black mass of locusts. We realised that they didn't know we were there. On they came, until, without warning, our guns opened up and the leading tanks began to brew up – exploding and bursting into flames as the first shells hammered into them. From that moment on it was mayhem with the armour desperately attempting to close with us. Then their infantry attacked. Unfortunately for them the ground around the road was dead flat. It was just a case of lining up the Brens and the Vickers: there was no way they could advance through the shit that was being thrown at them.

We stopped them but the next attack was not long in coming. This time, instead of attacking en masse, they divided up into small groups. Luckily for our small force, a couple of squadrons of the 2nd Royal Tank Regiment had arrived on the scene. There weren't many of them, but to us some was better than none at all.

The enemy knew that coming up fast behind them were the main divisions of the British. The only escape route, therefore, was straight through our lines. 'Wingy' Renton had vowed that, no matter what, there was no way we were going to be overrun.

When they finally attacked, it was a fixed-bayonet job. The artillery to our rear were by now firing over open sights. The enemy tanks were burning only yards away, in a few cases right on top of our positions. Their infantry attacked and it became hand-to-hand stuff. It went on all through the day: they attacked, were thrown back, they attacked again. On and on it went until about four in the afternoon when, all of a sudden, the noise started to die down. There were no more attacks that day. Our lines were still intact, a bit thinner it's true, but still holding.

The whole area to our front was covered in smoke from the burning tanks and trucks, the ground littered with the dead and dying. The air was filled with the all-pervading stench of burning oil coupled with the unmistakable smell of scorched flesh. There were constant explosions as the fires in the burning tanks reached the ammo. Mixed with all this were the terrifying screams of the

poor sods trapped inside their steel coffins. The cries of those poor
devils who couldn't be reached by the medics went on throughout
the night. None of us were the same men at the end of that day.
Our clothes were battle-stained, spattered with blood, oil and
filth, we were almost out on our feet through lack of sleep, and
still nothing had been decided. Would they attack again tomorrow? Would the white flags start to appear? How many of us
would survive the following twenty-four hours? Our line was
'Don't worry about it, it'll all come out in the wash'. That was what
we believed: everything comes out in the wash.

We were all pretty cheerful as we lay down for the night. We
huddled up together, getting what shelter we could from the
wind and rain. We had started out as six men and now there were
five of us. We had buried the unlucky sixth man, Taffy, a young
lad who had joined us only a few months before. He had come out
of the pits of South Wales, and had taken on the most important
task of being in charge of the brew-ups. Taffy was a comrade we
would miss, but overall we considered ourselves lucky: only one
dead. Our section corporal had a slight arm wound, nothing
serious, though.

The next morning was bright and clear, a welcome change.
With a bit of luck we might get a chance to dry our sodden clothing. The sun shone on the smouldering remains of the previous
day's battle. We could still hear the unearthly cries of the enemy
wounded. Why hadn't they brought them in? We never shot at
men collecting the wounded. We could only think that they were
frightened out of their wits.

The fighting started up again. First of all we came under heavy
shellfire, a barrage which lasted for about thirty minutes. Then
the mass of the enemy started to move forward, led by every tank
they could muster. Between the tanks came the infantry and the
hand-to-hand carnage started again. At about two in the afternoon their tanks were right on top of us. It was then that we learnt
how 'Wingy' planned to bar the way. He ordered our artillery to

open up on his own positions. The eyeball-to-eyeball fighting which had been going on between the infantry ceased like lightning as the soldiers of both sides threw themselves into the ground. The tanks were caught right in the open. They had no chance: tank after tank brewed up, some right on top of our slit trenches. The low walls of the redoubt that we had built had disappeared. After about ten minutes the barrage ceased, followed by a terrible silence. The only visible movement was the trails of smoke drifting over the area to our front, then, as our senses slowly returned, the agonising noises of the aftermath of battle began to filter through, the terrible cries of the wounded on both sides.

It slowly dawned on everyone, friend and foe, that the struggle had finished. Pieces of white cloth appeared everywhere. The fighting was over. We watched as the Italian General, Bergonzoli by name, came forward with a couple of his cronies and surrendered to our officer of the Rifle Brigade, Captain Pearson. Nobody cheered. We just sat on the edge of the remains of our now flattened redoubt; above us, an Italian tank with its turret blown off, inside three very dead men. Somehow we managed to summon up the will to brew up a tin of tea. This was our first experience of hand-to-hand fighting, actually killing another human being while looking into the man's eyes. In those two days of close fighting, we had learnt one of war's darkest mysteries: we had learnt how to kill with our bare hands.

12

We Meet the *Herrenvolk*

We were not to experience such close-quarters ferocity again until much later, when the battalion upheld its tradition in the finest possible manner, on a sandy stretch of ground at Alamein called Snipe Ridge. For the moment, though, we were given a period of calm. We were ordered to the base area next to the Suez Canal, about a thousand or so miles back from the front lines, for some leave, a refit and a nice long rest.

As we coaxed our worn-out vehicles east, passing us, going west, were the forces that were taking over where we had left off. Bright, shiny faces, fresh out from Blighty. Let those shiny new faces get on with the work; all we wanted were hot baths, clean clothes and plenty of good food, all washed down with liberal quantities of iced beer and whisky.

Every six months or so each platoon would get a short four- or five-day leave in Cairo. Having the whole platoon together meant that we always had company that we were at home with, and, of course, if any of us met up with trouble there was always a helping hand nearby. But this time the whole battalion was in the base area which meant that half of it would be in Cairo at the same time, mob-handed so to speak.

Once on leave, three or four of us would take a room together, but we never used the rooms, except to sleep off our drunken excesses. The floor space would be taken up with crates of beer and whisky, although, usually, we slept where we fell down. It was all good fun while it lasted.

We had not drawn pay for the last six months or more. Considerable amounts of credit had been amassed by us all. We soon found out that, in Cairo, money disappeared like water in the desert sand. It was during this short leave that a major scientific discovery was made, and, like all major discoveries in the field of science, it was made by accident. The true value of Milton's Antiseptic Liquid was realised while a repair job was being done on a cut hand.

The three of us – myself, Reggie Dennis and Tom White (naturally nicknamed Chalky) – had been drinking in one of the many bars that had sprung up in the centre of Cairo. The glasses were made out of beer bottles with the necks removed and Chalky had cut his hand on one. Reggie rushed off to the local Woolworth's and returned with the Milton's.

In our drunken stupor someone tipped over the half-empty bottle. The liquid ran all over the handwritten bill which lay in front of us on the table. We sat there in amazement watching the ink disappearing before our eyes.

It took Chalky (a right rogue if ever there was one) less than a minute to realise that our money worries were now a thing of the past. We got to work on our pay books. It was simple. We drew out, say, £90, went back to our rooms, got cracking with the Milton's, the nought of the ninety disappeared as if by magic, and, hey presto, we had only drawn out nine pounds. Draw out another eighty the next day, and so it went on. Pay sheets were only copied in duplicate, one copy was kept by the office truck in the field, the second copy went home to England by boat. I don't think that any of us gave a thought as to what might happen if we were tumbled. Tomorrow was another day, a day we might never see. We all knew the short life of an office truck under air attack, and if the duplicate made it on to a home-bound boat, the chances were that the boat would get torpedoed. The upshot was that in our short leave we would draw in the region of four to five hundred pounds, which we gambled and drank away. We carried on this subterfuge until almost the end of our stay in the Middle East.

At the close of April our rest period came to an end. The battalion was ordered west to Sollum. So, with brand new equipment, new clothing and some fresh replacements in the way of men and officers, we drove back up the old familiar track to 'the Wire', the border between Egypt and Libya.

When we arrived we found that those cheery, fresh faces who had taken over from us after Beda Fomm had been pushed all the way back to the original start line. Not by the Italians, but by the new, more fearsome Germans. We were about to make the acquaintance of Rommel's Afrika Korps. A nasty shock was on the horizon.

13

The First Failure

By the time we arrived back at Sollum, all the nice new kit we had been issued with was back to normal – filthy. We were told by those on high that we were to push into enemy territory to relieve our men trapped by the German advance to Tobruk. The battle was code-named Operation Brevity. All arms went to it with some zeal. The letters we were receiving brought more news of the bombing of London and the suffering that our families were going through. The chance to get our own back, in the only way we knew how, gave the lads the will to get to grips with the intensely hated enemy.

We were in for a surprise: the Germans had better weapons than us. The only real weapon we had that could really inflict major damage was the twenty-five-pounder. As for our armour, it was tragic. Brevity ended with both sides licking their wounds. To us lowly foot soldiers it seemed that some of our brass were still living in the age of Balaclava: 'Forward to the guns, men. Tally-ho.'

It was now the end of June. Back once more to the usual routine of never-ending patrols. One thing we knew for certain: nothing big was liable to happen until the heat of the summer months eased, which would be somewhere around the end of October or the middle of November.

In the meantime, we endured intermittent shelling, daily attacks by German aircraft and, worst of all, the incessant attacks of the hordes of flies that followed us around wherever we happened to be. It was only in the evenings, when the scorching sun lowered itself under the horizon, that we were free of this pestilence. These flies were by far the most tormenting evil we had to face. You could make an attempt to take cover from aircraft and shelling, and in an engagement we could always fire back, but any attempt to combat the fly menace was doomed to failure. What food we tried to eat during the daytime hours would be attacked long before it arrived at the mouth of the luckless eater; a slice of bread, when we were lucky enough to get such a luxury, would be covered by a swarming mass of the huge black brutes. Only the bravest attempted such a feat. We ate at night and early morning, and if we missed those two meals we didn't eat at all.

The patrols went out day and night. A day patrol would gener-ally involve at least two platoons. A night patrol would almost always consist of one or two sections, either six or twelve men.

The officer in charge of the platoon would announce that so and so section would be on patrol that night. Accordingly, off we would go, the truck would take us up to within a thousand yards of wherever it was thought the nearest enemy post was stationed. Then off the trucks to see what we could find. The idea was to keep as quiet as the proverbial mouse and to this end anything that might rattle or make any noise was removed; so no tin hats (which we never wore anyway), and anyone who had a cough was always excused these forays into enemy territory.

Very seldom was there any fighting during these nightly walks; they were undertaken in order to keep tabs on the enemy posi-tions. However, there were times when these patrols turned to our, and Jerry's, advantage.

I first experienced this when Mr Vernon, our platoon commander, detailed our section for patrol. Just before we set off, we were told that the lads who had done the previous night's walk were volun-teering to do our shift. The tale they came up with was that they had made contact the night before, but that the corporal in charge had lost his wallet and knew exactly where he had dropped it.

Fair enough, no complaints, you lot go, we get a good night's kip. Our suspicions were aroused the next morning when two of the lads who had been part of the patrol were as sick as pigs. It was then discovered that they had a crate of Schnapps in their truck. To cut a long story short, they had met up with these Krauts and, instead of doing each other mortal damage, had struck a deal: Schnapps and black bread in exchange for tins of bully beef and some English cigarettes!

It doesn't take much imagination to work out how these encounters happened. The six-man patrol creeps forward towards the enemy position, probably only a lance jack in charge. They become aware of movement to their front almost at the same time as the enemy become aware of them. Men being what they are, nobody is too keen to start hostilities. Some bright spark calls out:

'Oi, Fritz, you speakada English?'

To the normal British squaddie, this form of address would be enough for any foreigner to understand. The Germans, being European and not half-illiterate islanders, would have at least one of their number who would be able to converse in some form of simple English.

'What you want, Tommy?'

'Got any Schnapps?' A longish pause,

'Ja, you have English cigarettes?'

And so an arrangement would be made for a rendezvous the following night, to the mutual benefit of all concerned. These exchanges went on for about three weeks before some officer let the cat out of the bag. We heard that 'Wingy' threw a fit but nobody was ever hauled over the coals for these profitable escapades. One way or another, these unauthorised jaunts to add to our rations went on throughout the campaign.

One fine day there was myself and my mates Reggie Dennis and Albie, sitting by the truck (we were off the carriers for a spell), when our Company Commander Peddler Palmer's runner came over and told me and Reggie that we were to report to Company HQ at the double.

'What's wrong now?' says I.

'Don't know, mate,' says the runner.

So we jump in the truck and off we go.

'Perhaps it's our turn for a bit of leave,' says Reggie.

'We ain't so lucky as that,' says I.

We present ourselves to Peddler, who is being fussed around by his batman, a sort of officer's skivvy. We tried to remember what we had done wrong and why we were being hauled over the coals.

'Turner, give these two men a drop out of my bottle.' (Turner being the batman in question.)

Turner looks down his nose, thinking no doubt that we are below drinking with his beloved Captain. However, he duly supplies the two tumblers of whisky and slinks away muttering to himself that he doesn't know what the world is coming to.

As for us, we both supped up with speed, just in case Peddler suddenly came back to his senses.

'I cannot believe what I'm about to tell you two,' says Peddler. 'You are both going to South Africa for a tour of duty.'

Deathly silence on our part.

'You've both been picked out of the hat to join a party to escort prisoners of war to Durban. You leave tonight with B echelon. Make your way to Alex and report to GHQ. Why they see fit to reduce my sections I've yet to find out. The two of you had better get on your way. Dismissed.'

14

South Africa

It took us four days to make the journey to Alexandria, then on to Cairo, and from there to the Middle East base camp at Ismailia, the place made famous by the 1965 film *The Hill*. The film depicted, with absolute truthfulness, the daily routine of life in the infamous military prison. This was the first time we had seen the place but we had heard all about the goings-on there. All the fresh drafts from home and other stations received their initiation at this hell on earth. The bullshit was unimaginable.

Along with about fifty other men from other units stationed at the front, we were showered, had our hair cut, and were given the usual delousing (a very necessary operation). Then we were given new kit and long lectures on how to behave when we arrived in Durban.

'Never talk or associate with the natives.'

Needless to say, all this chat was going in one ear and quickly out of the other. All we wanted was to get on our way before some brass hat changed his mind. As it turned out we needn't have worried. After about three days we were introduced to the ship that was going to transport us to dreamland, a land free of bullets and flies.

It turned out to be the sister ship to the old First World War trooper, the *Hampshire*, the ship that had taken Reggie and myself from Southampton to Karachi. The only difference being that the *Dunera*, which had originally taken us from India to Palestine, was at least fifteen years older than the *Hampshire*, which made it a very old tub indeed. Reggie and I knew only too well what to expect once this ancient trooper hit the high seas, but at least we were not in the hold on this trip.

The hapless Italian prisoners were loaded aboard, and that night the boat slipped its moorings and we were off, down through the lower half of the Suez Canal, past the old coaling station at Aden and out into the broad expanse of the Indian Ocean. At midday the temperature reached 150°F. The days slid quietly past until we reached the Madagascar Strait. It was there that the seas hit us.

The storm was unbelievable. We had the nightmare experience of looking down and seeing the black sky, and then looking up to stare in abject terror at the foaming waves. The storm remained trapped in my memory for years afterwards, and never again would I be happy about voyages at sea. On top of the noise of the storm we could hear the wailing of the prisoners, battened down in the depths of the holds, all watertight doors clamped firmly shut.

After about seven days the ship finally made landfall off the coast of Africa. We tied up alongside a quay that was filled with cheering men, women and children. Before we disembarked we were told that we were to report to a general office in Durban every Monday morning. Other than that, we would be taken care of. It wasn't until we actually stepped on to terra firma that we understood just how we were going to be taken care of.

Two at a time we were thrust into waiting cars, not by the army but by South African families, and whisked off to their homes. I got separated from Reggie in the scramble and eventually me and another bloke found ourselves at a large, imposing residence way out in the sticks. The lawn of this establishment was almost the size of the regimental parade ground at Meerut. It came complete with an oversized swimming pool. As we swept into the grounds of this mansion we were waved at by a couple of African women who were sweeping the drive. It didn't look dirty to me, but they were sweeping it anyway. In no time at all we were ensconced in a small building which had been erected for this special occasion. We stayed with this family for the whole six weeks we were in Durban.

We had the use of a gigantic American Chrysler, freedom to go wherever we wanted and were invited out to parties every night. In some cases the female population even came to blows over who owned who, and they weren't all young women. Their mothers were also not slow in effecting a capture.

The family that owned this establishment went by the name of Anderson and they were very proud of their Scottish origins. They had a daughter aged about sixteen who insisted on escorting us to all the dances and parties.

We were only too aware that before very long we would be going back to the flies and filth and the killing. There was a short-age of eligible young Englishmen in the colony, and if the families could have married us off to their daughters they would have done so. Seeing that the Anderson family owned, or partly owned, the *Natal Daily News*, I would have been on to a good thing. But I refused to bite. Somehow I managed to put in place a mental barrier against personal involvement. I used to carry around the letters I had received from Freda and I would read those letters time and time again. More than anything, this exercise kept me in the real world. I was twenty-two years old and still a virgin.

I had never before experienced the absolute domination of one race by another. We would be at one of the many dances, and eventually, fed up with the never-ending lemonade, would launch out into the streets looking for the nearest bar. Once, a crowd of us finished up drinking in a house full of the native population, a real, genuine, knees-up. It must have been about three in the morning when the Red Caps found us lying in the gutter. After a few hours in the nick, we were taken before the military authori-ties and given a right dressing down. Some of us could still not stand upright, including yours truly. Once again it all went in one ear and straight out of the other.

The lad I was staying with went by the name of Les Dawlish, and he came from Yorkshire. One fine day, we were out in the Chrysler with another couple of lads when we were thumbed down by two women. They looked as if their sell-by date had long gone. They wanted a lift home: would we oblige? We pulled them both aboard and finally arrived at a farm, way out in the middle of nowhere.

Hardly had we got into the place when the two women started undressing. In no time at all, Les and one of the other lads were banging away in the bedroom. Having finished the first course, up comes the coffee and grub.

'Where's your husbands then?' I ask.

'Oh, them, look out of the window.'

Sure enough, almost on the horizon, were two men, slogging their guts out at whatever goes for work on a Boer farm.

'Don't worry about them, it'll be dark before they get back.'

Still I didn't bite, so it was left to Les and the other chap who hadn't had his turn the first time around to do the servicing for the second time. I was certain that these two women could have kept it up all day long and still come up for more. This couple were by no means out of the ordinary; it was quite common to be invited to someone's house for a party, and when you arrived the women would be in their dressing gowns ready for the fray. At the end of the six weeks Les actually asked me if I was queenie. I said that I didn't think I was. On the other hand, I was a lusty twenty-two-year-old: something must have been wrong with me. Think of the chances I missed!

When the ship took us back to Egypt after six – or was it seven? – weeks of heaven on earth, I couldn't restrain my emotion. As we pulled away I went below decks because I couldn't face the fact that this dream was ending. The trip back was in a much larger vessel, a modern passenger liner. Four days later we were back in Alex, having our last night on the town before getting back to normal.

15

Crusader

By the time we got back to base it was well into October 1941.
Reggie and myself had been ordered to Cairo to collect two new
vehicles and some kit. From there we were to make our way back
up through the desert to our unit. This was a journey of about
nine hundred miles, which we were expected to cover in five days.
Luckily the weather was getting cooler.

We scrounged a couple of days in the cesspits of Cairo and then
reported to the battalion base where we collected a brand new
carrier, a refurbished fifteen hundredweight truck and three lads
who had just got off the boat from Blighty.

We decided that in order to make better time we would try to
leave the coast road and cut over the escarpment to the Sofafi Fort.
This was not a well-known track. From the escarpment we could
see for more than ten miles and we watched with interest the
German and Italian planes bombing and strafing the long columns
of our supply vehicles. This went on all the time so we decided
that it would be safer to kip down during the day and move during
the night. Two lonely vehicles up on the escarpment, with no
cover, was too tasty a target for any stray enemy fighter. We had
the confidence to travel in this way because, by now, we had a lot
of experience of the desert, and, luckily, we didn't have an officer
or senior NCO to contradict us. We reported to Battalion HQ on
the evening of the sixth day. The holiday was over.

For most of the battalion our apprenticeship in the art of war
had been a gradual process. Since leaving India our weapons were

always at the ready and we had learnt that carelessness could bring sudden death. The Germans were very dangerous and we expected them to hit in the next few weeks. Would our apprenticeship give us the edge to survive this new threat? We knew things would get worse before they got better but we believed that we would win in the end.

Around 10 November the company was mustered for a talk by our Brigadier, one Jock Campbell, who was revered as a leader by all ranks of the brigade. He told us that Rommel was going to attack Tobruk, which was a thorn in his side. Australian forces had holed up in this small port and were resisting all attempts by the Germans to capture them. We were told that our commanders had decided to forestall Rommel's grandiose ideas by mounting an offensive which would end the German reign of terror and capture or kill the lot of them. This offensive was to be code-named Crusader, and it was scheduled for 16 November, in six days' time.

Jock Campbell wished us luck, rations were distributed and we were told to get as much rest as possible. There wasn't a lot of jollity. For the next few hours men sat and wrote letters, played cards and stacked up the gear that wasn't important to survival. This would be left with B echelon until the battle was over.

On the night of the 16th the rains started. We didn't have the luxury of tents and it wasn't long before we were all soaking. By the morning of the 17th we were on our start lines, and I would say that there wasn't a truly happy man to be found anywhere. Our fight would be known as the Battle of Sidi Rezegh, and it became the benchmark for all future battles. The next ten to twelve days and nights were to be the bloodiest and the most frightening the battalion had yet experienced both in length and sheer brutality. Other battles would be just as bloody but they were shorter and interrupted by periods of rest, moments when the battle went off the boil. This was not the case at Sidi Rezegh.

There were about six hundred tanks involved on both sides, not counting armoured cars, plus about twenty thousand men, all striving to kill, disable or capture the opposition. While this was going on the guns would lob shells into this maelstrom of men and machines hoping against hope that the targets they were firing at were the enemy; but, remember, a position held by the enemy at two o'clock could be overrun fifteen minutes later and the shells would land on our own lads.

The man in charge of the British Army was General Auchinleck, known as 'the Auk'. He was down in Cairo, fourteen hundred miles to the rear, unlike Rommel who was always right up in front with his leading elements. In the field our bacon would be saved by the brigadiers, men like 'Strafer' Gott and the afore-mentioned Jock Campbell.

The fight started at a fever pitch, and the mayhem and murder carried on until neither side had anything left to fight with. What remains vividly in my mind is the sacrifice of our tank crews, who were ordered to charge dug-in anti-tank guns. Most of them never got more than a hundred yards past the start line. We watched helpless while the 22nd Armoured Brigade was blown to pieces attempting to advance over dead-flat terrain into the mouths of the waiting guns.

As far as I remember, deadlock was reached on the evening of the 26th or 27th. Both sides had literally fought each other to a standstill. Between the start of the battle and the end, an area of roughly fifty square miles became littered with the burning and smashed-up remains of more than eight hundred armoured vehi-cles, hundreds of dead and rotting bodies and a dense pall of smoke thickened with the stench of rotting flesh.On the last evening we were told that we would pull back at first light. However, when we stood to at dawn, it was obvious that Rommel had anticipated us. He had withdrawn the battered remains of his forces and left the field to the British. We could hardly believe our eyes. During the night we had been on constant alert and could clearly hear the clanking of German tanks. We naturally assumed that Rommel was getting ready for another go.

As the first rays of sunlight spread across the battlefield all that was visible was the remains of the previous day's bloodletting. We couldn't see the enemy, nor could we hear them. The impossible had happened – Rommel had retreated. There were no shouts of victory, only a feeling of utter relief that there would be no more blood spilt this day. There were too many corpses littering the field of battle for any sense of general jubilation. We had stood our ground and had the satisfaction of realising that these so-called invincible Germans could be defeated at their own game. The order came for us to move forward until contact was made.

Next we got the order that the Support Group was to advance and to keep in contact with Rommel's rearguard forces, harass them and slow down their retreat, so that the regrouped remnants of the 7th Armoured Division could put them all in the bag – some hope.

We were only too happy to comply with the order as it got us on the move, away from the stomach-wrenching duty of collecting the corpses. In the heat the dead quickly began to rot, and the stench was overpowering. The worst thing was extracting the bodies from burnt-out tanks, leaning into the blackened turrets and pulling out charred body parts with hooks tied to sticks. And, as always, the flies – millions of them, feasting on the putrid flesh and adding to the general horror that goes with cleaning up a battlefield. Luckily, 2nd RB only got this duty once; usually it was up to the Pioneers to tidy up the mess.

We made contact the following day. We and our supporting group of artillery and their twenty-five-pounders gave the Germans as hard a time as we could. Sometimes we got in front of them, more often than not we gave them broadsides from their flanks. As a force we were far too small to engage fully. We could only swat at them, and this we continued to do over a distance of some five hundred miles until, one by one, our vehicles gave up the ghost. We had shot our bolt; our clothing had been reduced to rags, we had gone for days without a wash, we were living on a diet of hard tack and once again we were infested with lice. To say that we were browned off is to put it mildly. Somewhere between Benghazi and Tripoli, the word at last came over that we were to pull back. Back, in fact, all the way to Cairo, two thousand-odd miles away. It was the end of 1941.

By luck, our losses in men had not been heavy. We were almost up to strength, the proportion of new intake to the old regulars being about five to one in favour of the new lads. Once we were back behind the lines the older hands tended to keep aloof from the new lads fresh out from Blighty. As time went by and more and more new men were brought under the battalion colours, and the older men were either sent back for a base job or, luckier still, sent home, these attitudes gradually faded. Us three, me, Reggie and Albie, never termed ourselves 'old soldiers', but we weren't conscripts, we were regulars, and that made a difference.

It took us about three weeks to make the journey back to base. There we could spend all day in the showers. New clothing and new weapons were issued as a matter of course although as Riflemen we kept our old rifles, mainly because we knew that they were all zeroed in to perfection. Our rifles had kept us alive. We trusted them and didn't want to change them.

16

The Cloak and Dagger Stuff

After a week of cleaning up, each of the four companies was given five days' leave in Cairo, starting with us, A Company. What luck! We were transported to Cairo and then once again left to our own devices. First we went to the pay office and drew what money we had in credit, then we had to find lodgings. Easy enough, as we would be surrounded by the natives offering us 'Best bed in Cairo, Johnnie?' Then off to the nearest bar to get a drink.

The city was a den of iniquity; all the vices were on offer. Whisky was drunk in pint glasses, and the bands in the so-called nightclubs played Westernised music from behind wire mesh. The mesh protected them from the beer bottles that were thrown from all directions every time they played a wrong note. Fights would start at the slightest provocation. Nearly all of us had some form of armament so shoot-ups were commonplace. We thought it was more dangerous in the nightclubs of Cairo than it was in the desert. A lot of the older hands were still operating the Milton's dodge, so we always had plenty of the necessary.

The five days went by all too quickly and we returned to base by the Canal. About a dozen of us were sitting under the sweltering sun, being attacked by the usual hordes of flies and intent on a game of pontoon, when over comes the company runner. I was to report to the Battalion Office 'ack dum', which was army slang for 'at once', (we still talked in a form of pigeon Hindustani).

I presented to the officer in charge, who looked at me as if I was something the cat had dragged in.

'You seem to have made a name for yourself, Gregg.'

'Yes, sir? How's that, sir?'

'The office had to send a report into Cairo about the reserve dump you and your section discovered. You must report to 14 Military Mission at Telekabir Barracks in the morning. Take all your kit and don't ask me what it's all about. You know as much as I do.'

Off I went, completely mystified. We all racked our brains as to what 14 Military Mission might be. Nobody had a clue.

Next morning I arrived at Telekabir Barracks where I was escorted to a small room by a Red Cap who looked more like a tailor's dummy than a member of His Majesty's Forces. There I was told to wait.

The office was devoid of any furniture except an army-issue office table and a couple of straight-back chairs. All sorts of things were going through my mind. I wasn't actually worried, but I had a sense of foreboding, not having a clue what it was all about. Then in walks this bloke dressed in civvies.

'Rifleman Gregg?'

'Yes.'

'Take a chair.'

He brings out a folder from a battered old briefcase.

'You were in charge of a section on a recce about six weeks ago?'

'I've been on a lot of patrols.' I was being very guarded. What was he getting at?

'You pinpointed a fuel dump fourteen miles west of Benghazi?'

'Yes. There were six of us in the patrol.'

'But you, being the senior rank, were in charge?'

'I haven't got a rank, I'm just a Rifleman.'

'You were in charge of the recce?'

'I had the most service in.' I omitted to tell the man that I was only senior to Reggie by a matter of two hours.

'But you were more or less in charge?'

'I suppose so.'

'This took place some four hundred miles behind the enemy lines?'

'Well, we often operate in places like that.'

'How did you find your way back to your unit? What I'm trying to get at is the fact that you had to make your way inland over featureless desert and yet apparently you managed to find your way without too much difficulty.'

'Any of us could do it,' I said. 'And, as for being featureless, that's not exactly true. In fact it's quite easy.'

'OK,' says the mystery man, 'let's go and eat.'

He takes me into the Officers' Mess where I had the best meal I'd eaten for years,

'Do you always eat like this?'

I was beginning to get this man's measure now. Whatever he wanted of me it had something to do with a knowledge of the desert. Perhaps I was in for a cushy job with the brass? The upshot was that he wanted me to report to a certain Major Peniakoff who was located in a fort about a hundred miles south of Sollum. I was to assist this major, whoever he was, in any way that he thought fit. Still nothing about the actual work involved.

I would have to sign a form, says the man, then I would take a sergeant's rank. I would find my own way to Sollum and then be picked up by a detachment of the Long Range Desert Group. They would take me to the fort at Maddalena.

'Do you know of Maddalena?'

'Yes, I know how to get there.'

'That's it. I'm certain that you're just the man for the sort of job you will be undertaking.'

'Just what's that?' says I.

'Secret,' says the man.

With that I had to report to another office where a document was thrust under my nose.

'Just sign on the bottom line.'

It turned out to be an order threatening all sorts of trials and tribulations if I ever disclosed anything about the coming job. I signed it without a second's thought. I was then given a form denoting my higher rank (with more pay) and told to get up to the desert as best I could.

'But don't hang around' was his parting shot.

And so off I went to find some transport up to Sollum.

The man who had interviewed me found me later on in the day, in a bar called the Americana, a well-known drinking den in the heart of the city. He said he'd been chasing all over town looking for me. There was a plane going up to Sollum the next morning at 6.30 sharp and he wanted me on it.

Off I went to get well and truly sloshed. I was already beginning to have doubts about what I had let myself in for. I had been asked to take stripes before but that would have meant going to a different company, and I just didn't like the idea of leaving my mates. In those periods of constant danger, men get used to each other; you know what to expect and how far to go. The bonding in these close relationships makes life that much more bearable. As it was, I was beginning to wonder when, if ever, we would all be together again. So in the end I didn't get sloshed, just mildly merry.

The next morning, as the sun began to light up the sky over the city, I was transported to the small airfield at Mena, and in no time I was on my way in an old Blenheim bomber. The pilot, an Aussie of indeterminate age, greeted me:

'Jump aboard, Pom.'

His mate, another Aussie, instructed me to make myself comfortable, and to make sure that the guns were loaded, 'just in case'. I took one look at the pair of rusty old Brownings which served as armament and promptly dozed off.

When I woke up, we were lining up for the airstrip at Sollum.

17

The Libyan Arab Force Commando

The airstrip at Sollum was as basic as it was possible to get: a cleared strip of earth and a solitary mud-walled building which doubled as a storeroom and living quarters for the two RAF ground crew who manned the place. The old Blenheim roared off into the sky, leaving yours truly sitting on his bundle of kit munching away at his last piece of melted chocolate.

I had almost given up the ghost when a cloud of dust heralded the arrival of a patrol of the Long Range Desert Group.

'Been waiting long, mate?' was the cheery greeting and off we set for the long traipse over the desert to Maddalena.

Fort Maddalena was one of a series of mud and sand defence structures built by the Italians during their occupation of Libya in the 1930s. From these forts the local commanders would sally forth against the Bedouin tribesmen who constantly harassed their lines of communications. The methods used to subdue the tribes were brutal and simple. They would take the captured leaders up in an aircraft and drop them alive, down into any Bedouin encampment they could find.

Not surprisingly, the Bedouin hated the Italians. When the chance came to get revenge they gladly sided with the British forces whose representative came in the form of the rotund Major Peniakoff, a Belgian by birth, a Muslim by faith, and a devout Anglophile by nature. Popski, as he was known, travelled around the far reaches of the Western Desert, recruiting the Senussi Bedouin as information gatherers. The Bedouin, led by Peniakoff and his assistant, Sergeant Terry MM, carried on their clandestine operations under the name of 'The Libyan Arab Force Commando'. This was the unit I had been seconded to.

I was dropped off at the fort which I already knew from patrols with the Rifle Brigade. There was no sign of life. Just where was this mysterious major? I ran him to ground in a large room, sitting in a tin bath having water poured over him by a small Arab boy. I thought here was a man to whom the usual protocol of command meant very little. And I was right; he turned out to be a true man of action, who hated the German race with a white-hot intensity. He was also a man of few words.

The young Arab boy, Ahmed, was the sole survivor of an Italian air attack. Popski had found him wandering in the burning ruins of his home. The major had taken it upon himself to look after the boy, and in return Ahmed regarded the major as a sort of god. Everywhere the major went the boy went too.

The major finished his bath and while Ahmed cooked the evening meal he gave me a rundown of what he expected of me. His first question was straight to the point, no time-wasting: could I find my way to Siwa Oasis? I started to warm to the man. I said yes. Then he said:

'You can bundle up any clothing that bears any resemblance to a military uniform. In future you'll wear this.'

Ahmed brought in some rough linen underwear and a long Arab dress and a dirty length of linen to wrap around my head.

'If these boys see a uniform they tend to shoot first. They bury their mistakes.'

He went on to explain how he worked. He and his accomplice, Sergeant Terry, toured the outer reaches of the desert visiting small bands of Bedouin. From them they gathered information about the whereabouts of enemy formations, their fuel, ammunition and food dumps. In return for this they would hand over sacks of salt, sugar, tea and any equipment the Bedouin needed.

He said that he would send me messages telling me where to take the goodies he had promised. Any important information would be handed over to me by the tribe in question and I would then take it to the Long Range Desert Group operating out of Siwa Oasis. The LRDG would use the intelligence to inflict as much damage on the enemy as possible.

'And by the way,' he said before we got our heads down, 'don't get caught by the Germans or Italians, especially the Eyeties. They shoot spies.' I slept very fitfully that night.

In the morning Ahmed cooked a huge fried breakfast and the work started. I was to deliver the goodies to an encampment about a hundred and twenty miles west of Siwa. A guide would be at the oasis to see me in. I was then to return to the fort and hang around until the major or Sergeant Terry put in an appearance. If any enemy patrols started poking around I was to hide until they left. Then I was issued with a battered Austin A40 pickup.

'Better check it through,' says Popski.

The next morning, I filled the truck with fuel and water and set off to follow the almost invisible track to Siwa Oasis, about one hundred miles to the south. The major had already left, lumbering out of the fort astride a vicious looking camel, with Ahmed following behind on another. And that was me for the next couple of months, a glorified bagman, rendezvousing all over and far out into the desert, not being able to speak a word of the lingo, all on my Tod Sloan. Popski's advice, 'Whatever you do, don't get yourself captured', was always in the back of my mind.

After the first delivery I made my way back to the fort, expecting a couple of days rest before the major returned. Some hope.

Waiting for me at the fort were a couple of tribesmen. They had a message from the major, complete with map reference. At the bottom of the note was written one word: 'immediate'. This meant a journey deep into the southern edge of the Western Desert, five hundred miles there and back.

I started out after first light to get in as many miles as possible before the heat of the day made any form of travel unbearable. This became a pattern. Near midday I would look out for a spot which might give some form of protection and shade. In midsummer the temperature would reach almost boiling point, so during the hours of mind-bending heat I would lay low until the cool of the evening allowed the journey to continue. Once settled and camouflaged, safety from detection by marauding aircraft was guaranteed.

I arrived at the rendezvous at the end of the second day. The two Bedouin were waiting for me. Their camp lay on the outer edges of a small oasis and they guided me in with uncanny precision. I was greeted by the male members of the tribe who offered me tea. The tea was not the normal stuff, it was mint tea, and the method of brewing it consisted of pouring the boiling mixture into a container with roasted peanuts. After a good swill around the liquid was then poured back into the pot and boiled again. Then it would be poured back over the peanuts. On this occasion this ritual took about thirty minutes, but I have known it to last over an hour. It is a solemn process, a holy duty to an honoured visitor. After the tea came the feasting, mainly roasted lamb or gazelle and, of course, the time-honoured chapattis.

In less than four weeks, I travelled nearly four thousand miles. All the time I prayed that the pickup would not break down and maroon me, turning me into bleached bones. Then I discovered that the Long Range Desert Group had workshop facilities which I took advantage of to give the old Austin pickup a good going-over.

Back in the fort the messages continued to come in, sometimes from the major, sometimes from Sergeant Terry, all marked 'immediate attention'. On one occasion I came near to calamity. It was my own fault. I had begun to get careless.

The rendezvous on this trip was quite near the Benghazi–Tripoli coast road. The only sure way to find the encampment was to travel on the road itself, which was alive with enemy traffic. I arrived about three hours earlier than I had expected and was waiting about two miles off the road when I realised that I was in danger of being seen by enemy aircraft. So, instead of waiting until nightfall, I decided to throw caution to the wind, go in, get the job done and get out that night. The fact that I would be travelling along the road in a British truck was not all that much of a problem. The Germans had captured and were using quite a lot of our vehicles.

What almost did for me was a traffic jam. At first everything went fine. I only had two or three miles left to cover when one of their tank transporters came to a sudden halt in a position which made it impossible for me to round it. I sat in that pickup for nearly an hour expecting any moment to be accosted by an inquisitive German or Italian. It didn't happen and eventually I moved on. I made the contact in full view of the enemy traffic roaring east and west along that endless strip of black tarmac. I would never allow myself to get into that predicament again. When I told Popski what had happened, he just said: 'Why worry? You got away with it, that's the main thing.'

What probably saved me was that after a couple of weeks I had stopped wearing the clothes that Popski had given me and gone back to my general-issue khaki drill. I was covered in dust and looked military, so I was able to blend in with the general traffic on the road.

After some months of this dodging around the Blue (which is what we called the desert), I received a note saying the major would be at the fort on a certain day. As we ate our evening meal he told me the news:

'Terry's gone back to his unit. This operation is being run down, I have to report back to Cairo, you are to proceed to Siwa. Major Sterling wants a driver to assist their doctor. You can leave in the morning.' A man of few words, that's how he told me about my new posting. Next morning we said our farewells and wished each other a long life.

I don't know what happened to Ahmed; he was a nice kid. I suspect the major took the boy with him. Some months later reports began to circulate about a tearaway unit that went under the name of Popski's Private Army, a small force operating hundreds of miles behind the lines and doing violent damage to the enemy. Yes, I thought, that's the major.

18

The Long Range Desert Group

The cloud of dust bearing down on the fort signified the approach of the Long Range Desert Group truck that was to take me to Siwa Oasis to start my new duties. The LRDG was made up of odds and sods from New Zealand, Australian and British regiments. It was their job to get around behind enemy lines to cause maximum disruption and chaos.

I arrived in Siwa, introduced myself and was issued with a compass and enough maps to take me to Timbuktu if necessary. Then I was introduced to my new vehicle, a thirty-hundredweight Chevrolet, equipped with a box of rations, a twenty-gallon drum of water and two forty-gallon drums of fuel clamped to the floor. I had my own weapons and plenty of ammo. Then I was given a map reference and, without further ado, was sent on my way.

I knew the area I was heading for and made contact late on the second day. As soon as I arrived, I was told to get some food down me because I would be going straight back to Siwa, with three injured men. As I left I was given a few words of encouragement and told to look after the three men and to try not to shake them about too much. That was my first job with the LRDG. From late May to early October I crossed the lonely wastes of the desert, bringing home the lads who had been wounded, sometimes on my own, sometimes with the doctor. If they were in a really bad way another lad would be detailed to come with us to help out. My job was to get them from A to B in the shortest possible time. If the vehicle broke down and became immovable we would be marooned, hundreds of miles from any chance of rescue. However, the old American Chevrolet two-tonner took everything that was thrown at it. It just went on and on.

During the time I spent with the LRDG I never fired a shot in anger. My mates back in the Rifle Brigade were being slaughtered at places called 'Gazala' and 'Knightsbridge'. My main problem was enemy aircraft.

Once I collected a lad who had been badly shot up when his patrol had engaged a food and fuel convoy on the road west of Derna. I picked him up under cover of darkness but by the time I pulled out from the rendezvous it was getting light. This was bad news, and normally the whole patrol would have made tracks to the south and stayed put until the following night. But the lad was in a bad way. The officer in charge asked me if I thought I could make it. If the lad was to have a chance I would have to leave as soon as possible, so I did. I drove off, leaving the patrol camouflaging their vehicles to hide themselves from the aircraft that would come looking for them at first light.

I had gone about fifty miles inland before I was spotted by an enemy fighter. The method of foiling aircraft attack in the open desert is quite simple. The plane, or planes, would generally attack from behind. What you had to do then was a complete 180-degree turn to face the oncoming attacker. This put the plane at a distinct disadvantage: he couldn't dive towards you as he would finish up diving into the ground. So he was forced to fly over you, then he would bank round for another go, at which point you did another 180-degree turn to face him so that he was back to square one. This game of cat and mouse would end when the pilots began to run out of fuel. This was the only method of avoiding being shot up, and could only be carried out in an open, flat place like the Western Desert. Three times during that long day we were subjected to attacks, until, as night fell, I made a last compass bearing and reached Siwa. The lad lived to fight another day.

In the first week of October the whole outfit was called to the centre of the encampment at Siwa and told that, because of the seriousness of the situation at Alamein, we were to return to our units. I was going back to the real world. I looked forward to getting back with the friends who really mattered to me, my true mates who, through hardship, had learnt to put their life in trust in each other. Men who, like me, knew no other life but that of kill or be killed.

19

Back in the Fold

We set off in convoy to drive back to the Alamein line. Leaving Siwa, we swung north to cut across the Qattara Depression, a sea of sand chequered with patches of salt marsh and bog. It lay at the southern end of the British line which stretched twenty-five miles from the tiny railway station at Alamein on the coast, south to the escarpment which formed the edge of the Depression.

Although it was thought to be impassable there were ways through it, and, although it was not mapped, small groups could get through if they had knowledge of the area. We knew it like the backs of our hands. We crossed in two days. To get out of the Depression you have to climb a five-hundred-foot escarpment. We coaxed the lorries to the top, from where, spread out in front of us, we could see the northern coastal plain. It was unbelievable: none of us had been this far back for months, and normally it was an empty, flat, depressing place. Now, as far as the eye could see, the scene was alive with the movement of thousands of vehicles, some going west, others returning to base to bring fresh supplies. A whole army on the move.

We drove down, passing through lines of troops, almost all of them fresh out from Britain, white faces, white knees, some of them looking completely lost. We must have seemed like creatures from another planet, filthy dirty, unshaven, and our clothing falling off our backs.

Soon after we reached ground level we stopped to brew up our breakfast rations. We were sitting around the trucks, enjoying, for the first time in months, the luxury of resting without worrying that the enemy was creeping up on us. We were approached by an ultra-smart young officer, who protested at our presence and ordered us out of his lines. None of us took the slightest notice and just went on with our meal. He went on remonstrating with us until at last our captain stood up to have a go at him. The look of disbelief on this officer's face when the captain revealed himself had to be seen to be believed. He continued to shout, we continued to eat, and his men began to take a lively interest in proceedings. One of our lads, a New Zealander, fired a long burst into the air from the Brownings which were fixed to the centre of his truck. The noise was incredible. The officer threw himself gibbering on to the deck.

'What you doing down there, mate?' says the New Zealander. 'I'm only clearing the guns.'

We finished our meal and drove off to shouts and cheering from the surrounding throng. Those men would soon be as dirty and scruffy as our mob.

I finally made it back to my old battalion. B and C Companies were doing a stint up front. A and S were having a rest. Straight over to A Company and the first person I saw was my old corporal, Ted Cunningham, now a sergeant. What a man he was, a born leader with about seven years' service behind him, a real old soldier, and then some. I was greeted with the news that there was no carrier available for me so I would have to crew up with one of the others until something became available. So, over to Reggie and Albie. I was back with my mates. We were soon swapping tales and we all agreed that I had been very lucky and that I was a right skiver, having missed all the trouble at Knightsbridge and the withdrawal along the coast.

I was sent for by the new Commanding Officer, a chap by the name of Vic Turner, who asked me detailed questions about the type of operations that I had been involved in. He was completely different from 'Wingy', the old CO: much younger and less regimental.

The very next day I was to witness what was for me a personal tragedy. One of the lads, Frankie Batt, mentioned earlier, who had arrived at the depot in Winchester on the same day as Reggie and myself, was detailed to drive a truck with a supply of mortar bombs for the companies up front. He hadn't travelled half a mile when the truck exploded, hit by a shell or a misplaced anti-tank mine, nobody knew. I immediately jumped in the carrier and belted over to what remained of Frank's truck. When we got there Frank's body was still upright behind the wheel, and I thought that by some miracle he was still alive. Ted kept his eyes on the Krauts, while I eased Frank out of the cab only to watch in horror as the bottom half of the body slithered away onto the stones and sand. There I was, covered in Frank's blood, holding his top half against my chest and at my feet the mangled remains of his bottom half. I went berserk, I was told later on that it took three lads to restrain me, I was trying to drive the carrier at the Krauts with all guns blazing. I don't remember any of it. Somehow Ted managed to calm me down. We got back to our lines and within a couple of hours he had found me some clean clothing. How he kept his own cool baffles me to this day. Ted's actions were yet another striking example of the comradeship born out of extreme danger and hardship. Alas Ted himself had only a few weeks left to live – he was killed leading a carrier section in the later stages of the march to Tunis.

We held a short service out of respect for Frank, who had been liked by everybody. The day after, Reggie, myself and Albie were detailed to collect a new carrier. After we picked it up, we painted our old mate's name on the side and silently vowed that some Kraut was going to pay for what happened to Frankie.

Having collected the new carrier, we set about getting it fit for service, making sure that the floor was well covered with sandbags, that the trackpins were well burred over and fitting our captured guns.

So there I was, back among the lads who meant the most to me. We trusted one another, we understood each other's capabilities. For the first time since I had been posted away, I felt as if I was standing on secure ground.

20

Operation Breakthrough

A few days later I was ordered to report to HQ where the CO, Vic Turner, was waiting with Ted Cunningham. Turner explained that our casualty rate had caused a severe shortage of experienced NCOs. I had already turned down the chance of promotion and the three tapes given to me when I joined the major had now been taken back. Ted asked me whether I would reconsider my earlier refusal to have my name submitted. I replied that if I could be assigned to my regular platoon and have the same crew, I would. I was told that this wasn't possible because the shortage was primarily in C and B Companies. I thanked the Colonel and gave the same excuse that I had given before: I had joined up with my friends, and, God willing, we would live together. If He wasn't willing then we would all die in the same hole as equals. Vic Turner accepted this as good an answer as he had heard. On the way back to the platoon, Ted said that he was glad in a way as he wished to keep the same gang together. Dickie Bird, our platoon officer, wished me luck and seemed relieved that he wasn't going to have to train another team.

We had now been in the desert for two and a half years, all of it in continuous contact with the enemy. The days passed and we were soon back in the old routine of patrolling by day and night. The night patrols were generally non-violent; we might get a prisoner or two or come back with intelligence. The day patrols were a different matter. They would almost always end in an exchange of fire and usually there were casualties and, more often than not, bodies to be buried.

One morning the whole company was gathered together. We were told the sad news that General 'Strafer' Gott, who had been our much admired Brigadier and was now due to take over as Commander-in-Chief, had been shot down and killed while travelling by air from Alex and that we had a new CIC, General Bernard Montgomery. We wondered what he'd be like.

Later we met Monty when he did the rounds and introduced himself personally to nearly all the troops. We were impressed by his forthrightness and this inclined us to give him the benefit of the doubt. But the truth was, we'd had so many commanders-in-chief and we'd heard it all before.

Rumours had been flying around for some time about an impending assault on the Germans. Then, on 22 October, we were told that an attack would be going in the following evening at ten o'clock. Our job was to protect the engineers while they cleared gaps in the German minefields.

There were three gaps: ours was called 'Star', and the other two were called 'Sun' and 'Moon'. We spent the rest of the day punching star-shaped holes in old petrol cans. The cans would have lighted hurricane lamps put in them and would be hung from posts driven into the ground along the edges of the star gap. The post-driving teams would work just behind the engineers who were clearing the mines. A brass hat came round to inspect how we were doing and told us: 'Prepare yourselves for some excitement.' We wondered what he meant by 'excitement' and knew he didn't mean jumping for joy. We went away to make the usual brew and write our letters home.

Monty sent round his order of the day to pep us up. This is what it said:

When I assumed command of the Eighth Army I said that the mandate was to destroy Rommel and his Army, and I said that would be done as soon as we were ready. We are ready now. The battle which is now about to begin will be one of the decisive battles of history, it will be the

turning point of the war. The eyes of the whole world will be on us,
watching anxiously which way the battle will swing. We can give
them their answer at once: it will swing our way . . . Let no man
surrender so long as he is unwounded and can fight ... Let us all pray
that the Lord Mighty in battle will give us the victory.

Well, I can't remember that we enthused too much about the Lord
giving us victory. We were just hoping that Monty wouldn't make
the usual mistake of sending our tanks hurtling into the jaws of
Rommel's 88s.

21

El Alamein:
The Butcher's Shop Opens for Business

Friday 23 October 1942 started cold and dry. We spent the first part of the day finishing the hole-punching job we had started the day before.

We would be the first to go in and the tension was felt by everybody. The usual banter that you always got before a battle was conspicuous by its absence. We all knew that this night's events were to be something different. We were kept hard at it punching out the stars on the tins, although the total needed for the job had long ago been reached. It was that old army formula: 'Keep them at it, takes their minds off what's coming.'

As the day wore on we began to relax. This was thanks to the old regular soldiers who were still with us in considerable numbers. So we brewed up the tea and remembered the old reassuring line:

'Not worth worrying about, mate. Everything comes out in the wash.'

The carriers would have the job of protection while, behind us, on foot, came the Rifle platoons banging the iron stakes into the ground and hanging up the tins with a storm lamp inside. The tins with the punched-out stars were to be placed facing back towards our own lines to guide the lads along the path the advance was to take. Behind us would come the main infantry units which, once the minefields had been breached, had to fan out and get down to the dirty business of clearing the enemy front lines.

Behind these unlucky individuals would come the tanks in support.

At eight o'clock in the evening we were told to move up to our positions, carriers to the front, the Rifle platoons right behind us. To the rear the gunners were stacking up their ammunition ready for the barrage which was due to start at 10 p.m. sharp.

Along the twenty-five-mile front, between the escarpment and the sea, it was rumoured that there was a twenty-five-pound gun every twenty-five yards. Behind the twenty-five-pounders were the sixty-pounders and behind them the howitzers. Waiting in the wings was the navy, poised with their sixteen- and twenty-inch guns, all laid on to the unsuspecting Germans and Italians. The enemy would soon be at the receiving end of an avalanche of hot, exploding metal.

And so we sat, all with our own private thoughts. This was to be the like of nothing we had yet experienced. Everybody tried to cheer everybody else up while attempting to hide their own private fears. It may have been easier for the troops who had just come up, but us old hands were under no illusions. We were all shit-scared and trying not to show it. Once the flag went up it would be easier, that we knew. In the meantime, we waited and cursed, and waited and cursed some more.

It got dark, the wind rose and a slight drizzle began to fall. Men took what shelter they could, huddling against the sides of their carriers and other vehicles. Without warning, a Very light soared up into the night sky and, as it began to descend, the first guns opened up. The whole twenty-five-mile stretch of front shook with the concussion, and a thunderous roar enveloped us as shells began to churn up the earth over which we would soon be advancing. Then the bigger guns to the rear opened up, the heavy shells going over with a strange swirling sound. A continuous stream of heavy metal passed over our heads. Then we could see the flashes out to sea as the guns of the warships added their weight to the fray. Fear vanished. We, along with thousands of other men, waited for the barrage to lift. After about twenty minutes of this infernal din we were given the order to advance.

I remember the cheers which went up, as if the whole company had been released from a hidden restraint. In front of us and around us were the engineers, lying down on their stomachs searching for mines, prodding away with bayonets, desperately feeling for the touch of metal upon metal. We moved slowly forward, the lads behind us banging in the metal rods and hanging up lighted tins. Soon the whole area was lit up like Piccadilly Circus.

By now we were being mortared and machine-gunned quite heavily. The word got through that we would have to get in front of the engineers to give them greater protection. We were not to stop and help if a carrier went up; we must keep going forward.

Our eleven carriers went straight through, much to our relief. The poor sods around us who were taking a beating, even though they were keeping themselves lower than a snake's belly.

We had been at it for about an hour when our carrier lifted up on its haunches, and came back down with one almighty thump. A track had been blown off. All three of us burst out laughing, a nervous reaction to the realisation that we were all still intact. Reggie and I got down to cover Albie as he tried to repin the broken link. It doesn't sound much, but remember that we were marooned in the noise and confusion of the bombardment. We felt very vulnerable. It was a horrific experience.

By now the battle was going full blast, and there was us, completely disabled, moving about in the open trying to get the unwieldy track back on its runners. If it had been a normal skirmish a couple of the other carriers would have come to our aid, but not tonight. Everybody was going forward – you don't stop for anyone, that had been the order and that's how it was. The repair seemed to take hours but I suppose it was only about thirty minutes. When it was fixed we frantically drove forward to take up our position with the rest of the platoon.

As soon as we had cleared the first line of minefields we witnessed something that none of us will ever forget. Lit up in the sporadic flashes of the guns, moving forward without any hesitation, came a solitary piper, walking slowly, as erect as a flagpole. We watched this apparition appearing out of the smoke behind us and slowly disappearing into the rising crescendo of battle that raged to our front. Following right on the heels of the piper came his mates, the Jocks, in full line abreast, fixed bayonets and all, straight through us and into the inferno of smoke and fire. If anyone I have ever witnessed deserved a VC, that lad deserved it.

At first light the battalion had made its first objective, but nobody knew just how forward we had managed to get. The air was thick with dust and smoke, and the terrible sounds of the wounded, crying out in anguish as the lifeblood seeped from their torn bodies. The medics had been at it all night but all around us lay dead and wounded comrades and enemies, their bodies twisted into grotesque positions by the impact of red-hot flying metal.

Tanks were burning all over the place, and this scene repeated itself all along the front. Surely it would all be over in a few hours? We asked ourselves the question we had asked time and time before: just how much can a man stand?

We never found the answer. We were given the usual order: 'Hold the line until the next contingent comes up.' Every now and then things would stop as we took on fresh supplies, ammo and the like. We stayed in the battle for the next two days after which we were finally pulled back for a much needed one-day rest.

On 26 October we got new orders.

22

Snipe:
2nd RB Open the Gate

The battalion was to move forward under cover of darkness until we came within earshot of the German lines. As before, there was to be no hanging back to aid or assist anybody in distress. We were to move forward as steadily and as quietly as possible, no shouting and screaming, no revving engines.

At about midnight we moved off. After about an hour, and with constant halts to assess our position, contact was made with a small enemy force, some prisoners were taken and sent back through the lines. Then we moved forward again, unchallenged.

Eventually we were called to a halt. Dickie Bird, our Company Commander, came round and told us to unload everything from the carriers. We had reached the point of no return; this was where we would dig in and this was where we would fight.

''Ow long we going to be 'ere for, sir?' pipes up Albie.

'I know no more than you do, lad,' replies Birdie.

We knew the carriers could be turned into smouldering wrecks and we had no wish to be in or near them when that happened. Albie jumped in and drove it as far back behind our position as possible, to where we could unload all our long accumulated and treasured gear. Out came bedding rolls, all the grub and water, a couple of jerrycans full of petrol, two German heavy machine guns, four boxes of ammo, two rusting Brownings, a couple of Brens and our trusty Lee-Enfields.

Then we dug ourselves a nice trench, Reggie jumped in and made the inevitable brew, while Albie and myself concentrated on loading the ammo belts for the Brownings and the German machine guns. Dickie Bird came round at about four or five in the morning, and he stared into the bottom of the pit and said:

'Might as well send the rest of the battalion back, enough armament here to see off an army.' Then he broke the news that we were to sit tight and defend the anti-tank guns from all assaults by the enemy. We were right on the edge of the enemy positions; any attempt to fall back if things went wrong would mean our certain destruction. It also meant that any attempt to reinforce us would be doomed to failure. So began the legendary Snipe action.

The battalion had formed a rough sort of oval shape, along about a thousand or maybe fifteen hundred yards of line. There was a gap of about fifty yards between each section. We were on a slight rise of no more that five metres. We did not know it but we faced the German 90th Light Division, the 21st Panzer Division and the Italian Trieste Division.

At first light we poked our noses over the ridge. In front of us were hordes of Germans, sitting by their trucks and tanks, calmly eating whatever Germans eat for their breakfast. They looked at us in sheer amazement. The silence seemed to go on for hours, then they dived for cover.

For the next ten to fifteen minutes nothing happened. After about half an hour they made their first move. Two medium tanks and an armoured car approached the position. To our right was one of our anti-tank guns and between us and it was another carrier section. In front of the anti-tank gun was a rifle section, placed to defend it from infantry assault.

The three men crewing the anti-tank gun allowed the three enemy vehicles to get to two hundred yards, right until they could see the drivers' eyes peering through their front-vision slits, and then our gunners let fly. Within half a minute the three vehicles had disintegrated into balls of flame.

After that their infantry attacked and all hell was let loose. We were at the top of a sixteen-foot slope and this was their undoing. They were mown down, some of them no more than twenty feet away from our guns. This continued for a short period of time, then, as smartly as the attack had come in, it faltered to a close. Then there was one of those lulls. The Germans pulled back, we lowered our sights and made a brew. They sent in another attack, to no avail. Then another lull, another brew-up.

The position to our right had gone very quiet. Reggie crawled over to them; they were all goners, they had taken a direct hit from a mortar. Dickie Bird came over and told us to move our position further right to cover the guns. This we did and on the way we helped ourselves to all the ammunition and any food and water left by the unfortunate lads who had copped it.

A white flag went up from the German lines. A German NCO came to a point about forty yards away from us. Over went one of our officers, as cool as a cucumber. The German asked if we would allow them time to recover their wounded. We agreed. The German medics collected the wounded, leaving the dead scattered where they had fallen (which was common practice on both sides; there is no point in transporting a dead body from one place to another). Not a shot was fired, we made a brew and the CO repositioned the anti-tank guns.

Next we heard the telltale signs of more trouble. First the rumble and roar of heavy diesel engines warming up, followed by dust clouds as a force of about twenty tanks and armoured cars came rumbling towards us, closely followed by their infantry. Our anti-tank gunners allowed them to get close enough to make every shot count, then, while the guns turned the front rank of tanks into blazing hulks, we massacred the ranks of the poor sods who were slipping and sliding up the slope in front of us. None of us enjoyed what was happening; what kept us firing was that the boot could just as easily have been on the other foot, and, in the past, it too often had been. The battlefield gave us its usual choice: to kill or be killed.

Then came a second round of collecting the wounded, followed by another abortive attack. They lost even more tanks and a lot more men. An officer from our HQ squirmed his way over to us with instructions that, if possible, two of us were to drop back and collect fresh ammo and water. He said there were some tins of soya links if we wanted them. Soya links were an American attempt to recreate sausages out of soya beans. We hated them, but they were food.

Later, a young officer appeared, introduced himself and said that he had heard we needed a hand. One look at his nice fresh complexion told us that we had a novice on our hands. He had arrived from England on the last draft. His kit was unusually clean, but he seemed a decent lad and we needed more firepower if we were to survive through the rest of the day. Reggie helped him dig a hole while, down in the small weapons pit, Albie was preparing yet another brew, making the most of the fresh water that had come up.

We gave the new lad one of the Brens. He seemed taken aback by our apparently easy-going attitude and I had to explain to him the pros and cons of the situation we were in. Albie chipped in with the advice that, if he wanted to survive, 'When we put our heads down, you do the same, don't fire in long bursts and only press the trigger if you're sure you can hit someone, we're very low on ammo.'

To finish off I told him, 'Nobody wears tin hats around here. For one thing your head will roast, and another thing is that they make too much noise, the chin straps rattle and they clang when they get bashed.' Then Reggie chipped in: 'Don't worry, mate, the things are only useful for washing in.'

To his credit, the lad accepted all this banter and within an hour it was as if we had known each other for years. Between ourselves, however, we decided to keep our eyes on him. If he got hit and left a gap we would all be at risk.

There was no way out of our predicament. Retreat was not an

option. Our only hope was to tough it out until it got dark and we could be relieved. At least we were dug in, and had the advantage of cover over the attackers. The men who were bearing the brunt of the battle, the poor sods manning the anti-tank guns, were all above ground.

Around four in the afternoon we heard the big guns opening up, and the German lines to our front erupted in clouds of dust as the shells came crashing in on the poor sods lying there. More screams and shouts, along with the sound of flying shrapnel. It was the end of the peace and quiet we had been enjoying.

Then the German guns opened up on us. Although we knew that nothing short of a direct hit could cause any real damage, and that if such a hit happened we wouldn't know anything about it.

The bombardment went on for about fifteen minutes and then stopped as suddenly as it had started. As the dust settled, we realised that all was not well with the lads to our left. Two of them had been blown to pieces, and the only survivor was a Jewish boy who went by the nickname of Izzy. Izzy was one of those rare people who never seemed to show any fear. Very few men outside his close mates knew his real first name, and we just called him Izzy — a little East End Jew boy, and one of us. The death of his two mates had sent him over the edge. With a terrible scream he rushed from cover straight towards the enemy, his Bren gun blazing away from the hip. We watched poor Izzy go down, still loading another magazine into the gun. His body shook from the fusillade of bullets hitting him. The momentum of his rush had carried him right into the German lines.

Once again everything went quiet; another three men lost, another position to cover. We learnt that Battalion HQ had been straddled with a salvo of mortars and our CO, Vic Turner, had been wounded. Luckily he was still able to walk about and keep command. Our line was now riddled with gaps. I suggested to our young officer that we had better pull further to the right in order to give the anti-tank gunners more protection. He crawled back

to the command post with this suggestion and came back with
the news that the rifle position in front of our nearest anti-tank
gun had run out of ammunition and was out of action They
couldn't withdraw because they were in full view of the enemy, so
the whole of our part of the line would have to move to the left to
cover them. We reckoned that of the twelve guns we had started
with six were still in action.

Suddenly, coming down from the rise of a feature called Kidney
Ridge, about a thousand yards to our rear, were about a hundred
of our tanks in full assault formation. They swung round to our
left. Somebody had seen the danger we were in and had organised
a rescue. The German anti-tank gunners held their fire until our
tanks were within range and then opened up. Everyone watched
in silence and dismay as one after the other of our tanks brewed up
and the rescue attempt was abandoned. About forty tanks perished
in that doomed charge, proving once again the invincibility of
well-placed anti-tank guns.

Then came a massive infantry attack. However much we fired
into them, still they came forward, climbing over the corpses of
their comrades, shouting and screaming. We were literally blowing their heads off as they tried to clamber over the edge of the
rise in front of us. It had now got so bad that it was impossible to
touch the bare metal of our weapons. When, at last, it seemed that
they were going to beat us, they hurled their tanks at our few
remaining guns. The gun to our right was now only manned by
one lad, Sergeant Callaston. Vic Turner, in full view and without
any cover whatsoever, managed to reach the gun and worked as
loader to help keep it firing.

We were fighting hand to hand when, without any warning,
salvoes from our heavy guns started to crash all around us. There
was nothing to do except get our heads down and hope that the
enemy was sensible enough to do the same. They had had enough.
Those of them still able to move ran back to the cover of their own
holes while their tanks brewed up almost on top of us.

The air was filled with the smoke and dust of battle. The enemy dead were scattered all over the ground in front of us, cries of despair coming from the poor wretches who had survived, most of them mortally wounded.

Peace of a sort descended. Men of both sides squatted down on their haunches to count the cost. Smoke from burnt-out tanks and armoured cars turned daylight into darkness. Friend and foe, we were all in a state of shock. We sensed there would be no more action this day.

After about an hour, as it was getting dark, a lone German came towards our position carrying a white flag. He stopped about fifty feet from us, and our young officer went out to meet him. The German handed over the personal things that Izzy had been carrying on him. We all gave that lad a cheer as he went back to his comrades. All over our front the enemy were yet again collecting their wounded. Were these the evil men we had been told about? The men who performed atrocities wherever they went? In our eyes they were men of honour.

After it got dark, Dickie Bird came around to tell us that from midnight onwards we were to make our way to the rear as best we could. The battalion would re-form as soon as a roll-call satisfied Colonel Turner that we were all back in the fold. A Very light soared into the night sky. Tired and weary, with hardly the strength to hold our heads up, we gathered what kit we could manage, making certain that, above all, we had our rifles and guns. Then we drifted back the thousand-odd yards to the safety of our own lines.

It started to rain. The battalion managed to assemble about half a mile behind the front line. A company of the Service Corps had been detailed to dish out a hot meal for us. We looked a sorry lot, our bodies encrusted with the usual dirt and filth, our eyes bloodshot through lack of sleep. A lot of the lads had been wounded and wore bloodstained bandages. I remember that when Vic Turner addressed us, we all gave him a big cheer.

A senior Brigadier was also present and proceeded to spout the thanks of the High Command for what we had done. The Colonel, Vic Turner, was to be recommended for the VC, which would be regarded as a battalion honour, and some other medals would be dished out, mainly to the men who had crewed the anti-tank guns. This went down well and we let forth more resounding cheers. Whether we were cheering the lads who were going to get the gongs or just cheering ourselves for still being alive, I'm not sure – bit of both, I suppose.

So ended Snipe, a battle which cost Rommel more than fifty of his much needed tanks and nobody knows how many of his men. We had many gaps in our own ranks, brothers-in-arms, some of whom had been with the battalion for more than twelve years, men who could never be replaced and who would be sorely missed. It is my belief that we were never quite the same again. The mood of not only our own battalion, but of the whole 7th Armoured Division, which had borne the brunt of the fighting for the last two and a half years, changed.

We were no longer the harum-scarum force that we had once been. All of us were now more sober, and more cautious, with an unspoken motto: 'Discretion is the better part of valour.' We all needed a rest.

Within five days we were given new kit and were back doing the job we had been doing throughout the Western Desert campaign – annoying the Hun.

We chased Rommel past Benghazi, past Tripoli, pushing him back towards Tunis. Just past Tripoli we were pulled out of the line again and it was then that I left the battalion.

23

I Become a Birdman

As I previously observed, runners coming from the direction of Battalion HQ nearly always spelt trouble.

'Company to assemble in half an hour.'

Groans all around.

'Thought this was too good to last.'

We found the new Colonel sitting on a ration box (Vic Turner had gone back because of his wounds). Our Company Commander sat alongside looking a bit peeved.

The Colonel put us at ease. 'Sit down and make yourselves comfortable, men, and stop sweating. We're not going anywhere.'

Relief all around.

The Colonel gives us the gen. A new Parachute Brigade was being formed; each battalion was expected to supply volunteers to go back to Palestine to train for it. 'Anyone who wishes to volunteer step forward.'

The Colonel might just as well have been speaking to a brick wall. Jumping out of planes? What do they think we are, barmy? Following the long, unbroken silence the Colonel added that on arrival in Palestine the volunteers would enjoy two weeks' leave before taking up any training, and if, after initial training, anyone felt uncomfortable about the idea, they would be at liberty to return to their regiment.

No sooner had the Colonel uttered these words than the whole company, almost to a man, took a smart pace forward. Two weeks there and two weeks back and two weeks leave in between? It didn't take much thinking about. Neither did it take the Colonel long to realise the trap he had dropped himself into.

'Think again,' he spluttered, almost choking himself with laughter. 'Put your names forward and they will all be put in a hat.' Ten of us came out of that hat, including yours truly.

Three days later, along with a bunch of desert dodgers from another regiment, we were on an American Liberty ship in Tripoli harbour waiting to set forth on the morning tide. It was just our luck that, with the harbour full to bursting point, six German bombers came in at sea level, skipped over the harbour wall and plastered everything with delayed action mines, plus a few bombs. Half an hour later the three tankers were on fire, including the ship alongside us and to which we were moored. It was full of ammunition. One of the tankers capsized, covering the water inside the harbour with burning fuel. At two in the morning the ammo boat alongside us blew up.

All our American crew except for the cook had hotfooted it for dry land, taking the only serviceable lifeboat. We were left to man the hoses to keep the flames at bay which threatened to engulf us. The detonations of the explosions from the burning ammunition mixed with the screams of injured and dying men turned the dark evening into a flaming nightmare.

At dawn the navy arrived to set about clearing up the mess. A small crew boarded our ship and after getting us safely out to sea handed the ship back to the Americans. Then we set sail for Haifa. We didn't get there. The blast from the exploding ammo boat had split a welded seam along the keel. The ship was sinking lower and lower in the water. By the time we made it to Alexandria, she was wallowing about like a drunken camel and we finished the journey to Palestine by train.

Our destination was a town called Sarafand which we knew of old, but it had changed. What had once been a small township was now a huge military cantonment attached to an air force base.

The next few days saw us kitted out with all sorts of weird and wonderful clothing. After about four days, with no sign of the promised leave, the training programme started, run by a sergeant who had newly arrived from Blighty. He explained what we would be doing. We would start off with a series of route marches; we hadn't done a route march since our time in India! Then we would be taught how to land safely without breaking any of our limbs, and so on and so on.

None of us intended to be so foolish as to jump from a plane, so we asked about the leave we had been promised.

'I don't know anything about any leave,' says the sergeant. 'Perhaps you'll get it when you've finished training. I'll see what I can do.'

This didn't sound too promising; something was wrong somewhere, alarm bells were beginning to ring. We started the course but baulked at the weapons training. There was not a lot anyone could tell us about how to use a gun. What did they think we had been doing for the last three-odd years. So we had to go in front of the Commanding Officer, all forty of us. We explained to him where we had come from and what we knew of real fighting. Then we suggested to him that if he wanted to keep us, we'd like the promised leave.

The result was that we got our leave, but we had no hope of getting out of the commitment. It was suggested that we old hands form a Support Group with the heavy weapons, Vickers machine guns and three-inch mortars, and that this Support Group be attached to Brigade HQ. This suited us fine. We would all be together and wouldn't have to worry about looking after the untrained lads from Blighty. If it came to a battle the new lot might get into all sorts of weird and wonderful adventures and the last thing we wanted was adventures.

The training started. We threw ourselves out of planes, ate good food and enjoyed occasional short leaves in Tel Aviv. It was an enjoyable life; after all, we were now rich: we were getting two shillings a day extra.

It still worried us, though, that we were in a unit that was, almost to a man, made up of conscripts. As far as we could make out, not one of those who had come out from England, both officers and men, had ever fired a shot in anger. They had never experienced the mind-bending horrors of shelling and mortar fire, seeing your mates cut to pieces by machine-gun fire and being ordered to hold your fire while the enemy with his deadly intentions gets ever nearer. It seemed to us that the training we were getting was useless as a preparation for the horrors to come.

It also bothered us that we were regulars and they were conscripts. We Rifles had our history, the honour of the Regiment was woven into our training, and that was important to us. These lads had none of this. Would that make a difference when the chips were down? Only time would tell.

The first planes we went up in were small American two-engined Hudsons. These planes held eight passengers and the door was only a few feet behind one of the engines. When you jumped, with the aid of a healthy kick from the man behind, you were immediately hit by the blast of the slipstream. Fear of the unknown combined with the noise and then the sudden silence as the chute opened was very exhilarating, out of this world.

On our first jump we managed to land in the middle of a field of vines. A few of the lads suffered some very nasty cuts and bruises.

Next we went up in DC3s, Dakotas, a really super plane for the job. The stick of eight increased to a stick of twenty-two, a whole platoon.

The trick was to try to land within fifty to one hundred yards of each other. This turned out to be quite difficult, but we saw the sense in the idea. So we devised a plan, which meant jumping out of the plane holding hands and linked together. This was all right in theory but what happened was that the men who jumped last ended up on top of the opened chute of the men in front, which would cause the man on top's chute to collapse. This was OK at a thousand feet, because it would reopen but it was useless at an operational height of three to four hundred feet. So, no more holding hands. We got good, though, which pleased the staff teaching us.

Another first was our unorthodox manner of getting free from the harness before landing. We were told that we would practise dropping into water. The DZ (dropping zone) being an area of the Bitter Lakes, halfway down the Suez Canal.

'No need to worry,' says the worthy who's giving us all the gen. 'The area will be alive with boats and the water isn't deep enough to drown anyone who can't swim. Lift off at daybreak tomorrow. Dismiss.'

That evening some of us were sitting in the canteen talking about this coming threat to our existence. What, we wondered, would happen if the chute came down on top of us? We could drown. Then some bright spark came up with a suggestion.

'What if we're not in the chutes when they hit the water?'

We decided that we could hit the release buckle as soon as we jumped and just hang on to the harness until we judged it safe to let go, say ten to fifteen feet above the surface.

'Suppose we misjudge?'

'It's only water, what's the worry? Better than being dragged under by a chute.'

Another consideration was that only a few seconds' delay in leaving the plane would see us dropping in the middle of the Suez Canal, which we knew was fairly distant from the Bitter Lakes and much deeper.

Bright and early next morning, we were hauled out of our nice warm beds, given a huge breakfast and loaded into four Dakotas. This was the first real exercise away from base, and the longest flight so far. I don't think any of us were in a very happy state of mind. We adopted our time-honoured solution to too much worrying about our future prospects: we got the cards out.

We had only played a couple of hands before the dispatcher started to take off the big wide doors which two men could jump through side by side. Then on goes the green light. There's much shuffling of feet, sweaty palms, the cracking of bad jokes. This is the worst part of any action, the final wait. We knew from past experience that once the red light flashed on we would all push like mad to get out.

We jumped, the chutes opened and we realised that this was another cock-up. We were almost in line with the centre of the Canal. Bash the buckle, get out of the harness and hang on for dear life. In the distance the rescue boats were churning up the water doing their best to make it to where we were going to splash in. They had a long way to go. They just made it and only two chaps were drowned. By freeing ourselves soon after the chute had opened airborne, hanging on until we were a few feet above the water and then letting go, we had avoided the chutes pulling us under. Freed of its weight, it sailed on for another fifty feet before collapsing. It could go to Suez or the South Pole for all we cared.

The next morning we were all in front of the Commanding Officer.

'What gave you the idea about detaching yourselves in midair?'

One of our number was a real old soldier named Georgie Foulks. He was a corporal and this lad had seen it all.

'If you lot think for one moment that we're going to land in the middle of a bunch of Jerries still strapped to a harness you can f*****g well think again.'

Georgie boy was marched out for swearing at a senior officer. This didn't worry Georgie too much: he'd done more time in the nick than the CO had done time in the army. The CO agreed that the idea was sound. Recognising a good man when he saw one, he let Georgie go with a warning. Georgie wasn't too happy about this as he was hoping that he would get sent back to the Rifle Brigade. Our unorthodox method of landing was left to those that wanted to do it. It never became an official drill.

Next, we were shipped without warning to a camp near Tunis. I received a letter from Reggie saying Ted Cunningham had been killed taking part in a carrier attack near Cape Bon. Reggie and Albie had lost their carrier in the same engagement. I showed the letter around and we agreed that perhaps we had done the right thing volunteering for the Paras. After three and a half years of fighting, the most important thing now was to stay in one piece.

It was while on one of the many training jumps in the area that I devised a plan to rid myself of the dodgy pay book that I had been carrying around with me, the one with the Milton's Antiseptic smears all over it. It would accidentally fall out of an unbuttoned pocket in my jumping smock. I reckoned without Sod's Law.

The jump was quite normal. Out I went. Then it dawned on me that everyone else was passing me, GOING UPWARDS. My chute hadn't opened. I finally managed to open the chute at about two hundred and fifty feet by using my legs to force the lines apart. I was too low. I hit the ground with an almighty wallop, but unfortunately not hard enough for a spell in hospital and some leave. I did manage to lose my pay book, but in the excitement my helmet came off. I was put on punishment for not having it properly secured. I think the CO was getting a bit of his own back for some of the cheek we had handed out to him and his non-coms.

The chute failed to open because of my own pig-headedness. We had spent the previous day marching to the air force base, and had been left to our own devices as to sleeping arrangements. Instead of spending the night wrapped up in a single blanket, I took the chute out of its sack and wrapped myself in it. Result: a nice, warm, cosy kip. In the morning, I stuffed the chute back in the bag as best I could. In theory, as soon as I left the plane, out would come the chute and all would be well. Except that we had never had a lecture on the danger of static electricity. I had stashed the chute away while it was still damp with dew. Result: static electricity which caused the shrouds of the chute to cling together.

We realised that we would never be going back to our mates in 2nd RB. But we were in our early twenties and had no difficulty making new friends. More to the point, we blokes had injected our battle experience into the 10th Para Battalion. This would prove vital when push came to shove in the weeks ahead.

24

Sicily and Italy

The DC3s were lined up ready for take-off, destination somewhere in Sicily. A large glider force had left a couple of hours before and we were to follow them in.

This is always a time when men keep their thoughts to themselves. For a few moments their heads are filled with the people at home, families, dreams of the future. These are moments of peace before the hurricane of noise, fire and death descends upon them. It is always the same, as it was at this moment, sitting on the cold airstrip. Then the peaceful calm was broken. Everything cancelled, stand down. Men began to laugh and joke, the tension eased; the ferryman would have to wait for a new list of passengers.

We heard that the navy had shot the gliders and the planes towing them out of the sky. Then we were told that the planes had lost their way in the dark, which we didn't believe. In the Med, if the navy hear planes they open up straight away. It turned out that our glider force had flown over the fleet somewhere off Sicily. The navy had not been told about the operation. In the dark, they heard the planes and opened up, sending fifty gliders into the drink. So we never got to see the skies over Sicily. We eventually set off by ship for Taranto in the south of Italy.

10th Battalion (us) boarded an ancient British cruiser called the *Penelope*, nicknamed 'the Pepperpot' because of the number of holes it carried, scars of previous engagements. 156 Battalion were put on board an American cruiser called *Boise*, which, being the larger of the two ships, had our heavy equipment.

So off we sail to Taranto, the plan being for the two cruisers to sail into the harbour and unload both battalions who would then clear the town of any enemy. Then we were to form a defence perimeter around the outskirts of the town.

It might have worked but for the captain of the *Boise*. He decided that his would be the first ship in. So off he goes, Yankee Doodle sailing straight towards the harbour while we watched from about two miles away. He sailed straight into a minefield, and blew up. Luckily he didn't block the harbour mouth. Then we sailed in past the poor sods who had survived the explosion swimming about in the water. We threw overboard everything that could float to help them.

Penelope opened up with her six-inch guns to discourage any of the enemy who might be thinking about making a stand. The whole mob of us disembarked without firing a shot. After almost three long years we were at last in Italia.

There were no fanfares, no charging up beachheads, no fuss, no confusion. Loaded with our kit, we walked down the gangplanks, lined up on the quay and marched off into Taranto.

As we marched silently towards the centre of the town people slowly came out of their houses to follow us. Within a short time we were surrounded by what seemed to be the whole population of this small seaport, cheering, singing and even dancing. We were not prepared for this. Baleful eyes, catcalls, jeering, and possibly being showered with refuse, this is what we had expected. Even the hardest of us began to hand out our reserve chocolate rations to the kids, who were by now climbing all over us. We didn't stop, though.

Our objective was to secure the perimeter of the town, and this we achieved as the evening sky began to darken. We began to dig in; we were looking forward to a rest. But we didn't get much because for the next two days and nights the locals loaded us up with all sorts of fresh fruit and as many bottles of the local vino as they could carry to us.

How easy is it to feel like a hero? The short answer is, very easy. At last everything seemed worthwhile. These people were overcome by the sheer joy of being freed from the tensions of war. They had already rounded up the local secret police and information was coming in every minute about the positions and strength of the remaining German presence in the area. We marched off on the third day still surrounded by well-wishers, but with the helpful addition of a small band of local men who volunteered to act as our guides. These men were to prove their worth and their bravery when we came face to face with the enemy. They even insisted on hauling their own artillery piece along with them; it looked as if it had been dragged out of the local museum. Old or not, they managed to fire the thing when we met up with a small German rearguard. This small group stayed with us right to the end of our short stay in Italy.

25

Learning the Hard Way

We set off towards our objective, Foggia, where we expected to come up against some determined resistance. But except for a few desultory shots, nothing had so far happened to cause us any discomfort. Somewhere in front of us there was a force; how big it was we had no idea, and just where and when we would meet them was anybody's guess.

In the meantime a huge backlog of mail had been sent up. I had about twenty-five letters, some dating back almost a year. These letters were our lifeline to sanity; they kept our spirits boosted and, most importantly, gave us something to look forward to. Men would treasure these letters, sitting down of an evening to go over them. We usually shared them with the lads who didn't get letters, even when they conveyed the most intimate details. It was a kind of comradeship that probably only exists between people who live in permanent danger.

We all knew each other's families, wives and sweethearts, the children's names and if they were well off or living in the depths of poverty. We were a family. I don't know if the lads in the other companies who were new to the fighting behaved in the same way. In Support Group we kept to ourselves. The Commanding Officer of our battalion encouraged this attitude, probably thought it was better if we kept apart, so that we didn't undermine the lads fresh out of Britain with our private slogan, which dated back to Alamein: 'Discretion is the better part of valour.'

It was now quite late in the year, the days were still long and sunny and we felt on top of the world. It was like being on holiday; any thoughts of returning to the Rifles had long gone. I'd had a letter from Reggie who told me that the Rifle Brigade was in Italy as well and once again right up in the front line having a very tough time. When I showed the letter to the rest of the lads, we all felt sorry for our old mates and a letter was written to Reggie to show the men that our thoughts were with them.

One fine day we were making steady progress along a road which was nothing more than a well-laid track. The peace of this country walk was shattered when we heard shooting up front. The line came to a halt; we were well to the rear. Up comes a runner: 'Support Group to move up on the double.' The battalion was strung out for a distance of about half a mile, so it took us ten to fifteen minutes to get to the lead section, where, sure enough, there was trouble. Three of the lads stretched out, as dead as doornails, and the officer wounded. They had reached the end of the wood we had been crossing and without thinking had marched straight out into an open field, a field which stretched flat and exposed for about two hundred and fifty yards before the edge of the next piece of woodland.

The CO issued his orders: Support Group to get to the other side of the open field and sort out the opposition. We said nothing and did nothing. It was quite obvious to us that nobody would make it to the other side unless we found out just where the firing had come from. Silence: an order had been given, nobody had responded, what to do now? We explained to the CO that we were quite willing to deal with the situation but that we would do it in our own tried and trusted way, and it would take an hour or two.

At that moment a brigadier turned up wanting to know why there was a hold-up. When we told him, he blew his top. What happened next was an object lesson to them all, the CO, the officers and the rest of the lads.

'These Germans are no better than you,' shouted the brigadier.

'All you have to do is to show yourselves and show them that you mean business.'

Then he strode out of the wood into the full glare of the afternoon sun, complete with his red braid and his walking cane. The wind was blowing towards us and we heard the rustle of the incoming hail of bullets before we heard the sound of the shots. Next thing the brigadier was stretched full length in a pool of blood, the top half of his body torn from his trunk.

While all this was going on, Support Group had worked out how to tackle the problem. We filed off in two single lines away from the battalion and crossed the field about three hundred yards further down. As we had guessed, the force that had done the damage was a small rearguard detachment. It wasn't all that difficult to come up behind them and with no more ado shoot them to pieces. There were only six of them. It was all over in half an hour, nobody said a word, the battalion moved off, leaving one platoon to take care of the dead. That evening we were pulled up in front of the CO.

'I don't know what to do with you lot,' he says.

One of the lads suggested that it would be better if an experienced officer was put in charge of our detachment. We had already refused attempts to up-rank any of our group. Naturally we had a sergeant and a couple of corporals with us, but they saw things in the same light as the rest of us. We needed an officer to take responsibility; we knew that once we got this officer, we could look after his education.

Again we tried to explain that the battalion had been formed from raw recruits in Blighty and however good their training they were ignorant of the finer arts of combat. We had been fighting when most of the rest of them, officers and men alike, had still been at school. It wasn't that any of them were in any way lacking in courage, far from it. If anything, these young apprentices to the carnage of war were much more likely than us to obey an order to throw themselves into an attack.

But we knew the score, the dangers of making a wrong move.

We had always been taught that a fighting unit is only a fighting unit while it retains its strength as a unit. If the unit loses half of that strength it becomes a liability. If we were allowed to use our experience, like we had done in the wood, we could keep our casualties to a minimum.

The Colonel heard us out and the next day, lo and behold, we had an officer in charge of Support Group. When he came to us he was just a lowly second lieutenant; by the time we reached Foggia we got him his second star and he got promoted to first lieutenant.

Whenever we passed through a village we were treated like heroes. Flowers, gallons of the local vino and kisses from the local talent. This didn't seem like war. They would march by our side, oblivious to the fact that at any moment we might be greeted by a hail of bullets, or, even worse, mortars. They would cook our meals on the nightly halt, and, after darkness, they would bestow their favours for a bar of chocolate or, better still, a tin of bully. These were in the main happy, carefree days and we lapped it up.

This world was totally different from the desert. The filth, dust and sand which impregnated every pore of the body, the hordes of vulture-like flies and the desert sores and lice were all now only a distant nightmare memory. Here it was like paradise, all lush greenery, trees and lines of bushes, clear rivers and streams. It had its drawbacks, though. The desert was flat, you could often see the enemy sighting up their guns. Here there was too much cover for the enemy to hide in.

About this time I went through a very bad phase of the shakes. This very personal mental condition attacked me whenever I heard the sound of an explosion or the crackle of rifle fire. It must have been obvious to our group that I had gone chicken. I was saved by our sergeant. He took me off the Vickers and put me in a rifle section. And then, after about two weeks, a strange thing happened. I was in a lead section, a very dangerous position, and suddenly I realised that I was back to normal. What caused my mental revival I haven't a clue. I presented myself to the sergeant the next morning and told him how I felt. I was back on the

Vickers again, fifty pounds of dead weight over my shoulder and I was later told I was just as much of a nutcase as I was before.

We had covered about two hundred miles on foot, dragging all our gear behind us in collapsible prams especially designed for the job, saving us the aggro of carrying heavy packs. In spite of blisters we were fitter than we had been for a long time. The rations were better and we were showered with supplies of fresh fruit and other luxuries by the ever joyful local populace. All in all we were on to a good thing. With the sun shining and with no great danger of sudden death, the battalion steadily carried on, ever northwards.

About a week after the Brigadier's death, the four Italians discovered that there was a small concentration of Germans in a village about ten miles ahead. This time the Colonel sent a platoon from Support Group in front. Georgie Fellows, the corporal in charge, led the platoon forward, taking along two of our Italian friends. It took about four hours before they reported back that there was indeed a small force, but, in George's estimation, it wasn't much to bother about.

We put it to our new officer that he approach the Colonel and suggest that all four platoons divide up into two groups, work our way round the rear of the village and go in about three or four in the morning to finish things off. Georgie insisted to our new leader that he put the suggestion as if it was his own. Much to our surprise that's exactly what he did. It's a pity that I cannot remember the officer's name; he was only just out of his teens, quite a young man and it was all new to him but he was beginning to fit in quite well.

It wasn't really our job in Support Group to sort out these small detachments, but life had been so cushy that we looked on these little tasks as something to relieve the monotony. About midnight off we set, two platoons going to the east and two to the west. The two groups would join up at about two in the morning, somewhere along the road leading north from the village. By then, with luck, the Krauts would have their heads down sleeping soundly. Two of the Italians disappeared into the village to suss out exactly where the enemy had taken up residence. It was nearly three in the morning before they returned, and time was getting short. It would be light by five at the latest and by then we hoped to have the operation wound up. We silently crept into the village. There were only two buildings to take so we again divided ourselves into two groups. I remember most of all the simplicity of the affair. What I forget is just how tensed up everyone must have been at the time. There we were, on foot, behind the enemy, not really too sure of their exact number. As things turned out we just went into the buildings and woke them all from their slumbers; they didn't even have any sentries posted. Inside fifteen minutes they were all out in the village square, a couple of Very lights were sent into the night sky and the operation was over. Not a shot was fired.

That's how our officer got his second pip. It was also the end of our time in Italy. The German forces in the area had withdrawn to join up with their comrades in the Cassino area, where the real war was taking place. We had heard about the fighting at Monte Cassino and we thought we were well shot of it.

The news came that we would soon be going back to England. It was well into November. It looked like we could be home for Christmas.

While we waited, all sorts of entertainments were put on. We had been supplied with fold-up bicycles, one to each platoon, awkward things but they did have wheels. The Colonel suggested that a bike race would be a good idea and a course of roughly thirty miles was charted, a triangle with ten miles each side. I won this race by the astounding margin of twenty minutes. The local inhabitants treated me like a hero and I loved it.

Word came that we would be going back to Taranto to board ship. The next day a fleet of trucks came to transport us, but not to Taranto. Instead the objective was Bari, a small port on the eastern side of Italy. As the ship sailed out of the harbour that evening we were told that Taranto had been almost destroyed by German bombers, but all we cared about now was that, at long last, we were going home.

26

Home at Last

The continent that had claimed so many of my friends slipped by as our ship passed through the Strait of Gibraltar. The twinkling lights of the small townships along the Spanish coast were clearly visible. It was hard to believe that the inhabitants were not part of the war. For a second I thought about jumping overboard and swimming towards those havens of peace. The lights receded further and further into the distance until once again the black void of night overcame the ship. Only the steady thump, thump, thump of the engines disturbed my thoughts.

Men who would normally be laughing and joking were quietly leaning on the rails, staring into the distance. What thoughts were passing through their minds was anyone's guess. I know that in my own case these thoughts were very complex.

Our entry into the Irish Sea was marked by a decided change in temperature. It was bloody freezing. The port of Liverpool slowly came into view. Huddled up, with our hands deep in our pockets, we stood at the rails and glumly watched as the ship tied up. The freezing mist had by now turned to drenching rain. I thought that perhaps it wouldn't be a bad idea if the ship turned around and took us back to the sunshine we had so recently left.

These thoughts quickly disappeared in the general excitement as everyone slipped and slithered down the icy gangplanks and we clattered on to English soil. We were soaking. After a short march to the station, we boarded a train and were on our way to the town of Oakham in the county of Rutland. From there we were taken to our new base in the small village of Somerby, to a large stately home which would be our home for the next nine months.

In this remote area of Middle England the war might as well have been taking place on another planet. Those first few days were very easy-going; except for the morning roll-call, no other demands were made upon us. Just as well considering the vast amounts of the local brew that found its way down our gullets.

I had now reached the ripe old age of twenty-five and it was in one of the pubs in the main street of Somerby that I first set eyes on a completely naked woman. It was a Friday night, and this pub was full to the brim with servicemen, locals and a contingent of Land Girls. We had no idea what Land Girls were. Whatever they were, they could certainly put away vast quantities of beer. As the evening progressed and the noise and intoxication increased, one of the girls had stripped off and started dancing on one of the tables. The pub was in uproar, everyone was singing, cheering and shouting 'encore'. I was quite shocked by this display. I wasn't a prude: I'd experienced the fleshpots of India, Palestine and Cairo, not to mention Italy, where the local women were only too ready to donate their favours in exchange for a tin of bully beef or a bar of chocolate. Those women could be excused, they were on starvation rations. But this was a new experience, not only for myself but also for some of the older regulars. We had been away too long. This was the new England, a land at war.

I was still a virgin. In the desert women were hardly ever a topic of conversation. More to the point was the lack of decent food. One of my mates once said that when he made it home he was going to spend his time eating chocolate ice creams while sitting on the toilet and enjoying the luxury of pulling the chain.

Watching the girl on the table reminded me of the stories of the Roman militia fighting on the outskirts of Rome to save an empire that was disintegrating in a frenzy of mass orgies. Maybe I was being a bit far-fetched. It came as a relief to me the next morning when I discovered that I was not alone with these thoughts.

After a few days came the news that we had all been waiting for: two weeks leave with more to follow. The usual loud cheers, followed by letter writing. When I'd left England in 1938 I was a callow youth, not many years out of school. Now, after nearly five years of murder and mayhem, I was to be thrust into wartime London, and a world which had developed a new set of values. It could be said I had become a robot: do this, do that, advance, stay, withdraw. For five years I had been part of a group where survival meant acting together. 'Fitting in' with civilians who had minds of their own and were not used to doing what they were told was going to take some time.

I recall most vividly the moment I first saw Freda after I returned home. I knocked on her door and there she was with an apron around her. Naturally she said that she looked a sight, as if that mattered. Looking at her the world seemed to tilt. Although we had only really known each other for a few days before I went overseas I proposed to her almost on the spot and she accepted.

That was the first meeting with the girl who I was going to marry. Then came the walks and talks, the looking in furniture shops, the thrill of holding a woman's hand, the sheer thrill of being in contact with a dream, and, finally, of course, the wedding.

We bought the ring at Bravington's, a large jeweller's which had dominated the corner of the Caledonian Road at King's Cross for as long as I could remember. Everybody was making a huge fuss over me, and I suppose what with the red beret and the wings and a few 'I Was There' medals sewn on, I must have cut quite a figure. The wedding took place at the Central Baptist Church in the heart of Bloomsbury, with the silvery-haired Townley Lord presiding.

I cannot remember just how we wangled it, but after the wedding we got on a train at King's Cross, bound for Norfolk and the home of my old buddy Reggie. Everyone was there to see us off and wish us a happy honeymoon – Freda's three sisters, her mum and dad, plus all of my family except brother John who was now in Burma.

We had our wedding and our honeymoon and some wonderful days together – a brief trip to heaven. Then I returned to Somerby and real life. We were soon up to our old tricks, like the day our small bunch broke into the Headquarters Office and purloined a big batch of leave passes, and so while everyone else spent their weekends around the local pubs we would be on the train to London complete with our forged passes. The theft was never discovered.

It was decided that we needed a lesson in balloon jumping. The battalion was ordered off to Ringway, a huge air force base near Manchester. In groups of six, we were taken up to a height of five hundred feet in a barrage balloon. The basket had a large hole in the centre of the floor. On the command go you just slipped feet first through the hole. You dropped straight down, no noise, except the creaking of the balloon. It was so quiet that you could hear every one of the strings snapping as the chute opened. It was one of the most terrifying experiences of my life. Six men refused to jump. They were given twenty-eight days in the glasshouse and sent to obscure units to see out the rest of the war.

I got some more home leave, this time with official permission. Freda was pregnant and the joy and happiness of my new life was too great. Instead of catching the train back on the appointed day I decided to have another week. Well, I nearly had a week: two Red Caps appeared at the front door one sunny afternoon and I was escorted back to dear old Somerby where I got twenty-eight days in the glasshouse.

I never finished my sentence. On 3 June, after having done twenty days, I was rushed back to the battalion. Everything was in a state of uproar. Stores were being checked, hard rations allocated, ammunition stacked into containers as the unit was made ready to move at a moment's notice. For the next few days the battalion was split in half, one half being resident on the airfield at Cottismore, the other on alert at Somerby. The two halves changed about every other day.

We realised what was going on when we heard on the news that the Allies had landed in northern France. It was 6 June – D-Day. Rumours started to seep through that the initial parachute drop in the early hours of the morning had not been a success. We heard that the men had dropped too far away from each other, that there had been a mix-up at the dropping zones, and that it was all the Americans' fault. We were given short lectures on the need for close-formation jumping.

About the sixth or seventh day after the invasion we were rushed to the airfield and given the order to stand to. We were told we were going to jump into the Caen area. What worried us was the way the brass kept saying that the opposition were not worth bothering about.

The battalion stood to until it got dark. Then it was back to Somerby with a big sigh of relief all round. Apparently the fighting was too confused and the brass couldn't find a stable DZ. So we had another two to three weeks of alternating calm and tension. About half a dozen lads broke under the strain and were given their tickets to other units. There was no stigma attached; it could happen to anyone and we all realised this, especially me, who had come close to breaking myself and had only been rescued by the understanding of my mates. Quietly, we called them lucky sods.

The next stand to happened in August, when Montgomery was trying to stop the German retreat at Falaise. This time we actually boarded the planes. The first thirty or so took off and we circled over the Channel waiting for the rest of the formation to join up. Nothing happened. The flight landed and off we went back to Somerby. We were all sweating buckets, especially us poor unfortunates who had been circling over the sea.

It turned out that the DZ that we were bound for had been overrun by German forces just an hour before we were due to jump. So back once again for more intensive training, more practice jumps and more clambering over the neighbouring moorland. This was a very hard and uncomfortable six weeks.

About this time, the Rifle Brigade element in the battalion was called up in front of the Colonel. He had been sent a memo from the Army Pay Office stating that we were all some thousands of pounds in debt. He wanted to know if we could throw some light on the matter. He sat in front of us preparing for the biggest load of bull he had ever heard. Of course we couldn't help him. How could we get in debt for thousands of pounds? He knew the army better than us. Somebody had made a big mistake.

'No, we're very sorry, sir, we know nothing about it.'

If the Colonel had ever heard of Milton's Antiseptic Liquid, it was certainly not as an ink-eradicating fluid.

'How you all managed it I don't know, but I bet you are all as guilty as hell.'

He had us sussed as a gang of rogues, but he knew we had our uses.

After the war, I learnt from Reggie that there had been a major investigation in the Rifles but nothing had come of it. Everybody kept their mouths shut.

By this time Freda had acquired a couple of rooms over her sister's flat in Ellington Street in Holloway. We thought it was super. Surprisingly, given my record, I was allowed home on weekend leave and I was very happy to be away from my family and with Freda. We wanted to be on our own. The baby was beginning to show and I got intense enjoyment trying to feel the little movements inside her womb. Those were days of pure joy, perhaps the happiest of my life. But I knew full well that these interludes of sanity could all be shattered at a moment's notice.

The Germans were now attacking London with flying bombs and the more deadly V2 rockets. In the night, if I thought the bombs were coming too close, I used to drag Freda down to the Anderson shelter. Freda would never have gone down on her own; the raids never seemed to worry her. All I could think of were the shattered corpses I had witnessed. I didn't ever want to see my Freda go out that way.

One day in early September we were told the Brigadier was going to talk to us. We trooped into the mess hall, chattering and with the usual queasy feeling in our stomachs. Large-scale maps had been pinned to the wall and we were told that after this meeting we were all confined to barracks, no exceptions. Much shuffling of feet, everybody smoking their heads off. We were told about Operation Market Garden. It was explained to us that we were to capture the bridge across the Rhine at Arnhem. The Brigadier said there were no big German units in the area. Some bright spark summoned up the nerve to ask why we were being dropped four or five miles from the bridge. The Brig replied: 'Don't worry, it'll be a cakewalk. Good luck and dismiss.'

27

Market Garden

The first lift went in on 17 September. We went in the second day, which surprised us because our lot, the 4th Parachute Brigade, had the most battle experience in the division. Before we took off we were given a short, sharp pep talk by our Colonel, one Kenneth Smythe, known to all and sundry as 'Smithy', though not to his face, of course. He said that if any man wanted to pull out now was the time; no action would be taken.

'The last thing we want on this party,' said the Colonel, 'is passengers.' Not a single man stepped forward. We had suffered so many cancellations we all thought, officers and men, that if we didn't go now they might disband us. We filed on to our designated planes, dragging our cumbersome kit with us. The equipment included a huge kitbag which was attached to our webbing by a twenty-foot nylon cord. Into this bag we stuffed six three-inch mortar bombs per man, grenades, spare ammunition and our trusty .303 Lee-Enfield rifles. Depending what was in it, the bag could weigh nearly a hundredweight. You jumped with the bag in your arms and as you were coming down you lowered it to the end of the nylon cord, so that when you landed all your fighting gear was within reach. As well as the kitbag we carried more grenades round our waist, loaded magazines for the Sten guns, a hundred rounds of .303, and whatever else we could cram into any space left over.

There were five of us who had been together since Italy: yours truly, Charlie Downs on the three-inch mortar and his number

two, Norman Clarke (we called him Nobby); then there was
Paddy, who, naturally, came from Southern Ireland (he would
always emphasise the 'Southern'). Paddy was a giant of a chap. I
never witnessed him showing a moment of fear; nothing seemed
to trouble this super-tough Irishman. Then last but not least
Darkie Williams. We called him 'Darkie' because he was coloured,
not really jet-black, more half-caste. He came from Cardiff. Darkie
was my number two on the Vickers, the heavy machine gun
which, true to its name, was really heavy. The Vickers was made
up of the main barrel with water jacket, and the tripod upon
which it sat. Each part weighed in at about fifty pounds, not
forgetting the container for the water which kept this cumbersome death-dealing piece of equipment cool. All these bits were
stored in our various kitbags. We were one of the two heavy-
weapon platoons of Support Group.

After take-off some of the lads sat on the benches keeping their
thoughts to themselves. Our group passed the time as we had
always done in moments of crisis – got the cards out. Halfway
over the Channel I was cleaned out; luckily, before I had the time
to pay out any cash, the order came to hook up. We were at about
three hundred feet and below us we could see flooded fields.

All around the sky was packed with hundreds of aircraft. We
began to hear a noise like small pebbles being thrown at us. One
of the American aircrew said that this was only light ack-ack, but
we took no chances and began to squat on top of our kitbags!

Red light on. The complete stick formed up; the same drill was
happening in every aircraft in the fleet. Everywhere planes were
ejecting their human cargo. Quite a few seemed in trouble with
flames and smoke coming from the fuselage but you had to hand
it to these Yank fliers: they kept flying straight on course. Green
light on and we were out, falling to earth.

It was immediately obvious that something was seriously amiss
with the 'cakewalk' theory. The air around us was alive with tracer,
the ground was covered with a dense pall of smoke. As we floated

down, instead of the silence of the normal jump there was an absolute bedlam of noise: the crackle of machine guns and the blasting sound of heavy mortars.

At a hundred feet I released myself from the harness. I was now hanging on with one hand holding my own weight plus the kitbag dangling below me. Fifteen feet from the ground I let go and, by a stroke of good fortune, I landed in a slight depression. I watched the chute float away, chased by streams of tracer.

I dragged the kitbag to where I could manhandle it. Everywhere there seemed to be disorder and chaos, but actually this was the other paratroopers, like myself attempting to locate their different sections and platoons. Hundreds of men were floating down from the aircraft that still thundered overhead, as well as the heavy equipment canisters crashing in. To cap all this, men were being shot or blown to pieces by the 'no-resistance brigade' which included two panzer divisions that had been refitting only eight miles from the drop zone.

We managed to land within a hundred feet of each other, but all was not well: Darkie had been hit in the leg. Darkie and Paddy had landed on top of the machine-gun position that had got Darkie and when I reached them and saw what Paddy had done, I could hardly believe my eyes. Paddy had landed on his feet and had kicked one of the two Germans, practically severing the poor sod's head from his body. The other German, who was only a young boy, had collapsed in terror and was shrieking and gibbering with fear.

Nobby, always the gentle one, had got a tourniquet around Darkie's leg.

Crouching in the ready-made gunpit we had acquired, we waited for the green flare, which would indicate the establishment of Battalion HQ. There was no sign of it so, with nothing to do except keep our heads low, I made a brew using the quick-brew tin. Simply tear the lid off and, hey presto, you had a fire: a really handy invention.

While we were drinking our tea the green flare went up. We now had to manhandle Darkie, along with all of our kit, across five hundred yards of open ground swept by merciless machine-gun fire. We took the gibbering German's weapon, a very useful sub-machine gun, for our own arsenal and left him to his own devices. Bit by bit we crawled our way over, finally handing Darkie over to the medics, who by this time didn't know whether they were coming or going. Then one of the non-coms organised a roll-call. Over a third of the battalion was unaccounted for, which meant they were either done for or were lying wounded out there in the mayhem. At least we had survived the drop and were all together under some sort of control.

It was decided to get moving, and this we did, in two single files, one on each side of the road. This was the classic drill for urban street fighting. In spite of the battle that was going on, the Dutch civilians were coming out of their houses showering us with flowers. They obviously thought their day of freedom had at last arrived. I remember that even as they were standing in their little gardens, cheering, clapping and showering us with their gratitude, soldiers who had been walking along would suddenly drop to the ground dead or wounded. We had travelled about a mile when a halt was called. Change of plan: we were to secure the landing zone for the next drop. We had no idea how we were going to achieve this now that the surrounding area was alive with enemy tanks, half-tracks and infantry. A quick about turn, much grumbling, and back to the DZ. Support Group were given orders as to where we should mount our Vickers and the mortars. There weren't nearly enough medics to attend to the hundreds of lads who had suffered injuries; the whole of the DZ was covered with the wounded of both sides, as far as the eye could see. The first chapter of the catastrophe was being written.

Nobby was the next to go down. He was finished before he hit the deck. Other men were instructed to fill the gaps left by Darkie and Nobby. By now we were completely out of contact with the battalion. Word had done the rounds that the first wave in had made it to Arnhem Bridge, but that the Germans had got their wheels moving and were already beginning to carve us up into groups. There isn't much that a lightly armoured parachute division can do to repel two panzer divisions. For the next six days we would try to draw the German heavy stuff away from the bridge to help our comrades who were in position on the northern end. If we were lucky the rest of the grand plan would work and the main army coming from the south would break through before all was lost. By the end of the first day we must have been down to about half of our original strength. Having dug ourselves in, a roster was arranged in order that everyone could get at least a couple of hours' rest.

As darkness fell we took stock of the scene around us. What stood out above all else was the crazy positions that the gliders had ended up in. Some were upside down, some almost standing on their heads, others were blown in half, bits of wing and tail-plane scattered over a wide area. They looked like pieces of modern sculpture, or huge headstones in a vast cemetery. Inside some of those broken structures of wood and canvas were the remains of men who had breathed their last gasps of life while still strapped into their seats. And all around, the motionless bodies. Most of the lads in the gliders had been detailed for the job, whereas we were all volunteers. One way or another everyone said a prayer for the poor sods.

The next day dawned, wet and misty; none of us had slept, not even fitfully. All night the sky had been lit by star shells and the enemy attacks had not stopped for a minute. Fresh enemy troops had arrived, equipped with rocket-propelled mortars. These were very deadly weapons; they'd explode with a devastating roar about ten or twelve feet from the ground, spreading a hail of shrapnel outwards and downwards. There was very little protection from this lethal storm of metal. To make matters worse, the Germans were now sending in their tanks against which we were powerless, so we withdrew further back into the woods.

An unknown number of the 2nd Battalion were at the bridge and under severe and non-stop attack. These brave men were to fight on to the very last round. Unable to force our lads out of the houses where they were dug in, the Germans turned their artillery directly on to the buildings, pounding away until they were no more than piles of rubble. Even then the survivors would somehow scramble out and into neighbouring houses to try and fight on.

Late in the afternoon of the third day the word went around that everyone was to fall back towards Oosterbeek, where a perimeter was being formed. All attempts to get to the bridge had failed. The few survivors still there would have to fight it out the best they could.

We were down to what food we had on us and what we could salvage from the kit of the dead, both British and German, that lay strewn everywhere. We still had a few six-pounder anti-tank guns operating in small pockets here and there and these were taking a heavy toll of the German tanks.

It was street fighting all the way to Oosterbeek. I think that if we had had a sufficient supply of ammunition the whole battle might well have turned out differently. The truth is we were only meant to hold on for three days and nobody had realised that we would be up against armour.

In some parts of the battlefield we were fighting at distances of less than thirty yards, bayonet charge following bayonet charge, the numbers of dead and wounded growing all the time. I saw one German soldier sitting in the middle of the road shaking and crying for his mother; nobody took any notice of him, no shots were aimed in his direction. By now my mob had dwindled from five hundred to about a hundred and fifty. Even so there were still jokes about the predicament we were in.

The sergeant now in charge of the group, a lad from another battalion who I'd never set eyes on before, detailed someone to be my number two on the Vickers, which, by a miracle, we were still lugging around. I had been ordered to set it up to cover a party

Rifleman Gregg. A soldier boy and soon off to the wars.

Mr and Mrs Hamblin, my grandparents. Victorians at heart, they could have been invented by Charles Dickens. They were worried about my mother and were scornful of my absent father. Eventually, we went to live with them.

Some of my aunts and uncles on the Hamblin side. Grandmother is on the far right and mother on the far left. This is a long time ago and I can't remember who they all are.

© Hulton Collection

Our mothers didn't want us under their feet at home, so we boys lived and played on the streets and we all belonged to gangs.

© Popperfoto/Getty Images

I loved the excitement of motor racing. When I left school I worked in garages and would get taken to the circuit at Brooklands to help out. Here is one of my heroes, John Cobb, in his Napier-Railton – a fantastic car. Cobb established a lap record that was never broken.

© Hulton Collection

In the army I was soon fitter, better fed and better dressed than I had been in civilian life.

Strange things were happening in England. The pro-Nazi Oswald Mosely and his fascist Blackshirts held Hitler-style rallies and brought violent trouble to Jews in the East End of London.

© Imperial War Museum

By 1940 I was in action in the Western Desert. We were constantly under fire. We learnt about combat the hard way and realised that the German Afrika Corps was a very formidable enemy.

We lived out of the back of our carriers and lorries. This is me in typical desert kit, a far cry from the parade ground.

© Imperial War Museum

© Imperial War Museum

The chap in the beret is Lt Col. Vladimir Peniakoff DSO MC, aka Popski. I was seconded to him to carry messages. This meant driving hundreds of miles across the desert on my own.

After Popski I was sent to help the Long Range Desert Group, driving lads like these to field hospitals when they were wounded.

By the time I went back to my unit I had driven thousands of miles ferrying wounded men to temporary hospitals like this and not fired a shot in anger. My biggest fear was that my vehicle would break down and strand me miles from anywhere, doomed to become a pile of bleached bones.

Reproduced with kind permission of the Cuneo Estate

I got back to the Rifle Brigade in time for the Battle of Alamein. 2nd RB fought a vicious battle at a place called 'Snipe'. Our Commanding Officer, Lt. Col. Vic Turner won a VC. This painting shows Turner and co. dragging ammunition over to a six-pounder being fired by a very brave man, Sgt. Charles Calistan, DCM MM.

Major Tom Bird, DSO, MC

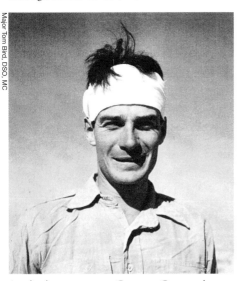

Another brave man – our Company Commander Major Tom Bird, DSO MC. His bandage covers a head wound he suffered at Snipe. He was scarcely twenty-four but we would have followed him anywhere.

In 1943, after nearly five years away, I got back to England. On 1 January 1944 I married the girl I had stood up just before I was posted abroad – Freda.

© CORBIS

Someone blundered. On 18 September 1944 we parachuted into Arnhem. It was the second day of the operation. We had been told it would be 'a piece of cake'. We landed in the middle of a battle. All around were the bodies of the lads who had jumped the day before.

© Imperial War Museum

We were to be relieved after three days. The light German forces turned out to be the tanks of 11 SS Panzer Corps. Fighting went on for nine days and the relief forces never arrived.

© Imperial War Museum

We fought with our backs to the wall, defending an ever-decreasing perimeter round the village of Oosterbeck. One good thing though: it was safer being dug in on the defensive than pushing forward in attack.

© Imperial War Museum

There is not much that lightly equipped paratroops can do against tanks.

© Imperial War Museum

In the end some of the lads got away but the rest of us were marched off as POWs. Over 10,000 of us airborne troops were dropped into the battle. When it ended on 25 September 1944, 1500 of us were dead or dying and nearly 7000 of us were prisoners.

© Getty Images

Nothing I had experienced in battle had prepared me for the horror and terror of the bombing of Dresden. The city endured three raids in twenty-four hours.

© Imperial War Museum

I will never forgive those who organised this raid, never. It made me ashamed to be British.

After the war I became obsessed with cycling, and was nearly chosen for the Empire Games in New Zealand. Here I am winning the Norlond Combine 25 in 1950 in 1hr 2mins and 11 secs. My racing career ended when I crashed and broke my shoulder.

I joined the Communist Party and retrained as a painter and decorator, replacing the Vickers machine gun with a spray gun. For a while I had a nice little business.

© Getty Images

Time passes. Soho in the sixties was a far cry from the place I had worked when I left school in 1933. In the early sixties I gave up the Communist Party and my part in the 'Great Game' and became a bus driver.

My craze now was the motorbike. I got a lot of enjoyment doing unpaid work at bike events.

In 1969 I married Bett at Rosslyn Hill Registry Office. I'm hoping to make a better go of it this time.

In 1985 a group of us began to attend motorbike rallies held by the FIM. This one was in Budapest. On the left is Tom and on the right Alec who, with me, were both members of a gang of four committed rally-goers. I am not sure about the lad second from left. Although they were all younger than me, I am the only one of the four of us who is still around.

My old friends in British security began to get wind of the fact that I was travelling behind the iron curtain. Soon I became a 'bagman', carrying shady packages and information between the East and West.

Nothing shady about this. One of the rally lovelies attending to what is left of my hair.

First pick-up in Dresden. For the rendezvous I chose a first-floor café with a good view of the buses coming and going. Always have your escape route planned – that's what Popski had taught me.

This was the best bike I ever had, my trusty 500cc Honda single cylinder.

Holidays with Bett, who has put up with me and seen me through some rough times.

A rally at a field in Sopron with the Hungarian Democratic Forum. This proved to be an historic event.

An army marches on its stomach, and the mayor of Sopron makes sure there is plenty of goulash.

We realised that, as honoured guests, we had been asked to cut part of the frontier wire between Hungary and Austria. Gang-of-four member Tom made the first cut.

Then I took my turn and got my five minutes of fame in the local paper. So ended my cloak-and-dagger days.

Comrades, the last three survivors of the Snipe action. On the left is Tom Bird who was my company commander, next to him is my friend Eddie Blacker, sadly no longer with us. I am standing next to Mrs Liddle whose husband had been a popular officer. He had recently passed away and we asked her to stand in for him. We were all 2nd RB regulars.

Explaining some of the finer points of Rifle Brigade lore to the then Prime Minister Tony Blair and his wife Cherie.

'Time-expired soldier man.' Me in Soho Square, my old stamping ground. Rick Stroud took this photograph in July 2010 while we were working on this book.

that was trying to find a way through the back turnings. I was later told that the party included the Divisional Commander, General Urquhart, who found himself trapped in a house and was unable to get out until almost the last day.

Once we were set up we discovered we only had enough ammo for a couple of short bursts. An officer volunteered to rummage around the area, and with the assistance of one of the lads found two full boxes of .303. For the time being at least we felt secure. With the Vickers back in action, no German was going to get within a hundred yards of us. Suddenly, the gun stopped firing, which was a bit awkward because a group of Jerries were advancing on us at a fast trot. The lad who had been feeding the gun had been hit. I heard him shout, 'I'm dead', then a fraction of a second afterwards he said, 'I can't be dead, I can still speak.'

He had stopped a bullet in his shoulder, and it had gone right through. Then he picked up another belt, fed it into the gun and that was the last thing that that little group of Germans knew. As long as the gun was in action and the lad by my side continued to feed in the belts of ammo it would have been a very foolhardy Kraut who attempted to get within spitting distance of our tightly knit group. In front of us Germans were falling like ninepins. What were we all thinking? Most probably something simple like 'better you than me, mate'.

We eventually made it to the perimeter at Oosterbeek which was to be our ever-shrinking home for the next four days. Those days produced unimaginable slaughter. The Germans had us in a vice, pushing us back and making our defensive perimeter smaller and smaller. Mortars and shells crashed down on us, each salvo leaving more lads dead and wounded. There was no food, no water, and no light at the end of the tunnel. Amazingly, we kept our morale up, even finding the time to crack jokes in the middle of the mayhem. All the fears that us clever dicks of the old brigade had about the new blokes enduring the rigours and sounds and sights of battle were proved wrong. We were all bound together by the instinct to survive, and everybody realised, even the rawest rookie, that the only way to do that was to protect each other at all costs.

'Don't panic, wait until the sods are almost on top of you, and then open up. That way you don't miss.'

It was about the end of the third day that real weariness started to hit us. We had been issued with a supply of Benzedrine tablets, to keep us awake. The pills affected our judgement – I am sure that under the influence of Benzedrine I charged into positions that, normally, I would have thought twice about. Some of the lads had over-proscribed themselves, which resulted in some terrible after-effects. We were surrounded by violent death, appalling noise, fire and horror and for the blokes who had overdosed this became even more exaggerated as the effects of the pills wore off. The one saving grace was that now at last we had gone from the attack to defence. This meant that we no longer had to lug around a load of extremely heavy gear. You dug your pit and awaited the onslaught. All you had to do was to keep awake.

28

The Witches' Cauldron:
Der Hexenkessel

Our perimeter measured roughly a mile by a mile and a half and in the middle of it was the Hartenstein Hotel. We had lost contact with the lads of the 2nd Battalion who were still battling it out around the bridge in Arnhem itself. We were running out of ammunition, although the small group of us around the Vickers gun got preferential treatment, perhaps because we were on the eastern side of the defence line and were taking the brunt of the attacks. There were a dozen men around my position, and we were in dire straits. I think the rest of the force was down to about twelve or fifteen hundred men, but I am not sure. If we weren't relieved within the next two days we would be defending ourselves with sticks and stones. We were aware that, while most of the Germans were treating prisoners well, we had also seen evidence of the massacre of prisoners by SS units. None of us wanted to be captured.

In spite of everything, we had no thought of surrender. We saw the battle now as a fight to the finish. There were as many Germans dead and wounded as our own number and, in the main, the few prisoners we had managed to capture and hold on to were very dejected. A lot of them had fought their way across Russia and said they had never experienced the ferocity of the battle they were now fighting.

Being dug into a defensive position had one advantage: the

number of casualties began to drop, and the main threat was now the incessant mortaring and shelling. It seemed to me that the enemy, because they were now the attackers, were sustaining more injuries than ourselves.

Day after day the battle raged, the dead and dying of both sides filling the ground all around us. Short truces were arranged to collect the wounded. The dead we left where they lay and the bodies, some of which had been there since the first day, were becoming bloated, stretching against their uniforms like balloons, a grotesque sight. Some of the lads who were in action for the first time found the sight of those bodies very difficult. In the end they got used to it, but they would never forget what they had seen. None of us would ever be able to cleanse our minds of the horror.

By the morning of 25 September it was obvious to everyone that the end was near. We hadn't eaten for two days, there was no water except what we managed to collect from puddles of rain-water, and then the word came round that there was to be an attempted breakout that night. A small British force had arrived on the other side of the river with collapsible boats that would ferry us across. No one was to move until told to do so by an officer. I wondered how many officers were left. At nine o'clock that night our forces on the other side of the river unleashed a massive bombardment on the German lines to our front. It went on for about an hour. Further to the north we could hear the rattle of small arms. We were now out on a limb, down to the last five hundred rounds of our ammunition

The Germans went on attacking us. This must have gone on until midnight, and then, suddenly, everything went quiet. No word had as yet come round to us, and we had just lost another two dead and two severely wounded. Our officer decided to send one of the lads to the rear to see if we could get some help for our wounded mates. After what seemed an age he returned. 'Can't find a soul', he reports, but he thought that the Germans had got behind us. If that was true we were surrounded.

Then it dawned on our dazed and battered minds: the breakout had come and gone, the bombardment at nine had been for covering fire; our own detachment, along with others who were lining the perimeter, had been left behind as a rearguard to cover the withdrawal. We were on our own. So what should we do? Did we keep together or split up? We all decided that the only thing to do was to split up into groups of three. The officer volunteered to stay behind with the wounded men and another chap, I believe from the 11th Battalion, agreed to stay with him. I've tried hard to remember his name, but when we weren't calling him 'sir', his nickname was always Birdie. Perhaps his name was Dick or Dicks; another Dickie Bird? I just cannot remember. Three of us crawled out and set off eastwards as a group.

29

In the Cage

We managed to avoid capture for two days. Other lads joined us and our group of three had grown to six when they finally captured us. It took about four hours by truck to get back to Arnhem; we hadn't realised that we had travelled so far. We were dumped in the centre of the town, which was a hive of activity, with German army transport driving aimlessly about. There were clusters of Dutch civilians sitting about with their hands on the tops of their heads – a very sorry sight. These poor devils had been rounded up by the Germans because they were suspected of giving aid to the British. The Paras were being treated completely differently. With no shouts or threats, groups of thirty at a time were simply told to make their way to the railway station where food and drink would be given.

The noise of battle had stopped; only the smoke and the terrible stench of rotting flesh, and the scorched, flattened trees gave any indication of the life and death struggle that had been going on for the last ten days. The Germans were just as filthy as ourselves. Many of them had been wounded and wore dirty bandages. Our clothing, too, was stained with dried blood, not necessarily our own but from our comrades who had suffered wounds, and who we had manhandled, and there were plenty of them.

When I finally made it to the station I learnt that the first contingent of five hundred had been sent off by rail the day before. The Germans were in a state of utter confusion, even panic. They were dashing about in their small military vehicles, their officers shouting orders. Our men were lying about all over the place, hardly able to keep their eyes open. Not surprising since, apart from catnaps, the majority of us had had no sleep since being dropped from the skies. To cap it all, we were starving hungry. Later on in the afternoon a huge lorry arrived and we were fed on bread and soup followed up with mugfuls of their ersatz coffee, a really horrible concoction made from acorns. It was the first hot food and drink that had gone down our throats since leaving the airfields of England.

We were told to remove our boots. The Germans must have thought that, having eaten, our strength would by some miracle return and we would all make a break for it. Although some of us had already been discussing the possibility of escape, I don't believe for one moment that such a break would have succeeded, we were far too weak and tired. Unshaven and unwashed as we were, who in their right minds would have assisted us? We must have looked a right murderous gang of cut-throats.

Just before dark, all the remaining prisoners were shovelled aboard the cattle trucks that had been waiting in the yards. In charge was a German who had only half of one arm and a heavily bandaged leg. He stood upright with the help of a stick, which he had cut from a tree. His hair was almost pure silver. This officer was directing operations without saying a word. He would just point his stick while balancing on his one good leg. 'Some geezer, that', we all thought.

The train journey to the POW transit camp at Limburg took two days, with a long overnight stop at Essen. About fifty of us were crammed into my truck, including a dozen Polish paratroopers, who had been part of the last drop on the third day of the action. It was clear that these lads had no intention of reaching the end of the journey. They were all very slightly built. They stripped down to their birthday suits and managed to clamber out of the truck's small air vent. This breakout happened in the dark, while the train was stopped at Essen. We couldn't follow, we were far too big. So we passed them their clothing and wished them good luck. Did they make it? We never heard.

At Limburg the respect and camaraderie that had been shown us by our captors at Arnhem vanished. The doors were slid open and with much shouting and cursing we were marched the short distance through the town and into the gates of our first *Kriegsgefangenenlager*.

Limburg was a transit camp. I remember very vividly the method used to keep order. At the first sign of trouble they would spray the captives with excrement from the camp cesspit. Not only would we be covered in the filth, but we would be sliding about on the muck that covered the ground. There have been periods in my later life when I have experienced various methods of crowd control, but never have I come across such an efficient one as hosing the trouble-makers down with their own shit. It works like magic.

In the camp, the different nationalities were kept apart in their own compounds. The only people who seemed to be able to roam about freely were the Poles and the French. They were the ones who appeared to have the jobs where it was possible to obtain supplies of food – I don't know why.

This harsh regime did not last long. After a week we were put on a train, the same system, fifty men to a cattle truck with a fifty-gallon drum in the middle as a latrine, and off we went to our second destination, the huge Stalag VI-B.

Limburg had been a floating cesspool, with no attempt by the prison staff to implement any sort of hygiene control. Stalag VI-B, by contrast, was highly organised. The organisation was left mainly to the British NCOs who closely followed the command structure of the British Army.

The high command were the senior regimental sergeant majors; their power passed down the chain of command to the corporals who would each have authority over a given number of men. It wasn't such a bad thing to have discipline imposed; it helped to keep us behaving in a manner befitting soldiers of the British Army. Of course everybody moaned and groused, but it worked.

We thought that the Americans and the French lacked discipline. Where we were made to wash and somehow press our clothes and shave every morning, a lot of these men lapsed into a couldn't-care-less state. The only people in the camps lower on the German hate list than the hapless Americans, and on whom ill treatment was frequently meted out, were the Russians; they could be shot out of hand for the slightest infringement of the rules.

The Germans drew the line at actually shooting Americans but they gave them the really filthy jobs, like cleaning out the cesspits. We felt sorry for these Yanks, but we thought that if our captors wished to take it out on somebody, better on the Yanks than on us.

After a week, the new arrivals were paraded on the football pitch and issued with a Red Cross postcard. A huge notice board had been set up, and written on it were the words we had to write on our postcard: 'We are alive and well and being treated well'. No deviation from the script was allowed. Well, at least it was something: it would lift the shadow of uncertainty from our families back home. So life went on – the food was horrible and the days were boring.

To help alleviate the boredom all sorts of lectures were organised. Some of the prisoners had been teachers and gave lessons to those inclined to listen; even languages were taught. Our small group thought that escape from the camp would be pretty difficult but, after the first four weeks, our main topic of conversation became ways of getting out of the place.

There were about two hundred of us airborne troops in VI-B. Early in November 1944 we were paraded and told that those who so wished would be moved to work camps. It was stressed that no war work would be expected of us. Names would be taken the next day. That evening the six of us approached the sergeant in command of our hut and told him of our intention to go for this offer. He went right up in the air. On no account were any of us to put our names forward for any work whatsoever.

WAR ORGANISATION
OF THE
BRITISH RED CROSS SOCIETY and ORDER OF ST. JOHN OF JERUSALEM

R.L.18.

President :   *Grand Prior :*
HER MAJESTY THE QUEEN   H.R.H. THE DUKE OF GLOUCESTER, K.G.

WOUNDED, MISSING AND RELATIVES DEPARTMENT

Chairman : THE DOWAGER LADY AMPTHILL, C.I., G.B.E.

Telephone No.
SLOANE 9696   *In replying please quote reference :*

7 BELGRAVE SQUARE,
LONDON, S.W.1

6913933. Gregg .V.
A.A.C.

2/4/44

Dear Mrs Gregg

We have received your letter of 23/10/44 in which
you make an enquiry for your husband

We are very sorry to hear that he has been posted as
missing, and should like to assure you that all possible
enquiries will be made for him.

If he has been taken prisoner, his name should come
through from the International Red Cross Committee at Geneva,
and his next-of-kin will be notified at once.

Please accept our sympathy in your anxiety.

Yours sincerely,

P.P. Margaret Ampthill

—— Chairman.

*The Red Cross must have sent thousands of letters like this one to the worried
families of missing soldiers.*

'Why not?'

'Because you're all better off under my control!'

I mentioned that if we wanted to escape, we had to get out of the
confines of the camp. I asked him how long he had been a prisoner.

'Since Dunkirk.'

I ventured to suggest that perhaps he might not be too proud
of the fact that he had been safely surrounded by barbed wire

while other men were risking their lives to get him freed. By this time he was really doing his nut. We left him ranting and raving.

The next morning the whole lot of us put our names down for work. I can still recall how overjoyed the commandant was. He had a 100 per cent success.

It was another week before the authorities lined us up and read out our names. We were all to be removed from the camp and split up into small groups of six to eight and then sent to small *Arbeitslagers*, as they were called. We wouldn't know where we were going until we got there.

Came the big day and now only four out of our original six were to stay together. We landed up at a camp in a suburb of Dresden called Niedersedlitz, housing about sixty men. It had one long hut, which included the kitchen and toilets, a small outside area for recreational purposes, the whole lot ringed by the usual barbed-wire fence. The camp was guarded by twelve soldiers who had mostly been posted back from front-line duties because of physical and mental injuries. Four or five of them were too old to be of any use to the army. The commandant was an oldish First World War naval commander, who turned out to be as reasonable as you could expect a German to be.

He gave us a lecture when we arrived and handed us over to the senior soldier in the hut, another sergeant who had also been in residence since Dunkirk. This bright spark promptly read us the riot act and informed us that all orders regarding the camp would come through him, also that he was in charge of the escape committee. I asked how many escapes had been successful.

'None,' he said, 'but bear in mind, if you wish to try, I want to OK the plans first.'

Had he himself ever attempted a breakout?

'No, I've got more sense.'

We went to our beds that first night determined that if it we were going to get away, this particular sergeant would be the last man we would involve.

30

The Work Camp

Life in the *Arbeitslager* was much more relaxed than in the huge camp that we had been transferred from. We were hauled out of bed at 6.30 for roll-call and to be given our work assignments for the day. After that we would have whatever breakfast was going and then be marched off by the guards. The workday finished at 5.30 in the evening, then back to the laager for the evening meal. The gangs always consisted of around a dozen men. If they were lucky enough to be working on a farm it was sometimes possible to scrounge a few potatoes or swedes or anything we could lay our hands on. We would share our bounty with our guards, who were often just as hungry as we were. This had the benefit of encouraging them to look the other way as we stuffed our pockets.

Another great job in the winter was shovelling coal from the wagons in the railway. This meant extra heat in the hut. Then there was the more menial task, *Gemeindearbeit*, labouring for the local council. In winter this usually meant shovelling snow. We would be issued with yard-wide wooden shovels. Starting at one end of whatever road had to be cleared, the *Postens*, or guards, in charge of the detail would line us up, point us in the general direction and set us off. Then they would disappear into a nearby *Gasthaus* and leave us to it.

Some of the men had been POWs since Dunkirk. They had their feet well and truly under the table, and knew all the wrinkles. They had made themselves indispensable and got 'the cream' – all the cushy jobs. Others, less lucky, grafted in local factories.

The work we were given had little to do with the war. We were bullied and chivvied by whoever happened to be in charge of us, but in the main it wasn't a bad life, better than the daily slaughter of the battlefield.

One day in the camp at Niedersedlitz, Rifleman Gregg encountered a nasty problem. I had been detailed to tidy up the rusty barbed wire that surrounded the laager and had cut myself. The wire tore a large gash down the length of my arm. A guard took me to the quack in the local village who doused the wound in antiseptic and then pronounced me fit for further duties. Four days later my arm looked like a barrage balloon. The old chap in charge said that the best thing was to send me to the area hospital. I was advised by some of the old stagers that I would be barmy to go to the 'Death House' as they called it.

'Stick it out, Vic. The worst that can happen is you'll lose your arm, you go in there and every new drug they've got will be tested on you. Don't be a mug.' Next day my arm was even more swollen. I had no choice but to offer myself to the infamous drug testers. I was taken into a sterile-looking room. An orderly stripped me to the waist and then in came the doctor. In a mixture of German and English he asked me if I was worried. Desert fighting had taught me that a person's character shows up in the eyes more than anywhere. A man's eyes tell you whether or not he is going to pull the trigger and kill you. I looked into this man's eyes and slowly lifted my arm.

'Do your worst, doc.'

Within two weeks it was as good as new. I was told later by the *Feldwebel* (the chief) that I had come very near to losing my arm. The treatment saved my bacon.

It was now late in November, and winter had set in. The intense cold, the thick ice, driving wind and deep snow were completely outside our experience. The Germans issued us with wooden clogs which were warmer for our feet, but we would never get used to the climate of Saxony.

Sometimes word would go around that Red Cross parcels were on the way; somebody may have seen a Red Cross train in the sidings or some such. The old hands told us that the parcels came about every two months. We were supposed to get one parcel per person, but it never quite worked out that way. These parcels contained all manner of goodies – tins of cooked ham, chocolate, sweets, tins of soup, sugar, cigarettes and tobacco. Sometimes we would find little notes inside, put there by the women who packed them. It was all good for morale.

I was now part of a group of four, and we were starting to feel the itch of freedom. At first we thought we should head for the Swiss border. We had no idea how far away it was, or how difficult it would be to find things to eat. The Germans were as hungry as we were.

We decided to save as much food as possible and try to break out at the first possible chance. We knew it would be difficult to attempt an escape in the grip of winter, but it was at least worth having a try. No matter how hard I concentrate I cannot remember the names of the other two lads; only Paddy the Irishman sticks out, not that Paddy was his real name, but all Irishmen were called Paddy. Just as anyone Welsh was Taffy, Scotsmen were Jock, a Jewish boy would be Izzy and anyone with a dark skin would be Darkie.

Then you had 'Chalky' White, 'Tansy' Lee, and 'Lackery' Wood. *Lackery* was Hindustani for wood, a hangover from the old British Army. No offence was meant by these names, and if you were given a nickname it stuck to the end of your service days and in many cases well beyond. It annoys me that the names of the other two lads still evade my memory, so I am going to call them Billy (somehow the name rings a bell) and Tommy.

Billy was quite small in stature. I think he had been captured in the desert west of Tobruk. He came from the Durham Light Infantry and had been given the choice of continuing his job down the pits or joining up. He was a fiery character, ready to put up his fists to anyone whom he considered was trying to take him down a peg or two. Size or reputation meant nothing to him. Billy was, in our language, a sure bet.

Tommy was quite unlike the rest of us. I distinctly remember Tommy if only for the fact that he seemed to be wider than he was tall. When he used to talk about his home life, we realised that he came from a different planet to the one we had been living on. When he talked we were for ever telling him to take the plum out of his mouth, all in jest of course. Having said all that, let me say this: Tommy never spoke down to us. He may have been a square peg in a round hole but he fitted in. Goes to show that it takes all sorts to make a world.

We had all silently agreed that Paddy was in charge. Nothing was said about this, it just seemed to happen, perhaps because he was the most determined of us four. We would discuss a possible course of action, Paddy would say his piece and that would be it. He was a born leader.

We decided that we would volunteer for the next snow-clearing job and see what happened. Naturally we didn't tell anyone what we were up to.

Now that we had decided to escape we began to store every spare morsel of food that we could scavenge from our ration. The Red Cross parcels saved the day. We knew we would have to make a break for it at the first opportunity and that with the weather being so bad, our chances of success were pretty slim. We had dropped the idea of Switzerland: it was too far away. Czechoslovakia, on the other hand, was only about sixty or seventy miles away to the south. All in all we thought we had enough food to last us for four days with luck, enough time to get to the Czech border. The next time we were put on snow clearing would be when we went.

For the time being we settled into the daily routine: get roused out of bed, swallow down the ever-present black bread and ersatz coffee, trudge to whatever work we were detailed to do, take the mickey out of the guards, scrounge whatever was going, and back in the evening to the daily slop and the everlasting card games.

31

Introducing an Honest Man

One fine day the camp commandant announced:

'I am pleased to tell you all, no work today.' Loud cheers. 'The new district commandant is coming to inspect the laager. Please don't let me down, I don't want any trouble.'

The commandant treated us with respect, and no one really had a bad thing to say about him. So we set to with a will, sweeping and cleaning; even the windows were given a wipe, no mean feat in the freezing temperatures. The work was still going on when, at about two in the afternoon, a small staff car came through the gates, all the guards saluting and clicking their heels. Unusually, there were no *Heil Hitler*s.

We paraded outside in front of a one-armed man leaning on a crutch, no slouch though, very upright. He had silver hair and I realised that I had seen him before. Without any hesitation he told us to dismiss and to go back to the hut where he would come later and introduce himself. He spoke perfect English – that is if you consider a strong Yorkshire accent to be perfect English. We hurried back to the warmth of the red-hot pot-bellied stove that was the heart of our quarters.

Half an hour later he came in and introduced himself as Captain Albert Jünger.

'First of all,' he announced, 'I have been a soldier all my life and I know all the tricks and all the excuses. I have been assigned to this job against my wishes. Behave yourselves and you can be assured of an easy passage. I can assure you all that being an officer in the German army is not a job for the faint-hearted. Give me anything other than a peaceful life and your feet won't touch. Any questions and any complaints?'

There were no questions, only the usual complaints about the food, to which he simply shrugged his shoulders.

'We get the same as you.'

After that there was a certain amount of good-humoured banter, and I asked him: 'How comes a front-line soldier like you gets a job of nanny to the likes of us? I last saw you, sir, at Arnhem.'

'Well, did you now,' he replied.

He was addressing the half-dozen or so of us who were still wearing our tattered and stained red berets.

'You red-headed bastards banged me up good and proper so they've sent me down here to keep you all in order. And that's what I intend to do. You may as well know that I disapprove strongly of the policy of sending you lot into this sort of camp. If I had my way you'd all be kept tightly sealed up where you can do no more damage.'

He said this without a hint of malice. He even smiled when he called us 'red-headed bastards'. He became even more informal.

'If you're curious about my English, my mother was born in Yorkshire, but my father was pure Saxony. If any of you can beat that for a combination I'd like to see the proof.' Then he left, saying, 'I mean it. No trouble.'

As soon as he disappeared the hubbub started, and somebody shouted:

'He's got you lot taped.'

Meaning us paratroops. In four years of captivity the long-service inmates had never seen anything like this man. They were used to the general run of misfits and rejects who typified the average bull-headed official common to the job. Captain Jünger was an unknown quantity. The four of us wondered just how far he would go if we went ahead with our plans. Paddy settled it:

'We've made up our minds, we go ahead, first opportunity, let him know that we take orders from no Kraut.' With that timely remark we settled down to await our chance.

It was nearly Christmas, and the same old boring routine. Get up, go to work, back to the laager, eat, cards, and bed, day in and day out. We began to think that we would be there until the bloody war ended.

About now, I received my first letters from home, routed through Switzerland via the Red Cross. I had two from Freda and one from my sister, Ellen, who was now in the ATS, and a couple from my mother. I was now a dad: my son Alan had been born on 11 November. The flying bombs were still doing a certain amount of damage, and my grandfather had died in Wales, to where he and my grandmother had been evacuated. But everything else was OK. The war would be over in a few weeks. That last bit none of us believed, but if it helped those back home to feel better, so be it. For our part we could only write the obligatory few lines, 'I am in good health, I am being well looked after'. Just as it was put on a board for us to copy, any additions and your letter went straight into the dustbin, so we wrote what we were told.

The camp commandant had arranged that the whole laager would put in a week's work at the local brewery; in return the camp would get a supply of beer, on the house, so to speak. Agreement all round on this one. Anyone who could be spared from the more menial jobs, like cleaning the city drains and other obnoxious tasks that the locals didn't want to do, was marched to the brewery every day for the whole week before Christmas. Quite a lot of unauthorised tasting went on, and it was quite a feat to stagger back to the camp at the end of the day.

It was quite obvious to us that the civil population had resigned itself to the fact that the war was lost. We could hear the far-distant sound of gunfire coming from the east. The Red Army might be getting closer, but life went on as usual. Red Cross parcels were delivered, and the guards brought a huge fir tree into the laager. It was more than we had expected. As far as it went, Christmas was quite an enjoyable affair.

On New Year's Eve it snowed very heavily, and we knew that in the morning we would all be turned out for snow clearing. That evening we held a short discussion. We had stored enough food to get to the frontier with Czechoslovakia. We had no idea what we would meet when we got to the other side, but at least we would be outside Germany. Surely we could then expect help from the locals. So it was decided: the next day would be freedom day and we all settled down to a good night's kip.

32

The Trial Run

We trooped out of the hut that morning, leaving the pot-bellied stove whose warmth gave us comfort and security. Outside the air was crystal-clear, and there was a slight but freezing wind. Our breath came out in clouds, and, as we walked, the foot-deep snow crunched under our feet. The temperature was below zero. The four of us waddled out to the roll-call wearing every bit of spare clothing we had been able to scrounge, including a spare blanket wrapped round underneath our greatcoats. On top of all this we had heavy, waterproof jackets. How on earth the guards didn't notice our enormous bulk is a complete mystery, but they didn't.

Niedersedlitz in those days was a typical old German suburb. It had a large, wide main road leading towards Dresden, and a smaller road running north–south. The two roads crossed in the centre of the village and it was there that we formed up. The main groups were to concentrate on the Dresden road and the two smaller groups were to work on the north–south road. It was impossible for the guards to maintain contact with everyone and they didn't expect to. We were given our instructions: *Mittagessen* (lunch) at 1 p.m., muster in the centre at 4 p.m. to march back to the huts.

So off we set, clearing the snow as per the book, the only difference being that when we reached the end of the street the four of us just kept on going. One of the other two lads wanted to come along but we only had enough food for the four of us. The two of them wished us luck and promised to attempt to hide our

non-appearance at the midday break for as long as possible, which
they apparently succeeded in doing.

At the end of the village we decided it was best to keep going
until we reached the next village. We would have to look for the
night's shelter no later than 4 p.m. Late into the afternoon,
Tommy, who had taken the lead, stumbled upon a single-track
railway line. It ran east to west and we tossed to decide which way
to go. We went west.

Somebody must have been looking after us because, just as the
light was fading, we found an old ramshackle hut, complete with
stove. Even the door was unlocked. The journey along the line had
taken us about three hours. We had made slow progress, our four
shadowy forms, half blotted out by the swirling snow, our bodies
bent forward, trudging ever onward through a cold lunar land-
scape, the railway line disappearing into never-never land. We
decided to lay low until dark, keeping well away from the vicinity
of the hut. Once inside our new lodgings, we had to get some heat
to dry our soaking wet clobber. Luckily we discovered a sack of
coal and some wood behind the hut and we dragged it inside. We
got the fire lit and the stove glowed red, heating the hut up like
an oven. Four very wet and bedraggled would-be escapees-cum-
nutcases dried out by the minute. Paddy had volunteered to
collect some snow to melt and we quickly discovered that a buck-
etful of snow melts down to a cupful of water.

It took us nearly half an hour to collect enough snow and then
we sat drinking our first hot mug of cocoa, supplied by the Red
Cross parcels. Soon we were cracking jokes, mainly at the expense
of the Krauts.

By now our escape would have been discovered and presumably
the word would be out for our arrest. None of us gave a thought
to the poor guards and what action might be taken against them.
After all, they had sort of put us on trust. We would have to keep
our wits about us in the morning, no doubt about that.

There was a map of the railway system screwed on to the wall.

Our track was a secondary line connecting Dresden to Freiberg. If we followed it we would reach another branch line heading due south. This would lead to the small town of Dohna which was only ten or twelve kilometres from the frontier. It was forty kilometres to Dohna: could we do it in two days? Time would tell.

Before settling down for the night we counted the rations. We had one long loaf of black bread, as yet untouched, three tins of Spam, three tins of rolled bacon, about a pound of assorted biscuits and American wheat cakes, two bars of chocolate, one untouched tin of coffee and some leftovers. Then we huddled up for the night. We decided not to put out a guard. If our presence was discovered we would have to kill whoever found us, and that was out of the question. Being disciplined for an attempted escape was one thing, but being called up for murder was another kettle of fish.

At seven in the evening the first trains started thundering through; they went on all night. We realised that the Germans could no longer move the trains in the day. Everything had to go under cover of darkness.

As soon as it was light we went out to collect snow for our morning brew, and the first tin of bacon was opened up. We spread the contents of the tin all over the top of the stove. The hut filled with smoke, but what a lovely aroma. Paddy dished out about a third of the bread; what with that and the brew, we couldn't ask for more. The meal would have to last us until we found shelter that night. The hut was warm and cosy; each of us, if left to his own devices, would probably have stayed put, at least until the day got warmer. But none of us would admit defeat in front of the other three. So we took the map off the wall and cleared every scrap of evidence that we had been in the hut, and, with a last look round our haven of rest, we set off, following the track due west.

Paddy led the way. Almost at once the snow started to fall, huge white flakes of the stuff. It would cover our tracks, but it was bloody cold.

33

The Second Day

Billy elected to take the lead on the road to nowhere. We let him get about three hundred yards before following his footsteps: what we were doing was treating the walk like a patrol, one man in front, two in the middle and a rearguard, in this case myself. This way, if the first man was caught out by a surprise attack then the other three had a chance to make themselves scarce.

Finding the railway line had been a godsend. It took us the best part of the morning to reach the junction which, it was obvious, was hardly, if ever, used. Underneath the coating of snow the rails were rusty-red. A small embankment on each side of the line helped us keep to the track. The rails themselves were hidden under two feet of snow.

We hadn't seen a soul since leaving the village. We were travelling now on the very edges of the Erzgebirge, an area covered in forest, hills and lakes. This part of southern Saxony is probably the most beautiful part of the whole of Germany.

We were confident that we could remain undetected until we came to cross the border. Then, and only then, would it be time to leave the safety of the forest and the disused line. We had about twelve miles to go; we thought this would take us until next day.

We were starting to worry about the state we were in. Cold was not a problem, but our clothes were getting wetter by the minute. We knew somewhere suitable to dry out would have to be found if we were going to be in any condition to tackle the third day's walk to the frontier.

Our route took us down a huge firebreak, about fifty yards wide. The trees and the swirling snow blocked out the light and it was getting darker by the minute. Billy stopped and suggested a brew-up but the suggestion was turned down. The temperature was below zero and Paddy insisted that we had to find shelter if we were to survive the night. By now our faces were encrusted with ice. To say that we were uncomfortable would be the least of it. We agreed with Paddy, so on we tramped.

Paddy went in front and we allowed ourselves the luxury of following in his footsteps. Luxury because Paddy was clearing the snow with his size-twelve boots. He had accepted the fact that all three of us were looking to him as leader, although neither by sign nor word was this mentioned. Suddenly one of us noticed that the line was going over a bridge. Billy scrambled down through the trees and shouted at us to join him. Our night's lodging had been found. Under the bridge it was as dry as tinder.

We set to gathering as much wood as we could. Lighting the fire was not so simple, because we were down to our last box of matches. We still carried the wooden shovels and they now came into their own. We cut one up to use as kindling and soon had a blazing fire. We had built a small shelter and set about collecting snow to melt. It was a very laborious task. We were safe until morning. If anybody came along that track in the night we would hear them miles away, and in any case whoever did come would be walking – should, that is, anyone be bold enough to venture this far out in the pitch dark.

Log after log was added to the bonfire, and soon we had a fierce blaze going. One by one we took off our clothes and in no time we were back to normal, as snug as four bugs in a rug, one and all settled down to our second night of freedom.

The third member of our little team said that we should take it in turns to stay awake in order to keep some form of watch. There was a heated debate about this suggestion:

'Don't be f***ing stupid. Who's going to find us here?' was the main argument. In the end it was agreed that the idea made sense. We would all do two hours each. This had the added bonus that the fire could be kept roaring away. We were nice and warm with food in our stomachs. We were certain that we would make it out of Germany. What happened after that was anybody's guess.

The following morning broke fine and clear. Like the morning before we all tried to delay leaving this cosy retreat as long as possible. Finally, we made the move, scrambling back up the steep incline to the line. This time Tommy took the lead with Paddy in the rear.

On through the seemingly never-ending forest, cracking jokes about anything that came to mind. Suddenly we were out of the forest and in open country, almost on top of a small village.

We were very close to the frontier, which was about six miles to the south. Keeping to cover as much as possible, we approached a line of small trees and bushes. Our excitement ran at fever pitch; each step taken was a step nearer our goal. Was this the frontier already? Tommy clambered through the by now quite dense bushes then, without warning, lost his footing and disappeared down a steep slope, followed in rapid succession by the rest of us. We hit the road almost simultaneously. We had fallen right into the arms of an army checkpoint.

The checkpoint was manned by a training battalion. They had no ammunition, but we didn't know that. The four of us sat down by the edge of the road while the Huns split their sides with laughter. It was a good try, we had enjoyed ourselves, but now would come the reckoning. We were bundled into an army truck and in no time at all we were back to square one where we were put under close arrest to await the judgement of our old friend Silverhair. We knew he wasn't going to see anything amusing in our adventure.

Captain Jünger turned up the next day trying to breathe fire and brimstone, but he couldn't bring himself to the point of explosion. Paddy and Tommy were transferred to another camp in the Chemnitz area, and that was that. Captain Jünger told us very firmly that if we tried to escape again, the very unpleasant consequences would be out of his hands. So we returned to normal duties. Back in the camp, the commandant hauled us both into his office, gave us a dressing down and promised me a job with the local cesspit cleaner.

Billy and I kept pretty much to ourselves for the next few days. We got over the disappointment of our capture. We had almost made it, in spite of the weather. We felt that we had made a point to all those who had sat out the war in the comparative safety of a POW camp. If we could get that far in the depths of winter, surely some of them should have at least tried.

34

Life in Dresden

For the next week or so I was allocated work inside Dresden itself, and so I got the opportunity to look around and take in the beauty of the place. For centuries, the city had been a centre for music and musicians from all over Europe. Their music haunted the streets.

Dresden was a city with something for everyone to delight in. It even had a magnificent circus and zoo. Dresden stood proud. The twisting, narrow side streets were still in the cobbled state they had been in for centuries past. As for the residents, they had a reputation for being independent to an extreme, and the area had been dubbed 'Red Saxony'. The POWs who were contained in the dozens of small *Arbeitskommandos* were given a degree of freedom unknown in other parts of the Third Reich.

Dresdeners were aloof from the war and stood by their belief that their city was unique and would never endure the fate that cities like Hamburg had suffered.

'Why would they waste their bombs on us? So we have a few toothpaste factories. Yes, we manufacture perfume and soap. Yes, there are a few installations which do war work but they are right outside in the suburbs.'

The rumour had gone around, and was believed by many, that if Oxford had been spared Dresden would be, too. Some shelters were built, most noticeably a huge one by the main railway station, and cellars were shored up. Dotted around the old part of the town, the *Altstadt*, were large water-storage tanks made out of concrete. Those were the only precautions they saw fit to take.

By the end of January, Dresden was filled to bursting point with fearful refugees fleeing from the atrocities being carried out by the ever-advancing Red Army. Added to this, the normal population of about a hundred thousand had been increased by the POWs and forced labourers from all over Europe, brought in to help maintain the public health system, the postal service, the rail system and the ever-increasing sewage problem. As the Russian army advanced, so every day more and more of these pitiful people were clogging up the roads and bridges leading into what they believed would be a safe haven.

The old *Feldwebel*, the lad in charge of the camp, must have decided that Billy and me needed some form of punishment for our foolish escape attempt. He put us to work in the sauerkraut factory. This was considered to be one of the worst winter jobs. Lorries from the fields delivered cabbages to the factory in huge frozen blocks, which had to be broken up by hand. Then the cabbages were cut up, and shovelled into a large vat. Having done this to the satisfaction of the owner, four of us at a time had to put on rubber boots and trudge around inside the massive vat until the cabbages were squashed to a pulp. It took four of us three hours to pulp each batch. The overseer would lock us in the vat room, with no toilets of any type. I had never eaten sauerkraut up to that date, and since that experience I probably never will.

That little number lasted until about the end of January, when I was told that I would be detailed for fresh work. The next morning I started my new assignment. Up to the gates comes an old boy complete with a farm cart pulled by a couple of bullocks, each sporting a huge pair of horns. This throwback to the Dark Ages was to pick me up every morning. In the evening I had to make my own way back to the camp. I asked the commandant if he wasn't a bit worried about letting me roam about so freely.

'Don't worry,' he says, 'by the time you've finished for the day you'll be so tired that you will probably be crawling back here on your hands and knees.'

I soon realised that the average Dresdener had never experienced dustmen as we know them. Every house had a huge pit at the back where all the household waste was thrown. Real stink pits. Our job was to empty them out. So we toured the city, the two of us sitting high on the seat of the wagon, below us the bullocks, grunting and steaming and defecating their way through the day.

On the first job of the day I'm given a six-foot-long pitchfork and told to get down into the pit and start shovelling the muck up to the surface. Eager to please, I jump in and practically disappear into the filth. The old boy stands there on top laughing like a drain. By one o'clock we had done three houses. In his own brand of German/English he shouts to me, *'Arbeit fertig*. Go we now home for food eat.' So off we go, first to the tip where we empty the cart and on through the city of Dresden right up to the banks of the Elbe itself.

If the bullock cart was something out of the past, the old boy's house dated back even further. It stood in the centre of a clearing in the forest, with the Elbe lapping at its foundations. It was an old timbered shack with a thatched roof, but not like the neat thatching you might see in arty-crafty England. This thatch was dried grass and weeds, drawn, it seemed, straight from the riverbed.

We were greeted by his wife, an apparition who looked like one of Macbeth's witches. I'm invited into the house and in no time at all the table is loaded with steaming bowls of stew and huge portions of fresh black bread. The old couple had no time at all for the authority of the state or anyone else, and the citizens of Dresden accepted their idiosyncrasies as long as they were prepared to empty the cesspits. He had stopped charging them money for his services long ago. He kept the pits clean in return for food.

I rolled back to camp with my stomach in agony. I had not

eaten so much for a very long time. The journey took me two hours. In my pocket I had a large German sausage and a full loaf of bread. Billy and I ate well that night and for many more nights after that. This happy state of affairs carried on for some three weeks until the old boy lent me his bike so he wouldn't have to come all the way to the camp every morning.

January was merging into February, the distant sound of gunfire had got noticeably louder with every passing day. The Russians could only be fifty or sixty miles away. It was my third day with the bike and I decided to make another bid for freedom. I headed off into the west. I had gone about a dozen miles when a lorry sent me sprawling into a ditch and put paid to my escape. Once again I was returned to the waiting arms of the camp commandant. Goodbye to that lovely job. When he realised that there would be no more lovely grub, Billy did his nut and called me all the names he could think of.

'I'm not having anything else to do with you,' he says, 'you're a nutcase.' I fully understood his reasoning.

Strangely, I wasn't punished for this latest escapade. The old boy got his bike back and another helper in place of myself. The next few days saw me cleaning out the cesspits in the camp, but this was a mild punishment which I had to endure until the old commandant could decide what to do with me. The decision was made for him when an urgent request came from the local soap factory for more workers.

On the day we were due to be marched to the soap factory, we were lined up for the morning roll-call, stamping our feet to ward off the cold. The sky was an icy blue, the early sun breaking up the winter mist. We heard the unmistakable sound of aircraft, and there, far above, were about two hundred of them. Some poor sods are going to get their balls blown away was what we thought, then we saw a Very light fired from the leading aircraft. We all, British and German alike, knew what this meant: they were about to unload.

The next few moments were very tense as the planes passed directly overhead, then we heard the unmistakable sound of air being displaced by heavy bombs. We all threw ourselves to the ground. I didn't hear any explosion; I was only aware of the earth jumping up and down. Me and the guard next to me were thrown in the air. We landed in a crater about ten feet deep, unhurt except for an insistent ringing in our ears.

Nobody on the parade ground had been hurt. Not so lucky were the poor devils who had the job of being the camp cooks. They had been preparing the morning slop, unaware of the arrival of the planes. One of the bombs landed right on top of them. Their remains were plastered over what was left of that end of our shed along with the guard whose job it had been to supervise the cooking. No work today.

Everyone, prisoners and guards, got stuck in clearing up the mess. Some timber appeared and by the afternoon the shed had been repaired. What remains we could find of our comrades and the German guard were scraped together and consigned to three wooden boxes. Silvertop visited us that evening and expressed his sorrow at the tragedy. He had already arranged for a small service of remembrance at the local church. The three men would be buried with honour. The camp commandant even raked up an old soldier with a trumpet to sound 'The Last Post' as the coffins were laid to rest in their German graves. That evening all the prisoners signed a letter of thanks to the commandant and to Captain Jünger for showing respect to our dead comrades. The following day, back to work as normal.

The *Seiffabrik* (soap factory) was about six kilometres south of the camp and we had to walk there and back. Because of the shortage of any type of fats, the 'soap' was really pumice powder, compressed into tablet form. I had been teamed up with a chap who turned out to be even more hare-brained than myself. He came from up north somewhere and had been captured in Italy, since when he had made two efforts to get away. We were detailed to go into a large outhouse, where we shovelled the pumice powder into a wheelbarrow, which was then wheeled up a ramp and emptied into the mouth of a huge mixer. When the overseer was satisfied with the consistency of the mix it was poured out of the machine ready to be put in the stamping machine and then the drier.

The pumice powder was piled up against one side of the shed; piled up against the other was about four tons of cement which another group of POWs were using to build an extension. The cement looked almost the same as the pumice powder. What followed was not my idea. It was the last mix of the day when Mad Harry, as I called him, suggested we give the mixer a ration of cement 'to see what happens'. I agreed to this madcap scheme. What happened was that, at first, the overseer couldn't understand why the usual consistency could not be attained.

'OK, leave it until tomorrow morning.' With that he switches off the power and we all march back to our respective camps.

Next day the overseer switches on the power. For about four minutes nothing, and then without warning all the ancient wiring began to smoulder and soon the whole roof was ablaze. The cement had set solid and jammed the machinery which in turn had shorted the electrical circuits. War shortages meant that spare parts didn't exist and the main fuses, which should have blown and cut off the power, had long ago been bodged with metal strips. The fuses didn't melt and the metal strips glowed red hot and set everything around them on fire. Soon the whole factory was ablaze. In no time at all the culprits had been traced, the police were sent for and they called in the local Gestapo. Harry and I were in deep trouble. As we were being booted into the police van the roof collapsed, sending up a triumphant fountain of sparks and flame, a tribute to Mad Harry's act of defiance. We were both taken to a large building in the centre of the city.

35

Thunderclap

Mad Harry and myself were dragged into the so-called *Straflager*. We were told that we would be charged and sentenced the next day. The building was circular in shape and so crowded that it was impossible to find room to sit down. In the centre of the hall were four forty-gallon oil drums, overflowing with excrement. The smell was something to be believed. The building had a large, circular glass roof. At some time it must have been a library or perhaps some sort of museum, at least that's what it reminded me of.

The room held about two hundred and fifty men of all nationalities, all condemned to death for crimes against the Nazi state. We knew that tomorrow our names would be put on the same list. Harry and I were in no doubt that if ever there was a place where evil things happened, this was it. The whole place looked and smelt of evil.

All the doors were bolted on the outside; we could see no way out. We got talking to a couple of Yanks who were in there for looting, a capital offence. They had been sentenced to be shot and they certainly looked real worried. These two unhappy men had been in the place for five days. They told us that roughly thirty of the inmates were taken out each morning, never to be seen again. This news cheered us up no end. Even so, we thought, where there's life there's hope.

It was now the morning of 13 February. At noon there was a general movement towards the door. Grub up! In it came, a huge drum of soup, no plates, no utensils. Some were too listless to attempt to join in the scrum. As for Harry and yours truly, we just looked on. Neither of us was all that hungry.

By managing to give a kick here and a shove there, we made ourselves enough room to get into some sort of lying-down position. Sleep was absolutely out of the question. What was going through Harry's mind I have no idea, but to me it seemed that, finally, all was lost. There was no point in agonising about what we should and shouldn't have done to avoid being sent to this place. In the end we spent what we thought might be our last few hours attempting to crack jokes, taking the mickey out of the other inmates and trying to convince ourselves that at least we weren't dead yet. We were doing our best to kid each other that perhaps we might get away with it, knowing, in the pit of our stomachs, that we'd had it.

At about 9.30 the air-raid sirens started their wailing. This failed to bring much response, then another, deeper sound made its impact upon our senses. The bloody planes were overhead. The drone gradually turned into a crescendo of noise until it felt as if the foundations of the place were coming apart.

We noticed that the sky, which we could see through the glass roof, was getting brighter by the minute. We could see long streamers of light slowly, almost hesitatingly, filtering their way down to earth. Inside the building it was as if all the lights were coming on. These were, of course, the marker flares drifting to earth through streamers of their own smoke.

It was at this point that some of the terrified inmates began wailing, then the wails turned to screams. I had to shut my ears to the demented noise.

Now the sky through the glass took on a deep red glow but there were still no real hard explosions. The flares hung in the sky for at least fifteen minutes, all the time the sound of the aircraft overhead increased in intensity, and then there was a short lull: the pathfinders had done their job and hotfooted it for home.

The lull was very short-lived, less than three or four minutes, and then it all kicked off. This time the noise of the incoming planes had a much deeper and heavier throb. The whole building shook with the reverberation of the aircraft passing overhead. Then the bombs began to land. The noise of the falling bombs was similar to the sound of a tube train as it rushes through a tunnel, but not one train – hundreds of them. A lot of the inmates were banging on the doors now, screaming to be let out, but those doors were stout and didn't give an inch. The guards had made themselves very scarce indeed. We were the last problem on their minds. By now the raid had been in progress for roughly fifteen minutes and we had not the slightest idea what was going on outside.

The next panic came when two incendiaries burst through the glass roof. This was a very nasty moment as huge shards of glass rained down into the centre of the hall. The incendiaries had broken up and large blobs of burning sulphur, or whatever those devilish things were made of, were coming down and sticking to the clothing and flesh of the prisoners directly underneath. It was impossible to kill the flames and thirty or more men suffered the agony of burning to death. Harry and I just sat by the far wall and let fate take its course.

Luckily, the smoke and fumes were drawn up through the shattered roof, so down at ground level the air was still clear. What began to worry us more was the fact that it was getting very hot. During all this Harry was still making a joke of the whole situation.

'No need to worry about tomorrow now, Vic,' says he. 'It's their own arses they're worrying about now.'

We were still crouched against our bit of wall thinking that at last the raid was over, when there was a tremendous crash and the wall opposite flew inwards. I had the sensation of being picked up bodily as if by some giant, invisible hand. The concussion and the force of the blast must have knocked me unconscious because the next thing I remember was being totally blind. Fortunately, this was caused by the clouds of dust and grit that closed out all light. I later reckoned that I must have been thrown the whole length of the building, about forty feet. I shouted out for Harry: no answer. At this time I was half buried under broken masonry but as I struggled to my feet it occurred to me that, apart from an excruciating pain in my back and legs, I was all in one piece. Nearly all of those who had been standing at the time must have been killed instantly, either by the blast or by the debris that came showering inwards.

As soon as the dust settled I somehow managed to grope my way over the rubble, along with the other lucky survivors. I began to look around, half expecting Harry to start cracking more jokes. Alas, when I found Harry he was lying completely motionless, half buried by the bricks and mortar that had been blasted inwards. Further examination told me that Harry was not of this world any more. He had the expressionless eyes that I had seen many times before on the battlefield. I knew death when I saw it. I managed to close Harry's eyes and pull some sort of cover over his twisted body.

Harry's sudden departure from the scene really knocked me for six. Here I was, in a situation in which at the moment there was no freedom of movement, without a companion to share my thoughts with, and all the time aware that life was being brutally extinguished all around me. On reflection, I suppose that these flashes of despair that were racing through my thoughts took me about the same amount of time as it did to realise that Harry was beyond help – a few seconds.

I sat down by Harry's side for some moments until I became aware that the roof of the building was in danger of collapse. With all the other survivors I joined in the dash for the opening and freedom. Outside we were met by an overpowering wall of heat, as if we had run into a furnace. People were rushing about screaming, everything engulfed in dust, smoke and flames.

By now the time must have been close on midnight, maybe

later, maybe a lot earlier, who could tell? Time meant nothing. The planes had gone, the raid was over – time to escape, something that wasn't quite as easy as it seemed. The fires were increasing in intensity by the minute. I was in the middle of a huge bonfire. On top of this, I had to contend with falling masonry. Everywhere buildings were collapsing in showers of dust and flame. The noise was indescribable.

This was my baptism of war as experienced by civilians, and I wasn't enjoying one moment of it. On top of all this, every movement I made was accompanied by terrible pain, as if a thousand knives were being stuck into my sides. Common sense told me that this could only be bruising caused when I was hurled from one end of the building to the other. It would get better in time; at least I was still mobile: no blood, all limbs intact. Put me down as walking wounded.

I had to take cover somewhere until the fires died down. Crouching in a shop doorway, as good a place as any, I took in a scene that was completely outside my experience. Terrified women, clutching their children, were scurrying out of piles of rubble that only a few moments earlier had been their homes. Everything was alight. All around buildings in full flame were crashing to the ground as if being pushed by giant hands, their timber structures destroyed by the inferno. The road was covered with bits of burning rooftops, more sections of which were crashing to the ground leaving trails of sparks in their wake.

Like everyone else, I was numb with terror. There seemed to be no way out of the ring of fire that we were caught in. Terrified or not, I do remember that I was calm enough to stand under that one small piece of shelter until the heat forced me to move. Small groups of people who had managed to survive the onslaught were moving about in twos and threes, all looking desperately for a way through the flaming ring. Keeping as near to the centre of the road as possible, I followed the direction of these groups, and finally ended up in a small, tree-lined square. The trees were in flames but at least it was a bit calmer and there was no danger of a building falling down on top of me.

I was starting to believe that, with a little luck, I would be able to extricate myself from this mess. Things would surely get easier in daylight

All the time the heat was getting more intense and instead of the fires dying down they seemed to be gaining in ferocity. The situation was precarious. The small square had quickly become so crowded that it wouldn't be long before people would be sitting in each other's pockets. This was not for me. Slowly and painfully, I moved towards what I thought was the outer perimeter of the conflagration, finally reaching a large open space; but this area was also getting crowded out, so I continued on until I found myself close to the railway station.

At first sight, the station, or what was left of it, seemed quite empty, then I discovered that nearly everyone was in the underground shelter. The doors had been shut by those in charge in order to stop overcrowding.

Nobody now seemed to be running; the initial panic had abated. Groups of people were stumbling around trying to find a way through the furnace that surrounded them. Buildings would come crashing down without warning, cutting off escape routes which may have been open only a few seconds before. As it turned out, the fact that the entrance to the station shelter had been closed turned out to be a lucky break for me and any others who might have tried to get in. There were some five thousand souls, trapped inside, mainly old and infirm people, mothers with their children, all crowded into a concrete sarcophagus. At some time during the raid the building on top of the shelter collapsed, blocking the doors and the only avenues of escape. One can only hazard a guess at the horror that must have unfolded after that. They were trapped in an oven and were slowly roasted to death. One could only hope that death came through asphyxiation due to the lack of air. Thinking about the barbarous ending of their lives could put the mind of a normal person beyond repair.

And so the night progressed. The heat out in the open became overpowering and still no signs of the fires abating. What was making things worse was the wind which had by now reached an intensity that I had never before experienced. It was howling like a tornado, sucking at my clothes as, somehow, I managed to make it back to the park.

A terrible death was being inflicted on thousands of families as they huddled in their *Luftschutzkellers* below the burning remains of their houses, all helpless civilians with not a fighting man among them. And this first onslaught was only the opening phase of the attack. This was genocide, ordered by high-ranking politicians, not by the armed forces. For myself, I will never forgive them. Never.

36

The Uppercut

The firestorm bombing technique had been developed in the big raids on Hamburg and other cities. It was not a weapon designed to destroy factories, rail links, marshalling yards and the like; it was designed purely to strike terror into the hearts and minds of the populace, and so destroy the will of the German people to go on fighting the war. The concept was simple, the thinking behind it fiendish. This is how it worked.

The first wave of planes, about four to five hundred, headed for the centre of the targeted city. Each plane carried incendiaries plus thousand-pound, thin-walled blast bombs. The objective was to set as many buildings on fire as possible. The scale and the ferocity of the attack would render the fire crews and relief organisations incapable of any effective means of assistance. The fires would spread rapidly from house to house, helped by the fact that most of the buildings in these old German towns were made of wood. The outside walls might be brick, but that was only a façade.

Once the fires took hold, the oxygen needed to feed the flames would be sucked into the conflagration; this quickly created a tornado. The wind would then suck every movable object, including human beings, up into the vortex. Then they would fall back, humans and otherwise, into the fires raging below. But this was not the end. The fire would suck everything back into the vacuum that had been created above the furnace. Objects would soar back into the air, up to a thousand feet, into the mushroom of smoke and flame which hung over everything. This is what I saw, and what thousands of men, women and children became the victims of, and we couldn't do a thing to help them.

About a couple of hours after the start of the first attack, fresh rescue services began to arrive from the outlying towns. A train-load of supplies appeared at the goods yards next to the demolished station. How the train arrived nobody seemed to know; probably it was there from the beginning. Wherever they could re-establish their authority, small groups of police and military rounded up any men they could find and sent them to the area around the station. Once there, they were kitted out with picks, shovels, crowbars and the like, and then sent in to try and save the poor unfortunates trapped in the cellars.

These groups were made up of all nationalities – British POWs, labour groups from France and Poland, Americans, even Germans. There was no sorting out; those collected were just sent in in groups to get as near as they could to the catastrophe and start work. You had to hand it to the Germans' ability to organise.

I can only describe what I saw from my group, but other groups must have seen similar things all over the city. By now it was well past midnight, the whole of Dresden was burning and it was impossible to get into the centre, the *Altstadt*, so intense was the heat. To make matters worse, the water mains had burst, flooding the roads. You walked in the water at your own risk – it was boil-ing – and on top of that the tarmac on the road surfaces had turned to sticky, melted pitch. I still had the wooden clogs which I had been given in the laager and these probably saved my feet from the blisters I was later to suffer on my face and hands. While we waited for the fury of the flames to die down, a halt was called to the rescue work, and instead we were fed by a female contingent going round in an army lorry dishing out bowls of hot soup.

You might ask: 'Why not just get out of the city?' The answer is that it was impossible. The rescue teams were encircled by their own rings of flame. Getting away would have been like jumping out of the frying pan into the fire. There was no escape; any person who was unfortunate enough to be in the city when the raid started was doomed to remain there until they were killed or the flames died down.

At about 1 a.m. the sirens started wailing again. Surely they weren't going to bomb a second time? In no time at all more flares were floating to earth like huge, dangling Christmas trees right over the centre of the city. It was difficult to understand why the flares were necessary. Their brilliance was dimmed by the inferno below.

The howling wind and the roaring flames manufactured by the firestorm made it almost impossible to hear the armada of aircraft as they swept over us. Bombs began to explode around us and all that anyone could do was to lie as flat as possible in the nearest doorway, or make use of whatever other cover was available.

The circle of fire had now consumed the entire old city. Whatever chance those trapped inside might have had, that chance was now long gone. They were all doomed. There was no way in and no way out. Some of the rescue workers who had the courage to attempt the impossible were simply caught up in the arms of the winds and hurled bodily into the inferno. We could only look on, covering our faces as best we could from the searing heat. The heat became so intense that we were forced to retreat even further back and all the time the fires grew in ferocity.

At daybreak all available personnel were sent back to the railway yards to start afresh. These yards were free of buildings and had become another island surrounded by flames. Apparently railway lines do not catch fire.

By now it was impossible to tell who was who; our faces and hands were blackened by the smoke and our clothing scorched to a brownish colour. One and all were treated as equals. Even seven hours after the second raid there was no sign that we were having any effect on the situation. The entire centre of the city was a raging furnace, and all attempts to enter this epicentre had been abandoned. We were sent to the area outside the *Altstadt* where the fires were not so fierce.

37

The Hammer Blow

From first light on the morning of 14 February, hundreds of POWs from the surrounding camps, along with gangs of foreign workers, were assembled around the perimeter of the devastated city. With our picks and shovels, we moved slowly across the mountains of smouldering rubble that had once been the pride of Europe.

All around us lay burnt and shrivelled-up corpses, some in groups, some lying flat in the roadways, literally stuck to the tarmac which had glued them to it when it melted, and then imprisoned them as it cooled and hardened. The atmosphere everywhere was polluted with the smell of roasted flesh. As if these mounds of bodies were not enough, we had to come to terms with an even worse horror which was revealed as we dug into the collapsed houses, trying to reach the cellars.

The scenes that we uncovered made some of the most hardened of us fall back in despair. The inmates of these cellars, if they hadn't been blasted to pulp, were shrivelled down to about a quarter of their normal size. In building after building men, women and children had suffered the same gruesome fate.

The bodies that were still in one piece were brought to the surface and piled up by the side of the road for later identification. But many were just a mass of blood, mud and pulped-up flesh. Some of the men were sick; quite a few were in an advanced state of shock. In the gang I was with, which numbered about two dozen, only half were able to carry on with the work.

For myself I must have worked on, carrying out the orders more like a robot than a human being. The nightmare that we were going through was an introduction to hell.

By now, everybody had assumed that the raid was over and that it would only be a matter of time before the rescuers would be able to break through the fire and get to the centre of the city, although we all dreaded what we would find when we got there.

Now and again we heard the sounds of shots. Strict warnings had been issued that looting meant instant death, by hanging, or by firing squad, and this is what we were hearing. Anyone caught with anything in their pockets other than their personal possessions was being dealt with on the spot, no ifs or buts.

Our work continued until sometime around midday when the sirens started wailing once again. The group I was attached to had grown to about fifty or so. We had reached an area near the park and upon hearing the sirens we were marched into it en masse. Inside the park was the city zoo which had already been hit and devastated in the second attack. A lot of the surviving and injured animals had freed themselves from the wreckage and were now roaming loose among the debris of smashed-up buildings. There were a small number of these animals, from tigers to small monkeys, lying about screaming with the pain from their wounds. These were put out of their misery by the guards with their rifles and small arms.

The demonic wailing of the sirens filtered through the roar of the wind and the crackling of the flames. They were still wailing when the American bombers appeared over the city. There were about four hundred planes and this time the bombing was more haphazard. A number of the groups were caught in the open and suffered heavy casualties. What caused even more damage were the smaller fighters which came afterwards. Apparently they had been told that they could come down to ground level with complete impunity, which is what they did, shooting at anything that moved. One of these planes hit the side of a house, crashed and burst into flames almost at our feet. We all gave a loud cheer and nobody moved to help that stricken pilot.

How could anyone justify this latest act of barbarity? For myself I felt ashamed that, being British, I was associated with this immorality.

Today, historians argue that the strafing did not happen. My memory may be playing tricks; it was, after all, one of the most chaotic and violent events I have ever lived through. But this is what I remember happening.

The third raid lasted about half an hour and, after the planes had passed by, the fires that had earlier started to die down were now blazing with renewed intensity. A new furnace opened up that the firefighters were powerless to deal with. Mercifully, this was the last raid, but it would be many hours before the flames died down and the terrible heat abated.

I spent three or four days with the team I was working with. I stayed mainly because, above all, we were being fed and sheltered. We slept inside wagons on the railway sidings and would emerge every morning to carry on the sickening work of sorting out the dead from the still smoking ruins. The railway sidings and marshalling yards were completely undamaged – not one bomb had landed inside the boundaries of this important transport facility.

By now I was worried that as soon as things began to get back to some semblance of normality I would be returned to another *Straflager* to face execution – not a pleasant thought.

So one morning I managed to stray away from the group and make my way against the tide of refugees which was still flowing in from the east. Over the Elbe bridge, ever eastwards. As far as I can remember I spent the better part of three days on the road, scrounging morsels of food wherever I could. Then, without warning, I found myself among a motley mass of troops: I had made it to the leading elements of the Russian forces. Of the German army there was no sign, only this mass of Russians.

It was a scene of utter chaos. Without any apparent source of command, there were just Russians, thousands of them, moving west across the fields, through the villages, always west. It was an incredible sight. Now and again there would be a burst of machine-gun fire and some sporadic rifle shots. What was being fired at I never found out. One thing was certain: no German forces were opposing them in this sector.

I could do nothing more than sit down among them and scrounge food. I tried everything I could to get them to understand that I was a British soldier but there was no way of getting through. I was stuck.

As for my appearance, I hadn't shaved for about a week at least, or washed for that matter. My clothes were hanging in threads and scorched to such brittleness that the slightest touch caused what was left to disintegrate into dust. Large, painful blisters had begun to form on my face and hands. The good thing was that I was alive, even if I was nearly naked. Getting food was all that I worried about. Something would come out in the wash. It always did.

Later, I worked out why it had been so easy to get away. All the spare manpower that the German authorities had was being used to divert the flood of refugees coming from the east away from the city. Once over the main bridge all I had to do was to keep going against the human tide. The nearer I got to the invaders the easier it turned out to be. In fact, once I was within striking distance I could have just sat down by the roadside and waited for them. It was sheer hunger that drove me on; nothing else mattered but food. So I left the smoking ruins of Dresden behind me as, mile by mile, I made the exhausting and painful trek to freedom.

38

It's All Over Now

I spent the next six or seven weeks with the Russian army. The big battle, the bloody struggle for Berlin, was in the north. I was away from the fighting with the Ukrainian Front army which was heading for Leipzig. Once I was whisked off to an interrogation area. Who was I? How had I arrived? I didn't understand a word until a German officer who was acting as a sort of liaison got hold of me. With him was a Russian officer who was able to speak a sort of pidgin English-cum-French. They said they didn't know what to do with me; not only was I disgustingly filthy but also the blisters that now covered my face and hands had begun to burst. Then they gave me a pair of Russian trousers and a jacket and sent me to have the blisters dressed. I was told that I could travel along with them if I wanted – not in those actual words, but that is what was meant. I thought this was a very good idea. After all, they were feeding me.

Watching the Russian army on the move was like watching a giant crowd leaving a football stadium after a match. They would move forward no more than about six or seven kilometres a day, stop and do the same again the next day and so on and on. Thousands of men on the move, spread over the hills like ants, with no apparent order or discipline. Only the front waves of this human avalanche seemed to be armed. Behind them, straggling along, came thousands more men, walking straight through anything that stood in their path – villages, towns, anything. Any opposition was crushed by the sheer weight of this vast Russian tide.

For my part I got into the good books of the dozen or so men I had attached myself to. One morning they couldn't get their truck, an American Chevrolet, to start. I realised that the Russians knew very little about even basic forms of maintenance. If a truck stopped they either stuck a horse on the front, if they had one, or men were detailed to pull and push. I knew all about the quirks and fancies of these particular engines. To get the Chevrolet going I just had to clean the plug leads, dry out the distributor and away she went. From then on I could do no wrong, and found my services in great demand. At least I was earning my keep.

Then the armies of the East and West finally joined hands and I met up with two Canadians. On Monday 7 May 1945 news came through that the Germans had finally capitulated. The war was over, although nobody would have thought it from the noise of small-arms fire all around.

That night the Russians ran amok and brought terror to the city we were in. Most of the population tried to escape to the west. I will just say that the Ukrainian forces behaved in a very gruesome way, a way which would not have been tolerated in our own army. The Russian troops showed no compassion towards the German population and seemed to take looting and raping as their just reward. One of the many things I saw was a Russian officer shooting a German for not obeying his orders quickly enough. It was a terrible time for the civilian population. I will leave it at that.

I wished my new-found friends farewell, we drank mugs of the firewater of which they had an inexhaustible supply, then, with the help of a Canadian despatch rider, I made my way to the British command centre.

My particulars were taken and I was directed to the mobile showers, given new clothing and had my blisters dressed by the medics. Then I was given a bed in a huge marquee that had been set up for the benefit of the stragglers who were arriving every hour of the day. After a week in this place I was put on board an old Wellington en route for home. In no time at all I was treading English soil once again. Somehow, I had survived.

Once back home I was sent to a camp to be sorted out. I got asked the usual crap: Who was I? Where had I come from? How had I managed to get there? I was told to collect my due pay and was given indefinite leave. I would be contacted about where and when to report back.

Now I was really going home, and I was still in one piece. I had to prepare myself for a life in the company of those I now hardly knew. Many a homecoming long-serving soldier must have had the same qualms as I had. Dresden had made me feel like a murderer; it had altered my whole idea of war. Never again was I to view it as a glorious adventure. On the train going home there were a load of the lads, living it up. I don't remember saying a word to any of them. I must have seemed a right miserable sod.

39

Demobilised

By the time I arrived at Waterloo station my mood had changed and, like the other lads, I was excited to be home. I was wearing all new gear; the only original article of clothing was my old stained red beret. I had managed to hold on to it through thick and thin and, to tell the truth, I was very proud of it. What made the battered red beret even better was that I still had my old RB badge pinned to the front of the wings. Like most of the lads who had come into the Paras from other units, my true allegiance was to my parent unit.

I left Waterloo and walked, weighed down by all my worldly belongings, all the normal army kit. I lugged it through all the familiar places, across Waterloo Bridge, up the Aldwych, along Kingsway and on to Russell Square, my old stamping grounds. My impatience to get home finally got the better of me and I took a tube to the Caledonian Road. In no time I was outside the two small rooms on the second floor of our tenement house in Ellington Street.

By now I was a bag of nerves, but the love I was greeted with is something I shall never experience again. Though I enjoy the deep love of my wife Betty, I am haunted by the memory of that first greeting and being given my son Alan to hold. In the last stages of pregnancy, Freda had seen the armada taking us to Arnhem as it flew over London. This had upset her and Alan had been born several weeks premature. He was now a beautiful strapping baby.

The excitement of it all was overwhelming. I was treated as a conquering hero and made the obligatory visits to our families,

friends and relations. I wanted nothing but to stay in this haven
of rest and safety forever. It was all over. I was home. The days and
weeks flew by until I received the orders to report to an army
depot at Tidworth for assessment.

I reported to the camp and was put in a bungalow on my own.
I couldn't work out why. I couldn't understand what it all meant.
I expected to be returned to my old unit, 10th Battalion The
Parachute Regiment. After two days it came up on the detail
board that I was to be interviewed the next day.

The report I had made at the reception centre in Germany had
followed me. The questioning started. They wanted to know why
I had been with the Russians for all those weeks. Why had I gone
east and not west? I asked the two officers who were questioning
me if they had any idea of the situation I had found myself in. Had
they any clue of what had really happened during those horren-
dous days in Dresden? All they were interested in was 'Why the
Russians?' On and on they went, like a stuck gramophone record.
'Surely you could have just as easily walked towards our own
troops?'

At that point I must have lost my temper completely. In the
end I was given orders to report to a Royal Artillery camp at a
place called Tregantle Fort in Cornwall. I was given a railway
warrant to Plymouth, and told that transport would be laid on to
pick me up. My request to be allowed to rejoin either the Parachute
Regiment or, failing that, the nearest Rifle Brigade unit, fell on
deaf ears. Two days later found me reporting for duty at the fort.

Tregantle is as remote a place as one could ever wish to find, an
old fort stuck up on the moors ten miles to the west of Plymouth.
To get to it you had to cross by the old chain ferry at Torpoint.
Even on the sunniest of days it seemed to be hidden by clouds of
clinging mist. At Tregantle I was kept practically incommuni-
cado. All the other men had similar tales to tell and none of us
could understand why we were there. I demanded an interview
with the Commanding Officer and told him that I wished to

complete my service for the full twenty-one years. His reply completely amazed me. He wasn't a bad bloke; all he knew was that I had been involved with 'the enemy' and that I was to be given my discharge papers with 26 Group, the next batch of men to be demobilised. This would happen within the next two months. I asked what was meant by being 'involved with the enemy', thinking that he meant the Germans. 'No, not at all,' he stated, 'it means your involvement with the Russians.' This took me completely aback. I realised that to argue would be so much wasted effort. All I wanted now was for the next two months to pass as quickly as possible.

I had one home leave from the fort and soon enough I found myself in the discharge centre at Plymouth. I was fitted out with a brand new civvy suit, shoes and hat. Then I was given a kitbag full of my army clobber and told that I was on the 'Class Z Reserve'. I was to maintain my army kit in good order for further duty should this become necessary.

Then it was on to a crowded train with all the other lads who had been demobbed. They were all singing away, happy and relieved to be out of it. Halfway home I slung the kitbag out of the carriage window. I arrived at Paddington without a stitch of my past in my possession. I had ditched the last remnants of a nightmare. The friendship and comradeship that had been an essential ingredient of life had disappeared, and had been replaced by a military authority that I couldn't understand. I was totally free. If they wanted me again they would have to drag me through the streets screaming. I was finished with the army.

And so ended the second stage of my life. There was no glory, no thanks. Yes, I had a few medals, but they had gone out of the window with the rest of my army gear. I realised then that all the human endeavour that had gone into the last six years didn't mean a thing to the powers that be.

I kept returning to the memory of those comrades who had not made it home. Only the fact that the regime of Hitler and his

Third Reich had been defeated made any sense. I was going home
to the ones who really cared, and from now on I would get from
life what I could. No son of mine would ever go through the
horrors I had witnessed.

So that's how it ended. Instead of the natural joy that might
have been expected, I walked out of Paddington with a chip on
my shoulder as big as a house and a grievance against authority
that was to govern and shape my future.

This is the army's last word on yours truly.

PART THREE

40

Coming to Grips with Life

Like every soldier back from the war, I wanted a safe, steady, job, preferably with a pension at the end. And, like many men of my generation, I was still thinking in terms of the 1930s.

My first job was with the Post Office as a night telephonist on the National Trunk Service. This, I was told, was a job for life: no need to worry about the future! At first it was a struggle. I had to memorise the codes for all the towns and cities in the British Isles. This took me about two months and then, all too quickly, the job became a full-time bore. One of the first things I noticed was that a lot of the men sitting alongside me were calling each other 'dear' and 'darling'. I soon cottoned on to the fact that this employment was a refuge for a host of queenies. Not that I minded; I had long ago learnt not to judge men by any label attached to them. They either stood up to be counted, or they were passengers. They didn't bother me and I didn't bother them. They must have known I was not one of them. In any case I wanted to keep myself to myself. If I was asked about the war, I was noncommittal. True to form, I soon decided that the job was not my kettle of fish. I went to the supervisor and told him I'd had enough.

Then I got work on various building sites, paid daily. After a few months working here, there and everywhere I took a government course in painting and decorating. The courses lasted six months and were designed to assist ex-servicemen like me to get back on their feet. The level of instruction was of a very high calibre, and, when completed, I felt that I was capable of taking on any job offered, and I did.

In those days it was easy. There was such a shortage of labour that you could be sitting in a café having a break and a foreman would come in: 'How much you lads getting paid over there?', pointing to wherever he thought we might be working. He would up it by a penny or twopence. The average rate was about four shillings an hour. It was quite normal in those days for a London building worker to change employers twice a week. And there was no problem about going back to the firm you had left. Building firms doing bomb-damage work were paid by how many men they had on the job, not by the amount of work done. A gang could be working on a particular job, the foreman would come round and tell us to drop whatever we might be doing and get round to another job smartish. This meant the guv'nor of the firm had been told that an inspector was on his rounds to check on the number of men on site. The scramble to repair the damage done by the Blitz was one big fiddle. Builders made fortunes and we all took our cut.

The most profitable method would be to get in first on a job, get up on the roof and strip all the lead and copper, then wheel it around to the nearest scrap merchant on the handcart. Lorries and vans in those days were an unheard-of luxury, so every gang had its handcart.

The memory of those days makes me feel very emotional. For Freda and myself they were the happiest years of our lives. We had peace after years of hardship and danger and we had our boy Alan.

After a few months working on sites around the West End of London I was offered a job with one of London's most prestigious firms, Hamptons of Pall Mall. This firm did all the big government jobs. I was put to work in Buckingham Palace. Everywhere the gang went there would be a Palace flunkey, keeping an eye on us, worrying about the family silver, no doubt. It was on this job that one of the lads lent me a book: 'Read this and learn a thing or two.'

The book was Robert Tressell's *The Ragged Trousered Philanthropists*. (Tressell himself was a house painter.) 'Written donkey's years ago,' says the old painter whose book it was. 'You tell me if you think things have altered.' That book was an education and I still sometimes turn to my tattered copy if I feel I need an antidote to the latest political propaganda.

One day I was asked if I could do boat work. 'Boats' was the name given to the cradles that are used to get at the outside of high buildings. They weren't the smart motor-driven jobs you see today, more like Heath Robinson devices slung on ropes and poles: very precarious.

'Sure I can do boat work. How much extra?'

'Twopence an hour.'

So all was going well, I was earning a bomb and quite satisfied with my lot. Then one fine day we get a new bloke on the gang.

'Yes, I can manage a boat, worked on them all my life, guv!'

The usual spiel. There he was right next to yours truly.

By the time he had his gear into his boat I was fifty feet below him working away and simultaneously chatting up the inmates of the flats, in many cases very lonely women. Meanwhile, the new recruit was slowly making his way down to working level, foot by foot. It didn't take long to realise that he had never been in a cradle before in his life. He was just below me when the side of the cradle he was tying up slid down to the perpendicular. Luckily for him the other side held. There he was, about a hundred feet above the ground, hanging on for dear life, and screaming away, making enough noise to awake the dead.

In no time a crowd had gathered below looking no doubt for something interesting to happen, like the lad crashing to the ground. As I was the nearest to him it was up to me to attempt to get the lad out of trouble. I began to swing my cradle sideways, to the left and then to the right, left again and right, backwards and forwards until I had enough momentum to grab hold of the rope attaching his cradle to the roof. There was a danger that the poles holding my rig would come crashing down, taking jolly old me with it. I had to let go of my cradle and somehow get a hand on to his ropes and climb into his boat. This I did. Helped by brute strength and more by luck than judgement. I managed to hook the rope on and get the boat levelled off. By the time I got him back to earth the lad had gone completely berserk.

Life wasn't all work. One Sunday I went for a ride on my bike up through Epping, just for a morning out. I met a chap I used to go to school with who introduced me to some lads from a cycling club. After that, I got a proper bike of my own and started to train with them twice a week. We would do eighty or a hundred miles a night. It wasn't long before I discovered that I could easily outpace them all. I started to enter races and in order to get in training I began to look for jobs that were a long way away so that I could cycle to them and get in the miles. It was about this time that Freda and I decided to have a holiday. I acquired an old second-hand tandem, complete with a small sidecar. Then up to the old Caledonian Market where we purchased an ancient army bell tent and we were ready for the off. All our gear was tied precariously around our latest acquisition, half over the back wheel and the rest jammed into the chair. Young Alan was shoe-horned into the space that was left.

A comfortable three-day trip down to Portsmouth, and then along to Eastbourne and home, that was the plan. One evening, nearing Littlehampton, we decided to camp on the dunes. Tent up, cook the evening meal, Alan dashing here there and every-where, revelling in this new-found freedom, and so to kip.

The next morning, the sun had hardly risen when, to my alarm, I heard a very familiar sound, popping noises going off in the distance, followed by a rustling sound going overhead. I shook Freda out of her sleep.

'Hold Alan down and keep down yourself.'

'Whatsthematter?'

'Somebody's shooting at us, that's what's the matter.' I scrambled out of the tent to suss out the situation.

We had pitched the tent in a gully, right in the middle of an army firing range, and, to make matters worse, we were nearer to the butts than to the sods who were merrily firing in our direction. I went back to the tent to tell Freda of the perilous situation we were in, and told her to keep well into the gully. Then, somehow, I had to make my way to the firing line. When I finally got there the officer in charge blew his top. I waited for him to calm down and then asked him, quite casually, if it wasn't his responsibility to check the area first before commencing firing. I was beginning to enjoy myself, telling this pompous halfwit how he should do his job. We increased his embarrassment by taking the rest of the morning to pack our gear.

I had been in the army from the age of eighteen to twenty-seven. Perhaps the years I had missed were coming back to me. I began to disregard my family responsibilities and flung myself into cycling. I badly wanted to win. Getting to the top was all I wanted. This meant that training became an obsession, and I mean *hard* training. My normal routine would be at least a twenty-mile ride to work, further if I could get it. Then I'd get home in the evening, eat a meal of brown bread and dates, douse my body in evil-smelling embrocation, then go out for a hundred miles' roadwork. Then back home all sweaty and dog-tired for a sluice down, followed by a massage and then sleep like a dead man. If I was racing at the weekend, sex was out of the question any time after mid-week.

I never gave a thought as to what this routine was doing to Freda. I was drugged by success and that was all that mattered. I didn't notice the first-class wrecking job that all this was doing to my marriage. And there was something else. I soon became one of the idols of the female followers of the sport. Need I say more! I do not for one moment think that in this respect I was a one-off. The moral of the tale is, if the top has to be reached, get there, and once you are there remember all the people who love you and support you, who have made their own sacrifices for you. The way I went about it was the wrong way. I was well on the way to achieving national recognition as a racing cyclist and was even shortlisted for the British Empire Games to be held in New Zealand. I was training hard and spending less and less time with my family. I was becoming a person of note and the lights of success were blinding me to the warning lights that were flashing at home. In the end I never did reach the pinnacle.

My work towards becoming a leader in my chosen sport came to an end when I crashed halfway through a hundred-mile time trial. Somehow I rode to the University Hospital in Gower Street, which was about fifty miles away. The quack told me, 'Nothing to worry about, it's only a sprain.'

Three days later an X-ray revealed that my shoulder joint had come apart.

'You can either let it heal up in its own way, or we can screw it together.' I had six weeks off work and no screw. That episode ended my cycling days. Then I found a new interest: the trade union.

I had started working for a big south London decorating firm, and in no time I was sent down to the Festival of Britain site on the south bank of the Thames. This was a huge undertaking and I was employed as a sprayer. But in order to get on the site I had to get a 'ticket' – a trade union card.

To get one, I had to find a member who would propose me. Then I had to present myself to the local King's Cross branch of the National Society of Painters where the other members would ask me any questions about the trade that they saw fit. My answers satisfied the branch members so I was seconded and voted in. After that, like everyone else I had to attend the fortnightly branch meetings. If you missed one without a good excuse you were heavily fined. That's how it was with the craft unions; the ordinary general workers' unions were much more flexible and accommodating.

When I came home from Europe I was violently anti-communist in outlook. The scenes I had witnessed during my short stay with the Russians, even though I was friends with the lot I was with, left me with a revulsion for anything Russian. I discovered very quickly that the branch I had joined was practically run by Communist Party members and I lost no time in making my feelings known. I wasn't jeered; I wasn't laughed at; instead the chairman simply said that there was a vacancy for a minutes' secretary. He asked whether, if I was nominated and voted, I would be willing to take on the job. I accepted the challenge.

I was now on the committee of one of the most influential London branches of the National Society of Painters. Events began to occur with lightning speed. At all big building sites there was always a small communist working group. Part of their job was to sell the *Daily Worker* every morning at the site gates. Sitting in our dinner shed I happened to pick up that day's copy. Splashed across the front page was the story that the newly released German war criminal and steel magnate Alfried Krupp was to have his confiscated fortune returned – £50,000,000. This couldn't be true, I thought. It made it worse that Krupp was an arms' manufacturer. Some other business I might have been able to stomach, but not arms. I looked through my *Daily Mirror* – nothing – then through the *Daily Express* – nothing. The story was a load of communist bullshit, that was my conclusion.

To my horror, it turned out to be true, most of Krupp's fortune and businesses were being returned to him. The next day I let it be known that I wished to join the Party. I might not have done this if the Labour Party had opposed the plan to give such a huge sum back to Krupp, but the only opposition was coming from the Communist Party. Two weeks later I was told where I could attend if I wished to think about joining. Life was getting interesting.

41

I Become a Red, but not Under the Bed

With Freda's blessing, and with some trepidation, I presented myself one evening to the local Holborn Communist Party branch. The comrades were discussing some speech recently spewed forth by Comrade Stalin. I dutifully listened to the discussion and was asked my opinion. I immediately blotted my copybook by asking them if they really took all this propaganda and bullshit at face value. Consternation in the room.

'Why don't you agree with the statement, comrade?'

'Well, for a start I don't accept that any one person is infallible, and secondly I refuse to believe the statements of those who hold the reins of power.'

Deadly silence. Who was this person who dared to challenge Comrade Joe, the holy fount of all wisdom? Then I realised that some people in the room agreed with me. Thrusting myself forward as the devil's advocate came quite naturally to me. I have never believed what I am told, only what I can see with my own eyes. So I became a member of the Communist Party.

Freda and I moved away from Islington. I don't know why, because we were very happy there. We stayed for a bit with Freda's mother in Collier Street, off Pentonville Road. Then we moved on to two rooms above my mother's place in Kenton Street. This was not a success. Finally, Holborn Borough Council offered us a requisitioned flat in Bedford Way, right next to Russell Square, where we had our second boy, David. Freda and I had by now discovered that married couples have rows. Freda, being part Irish, generally came off best in these sometimes noisy eruptions, not so much to prove me wrong but mostly because she would invariably be in the right.

Freda too joined the Party and together we would go on all the rallies and protest marches. We went on one massive London demonstration in Whitehall, against German rearmament (where we discovered that the most effective means of dealing with mounted police was to throw handfuls of small ball bearings under the poor horses' hooves). Freda and a few of her friends decided to carry on the demo inside the Houses of Parliament itself. They got into the public gallery shouting, 'Shame, Shame', and scattered leaflets into the Chamber. They were locked away in the cells for the night. The following day they were all bound over to keep the peace for a specified time. No fines were issued. They spent the dinner hour after their release celebrating in a local pub. Freda returned home slightly tipsy. I was very proud of her, and that evening we went to a small party in honour of our women comrades.

We decided that we would try to get on the London County Council housing list. We ended up in a flat on the Bourne Estate off Gray's Inn Road. It was much smaller than the flat in Bedford Way, but at least we were out of the clutches of the Tory-run Holborn Council. We found ourselves in a totally different world.

The Bourne Estate was owned by the London County Council. The buildings were old and there was a strong sense of community among the tenants. On 22 January 1953 Freda had given birth to our third child, Judith. Her arrival gave us a lot of joy. We now had two lovely boys and a little girl. Life was wonderful.

It was on the Bourne that I first crossed swords with the law. It was the middle of summer and I had come home during my lunch hour. We were both sitting by the open window when Freda said she could hear Alan crying. Looking out of the window, I saw below a man throwing punches at our seven-year-old boy, and holding on to his coat to stop him running away. Like lightning I jumped out of the window and landed on top of him. Without further ado, I attacked, the only way I knew how – violently. I was protecting my own. The man was carted away in an ambulance while his wife had gone to the local cop shop to accuse me of assaulting her husband. Our local bobby came round and asked if I was the one the woman was complaining about. After I told him what had happened he said to me, 'Go and hide yourself. Nobody but meself knows who the culprit is and I'm not going to say a dicky bird.'

All this seemed very strange to me. As far as I was concerned I wasn't in the wrong. So I began to argue the toss. Eventually another policeman arrived and I was taken to the station and charged with common assault. I spent the night in the nick and went up in front of the beak the next morning.

My local trade union provided a solicitor, Mr Sedley, to represent me. (Sedley went on to become a High Court judge.) The magistrate heard the evidence and decided the public must be protected from scoundrels like me who attacked ordinary citizens without provocation.

'Fourteen days! Take him down.' Whereupon Freda fainted.

There was a huge local outcry over my conviction. The policeman who had advised me to scarper visited me in Brixton prison and told me that the magistrate, one Mr White, and the man I had put in hospital were members of the same Masonic Lodge. I came out on appeal, failed, and went back to finish my sentence.

In Brixton I had to go in front of the governor who told me how harsh things could be if I failed to observe the rules. He was taken aback when I told him I had experienced conditions far worse than he could ever imagine and that there was nothing in the British prison system that would cause me any sleepless nights.

Even in prison I could not stop my bolshie ways from surfacing. I was given the task of sewing mailbags, eight stitches to the inch. After an hour of this I approached the prison officer.

'Before I do another inch I want to know the rate for the job,' says I. Utter silence throughout the shed, and next morning I'm in front of the governor again.

'I know why you're in here and I can well understand your beef. Finish the rest of your term and keep your nose clean.'

I didn't go back to the sewing game; instead I got a cushy little number taking the library books around the cells. On the fourteenth day I was a free man again. That charge of assault was to ruin any chance I had of playing a part in local or national government. I had a record, and it remains with me to this day.

My next venture into the world of work started when I went into the road transport industry, a place where, as long as you were able to drive a lorry, find a load when away from base, go without sleep for six days at a time and not ask too many questions, you earned decent money.

In the fifties and sixties the road haulage business worked like this: you would get a load, usually ten or twelve tons of reinforcing steel, and drive it to wherever it was destined – Manchester, Birmingham, Timbuktu, it didn't matter so long as it paid.

You'd get there first thing in the morning and bullied, chivvied or pleaded with the foreman on the site to get you unloaded asap . . . Then you had to find a load back. Running empty was a quick way to lose your job.

This was not difficult. In all the big industrial areas there were transport businesses specialising in sending stuff all over the country. As long as they knew you by sight a ticket would be issued, and off you went to the depot to load up. On the way back you'd have a kip in a lay-by, and arrive back in London or wherever in the early hours of the morning. Then you got unloaded in the morning, off to load up again and so on. Drivers always carried two sets of log sheets, one set for the police if you were stopped, and one for the firm, both sets bent. Fraudulent, as the police would say.

We were paid by the hour. They reckoned you travelled at twenty miles an hour, and added six hours for loading and unloading. If you managed to get in two London to Newcastle trips in a week, at six hundred miles a go, you were in the money. Haulage firms didn't worry about cards, stamps, or income tax – that was for the birds. It was all one big fiddle.

The A5 was the main trunk route between London and Manchester, the busiest road in Britain. It was the custom in those years to do all trunking, as it was called, by night. From London the drivers would start their journeys around nine or ten in the evening. They would charge up Barnet Hill in north London before eleven, out through St Albans and on to the A5 proper. From midnight onwards the drivers of these juggernauts would be struggling to keep their eyes open as they drove their overloaded, badly maintained wagons to all points north. That was the romance of being a heavy goods driver in the years following the war.

I stuck it out for about seven years, away all week and not seeing my family from Sunday night to the following Friday. There was such a demand for labour that it was almost impossible to be out of work.

It was while working on the lorries that I made my first trip behind the Iron Curtain. I stuck David on the back of my battered old Triumph motorbike, strapped on all our gear and off we went, complete with visas. That was some trip.

It rained heavily all the way through northern Europe until we crossed the Brenner Pass into the sunshine, on through Ljubljana and down to the southern coast of Yugoslavia. The trip took us three weeks and to remember that country as it was, and what became of it after Tito died, the massacres and ethnic cleansing, just about breaks my heart.

I did this trip for the second time with Judith on the back. We had a nasty moment when the bike slipped off the road on a hairpin bend and slid down the mountainside but luckily we had managed to bail out. The local peasants retrieved the bike for us and on we went on our merry way. The lorry-driving-cum-gypsy way of living ended when I had a visit from two strangers.

I was driving for a firm in Stratford at the time. An incident had occurred which resulted in four of us being charged by the local police for a breach of the peace. Three days before we were due to attend court we were sitting in a café in Greenwich when one of the lads comes in and says that two geysers are sitting outside in a car and they want to talk to me. All and sundry do a scarper from the café thinking that it's the law, except, of course, me. I go to the car to see what they want.

I'm invited to sit in the back, given a history of my activities with the Party and a rundown of some of the measures that could be taken against me. Then one of them asks: 'How come a man with your military history allows himself to get mixed up with a bunch of commies?'

It seemed they knew about my involvement with Peniakoff, Major Sterling and the Long Range Desert Group. They implied that I would soon be offered a job which it might be in my interests to accept. To encourage me they said that I could forget the court case. It had been written off. Unusually for me, I managed to keep my mouth firmly shut during this conversation. Then I was out of the car and they were gone. I told nobody about this event, not even Freda. The court case was dropped and I waited to see what would happen next.

42

The Moscow Narodny Bank

One Saturday evening the comrade in charge of the Road Transport section knocked on the door. Saturday was the one night when I could be certain of being at home and all of us, the kids, Freda and myself were sitting round the table enjoying our evening meal. All chatter stopped as the comrade entered and introduced himself. It turned out that the London area committee had been asked to find a suitable and politically reliable comrade to take the job of chauffeur to the chairman of the Moscow Narodny Bank. Was I interested? It meant I would be home every night, I could negotiate my own wages and would have no more charging up and down the roads of Britain. Freda and the kids thought this was a great idea, but I was not so sure. But I agreed to report to Finsbury Circus the following Wednesday to meet the chairman of the bank.

My interview coincided with my weekly pickup of ten tons of carbon black. There is no load more detested by haulage men than carbon black, a sooty mixture that is used to make tyres and other rubber products. Looking at, or even thinking about, this obnoxious material turns you black; we used to get a £20 bonus for handling it. Early that Wednesday morning I put a clean jacket in the cab and shot down to Millwall to load up. I was pretty sure the jacket wouldn't stay clean for the interview but it was all I could think of.

I loaded up and drove the lorry straight into central London to Finsbury Circus, where the bank was situated. The way I looked at it was this: I hadn't asked for the job, I didn't want the job, and so if they wanted me they would have to take me as they found me, and today they would find me in a giant artic full of soot.

I parked in a cloud of swirling black dust that soon began to settle on the shiny Daimlers and Rolls-Royces parked along the street, much to the disgust of the chauffeurs cleaning them. When I went into the bank I was struck by the noisy clatter of typewriters, the hum of conversation and people walking about from desk to desk, the normal atmosphere of a large, busy office, but something very strange to me. As I entered, the noise stopped. People turned around at their desks to look at the strange apparition. Up comes a beady-eyed individual demanding to know who I am. I explained that I had an appointment with the chairman of the bank, but didn't know his name: 'Just tell him that I'm here from King Street' (which is where the Communist Party had their HQ). Beady-Eyes motions me to follow him, which I do, leaving a trail of sooty black dust in my wake.

I'm ushered into a long, wide room, furnished with an impressively long and highly polished hardwood table lined with chairs. On one wall a six-foot picture of the genial, pipe-smoking Stalin and on the other a smaller one of Lenin. At the head of the table sat a scruffy looking bloke, no collar or tie and an old-fashioned striped shirt. This was the governor of the bank, Alexei Chernuzube. He couldn't speak a word of English so Beady-Eyes had to do all the translating. This man took one look at me and burst into an uncontrollable fit of laughter. Beady-Eyes says that the governor wants to know if I can start the following Monday and not to worry about the wages because he is sure a little matter like that can easily be sorted out. 'Is that it?' I asked. 'Yes,' says Beady-Eyes and tells me not to turn up looking so scruffy next time.

Next thing, I'm back in the yard, load delivered, telling my boss Ernie Lewis that he's going to have to find a new driver. Freda spent all the weekend pressing what went for my best suit. When I left for the bank that first Monday she told me: 'Behave yourself and try to give some consideration to others.'

I presented myself to Beady-Eyes, whose real name was George Matthews and who acted as secretary to the bank. He took me to the chairman. Chernuzube wore the same outfit in which he had interviewed me but now he had three days' growth of beard. I decided to tackle the question of wages. I was told that the last driver earned the princely sum of fifty pounds a month, about the average wage in those days.

'I cannot work for less than seventy-five a month.'

'That's only five pounds less than I get,' says Georgie boy.

'I'm used to earning well over a hundred a month. I'll accept a loss of twenty-five pounds seeing that it's a clean job, and I'll throw in the first five hours' overtime free.' By now we had been joined by one of the senior Russian staff. This lad had a rudimentary knowledge of English but it turned out that this was their first ever experience of wage bargaining. I said to George:

'Who determines your wages, then?'

'We leave it to the chairman.'

'And you're a Party member?'

'Of course. All the senior staff carry a card.'

'Tell him that it's seventy a month or I walk out.'

I got the seventy along with black looks from the rest of the so-called loyal staff.

After I had been there about two months I decided that seventy wasn't enough and put this to the chairman through his new personal secretary, a pretty little thing who had just arrived from Moscow. The chairman told me to put my living expenses down in writing, and then he would decide if my claim was justified. This I did and, without any sign of a grudge, he agreed to pay me my original asking price of seventy-five pounds. I asked him why it was that the rest of the staff were paid what seemed to me rather a low wage. He answered, through his new secretary: 'When they summon up the guts to come and ask, they may get more. We don't hand out money for nothing.'

Chernuzube didn't know much about banking (and even less

about wage bargaining); he was there to keep the bank in line. I learnt from one of the staff that he was in the GRU, Moscow's foreign intelligence service, although it would be a while before I understood the implications of this revelation.

The chairman's car was a Humber Snipe, a popular executive vehicle of the day. It cornered like a rocking horse and took the length of a landing strip to come to a halt. I could do the journey from the bank to the embassy inside fifteen minutes, sometimes less. Chernuzube would sit in the back of the car laughing his head off as I mounted the pavement trying to fight my way through the traffic jams. He loved it. I served the bank for about seven years, from 1955 to around early 1962.

For the first four or five months the job was fairly humdrum, backwards and forwards from the bank to the embassy, sometimes we went off to the trade delegation building at West Hill in Highgate, and sometimes down to the Surrey and Millwall docks. As you might have guessed, I was soon bored and thinking about jacking in this cabbage-brain occupation.

The embassy had a house in Hazlehurst in Kent, and the British Foreign Office allowed the Russians to use this as a weekend retreat for the various Soviet agencies in London. Normally they had to stay within fifteen miles of the centre of London. I would take a party down on the Saturday, and then pick them up on the Sunday. The house was well set back inside the grounds, away from the eyes and lenses of the Fleet Street press that camped at their gates.

One Friday night as I dropped Chernuzube at his flat in West Hill, he told me that he would be going to Hazlehurst on the Sunday morning. I was to pick him up at eight sharp. I arrived bright and early. Cherny gets in.

'Trade delegation.'

Off to the TD, just a few yards up the hill. In climb three of his compatriots, one of them a huge specimen with an unpronounceable name. I knew it started with 'B' so I used to call him Britvic.

I drove them all to Hazlehurst, where they spent the day getting tanked up. When it came to going home, they were well past the walking the white line test, and I wasn't exactly sober myself, but at least I could see straight.

We were just coming into the suburbs when Cherny tells me to stop at the next eating house. Quite unusual. Out they stagger, all four of them singing away in Russian. I sat in the car and prepared for a long wait. Not to be. By a stroke of ill fortune the establishment happened to be owned and run by a Polish family, and the clientele were almost 90 per cent Polish. The Pole at the counter refused to serve Alexei and his chums. I heard shouting and sensed that perhaps all was not well. In I went. Chernuzube had his coat off and was having a right go at the Poles who, in turn, were calling the Russians the scum of the earth. I arrived to see Chernuzube hit the floor. I got three of them out into the car and then went back for Britvic, who was holding a gang of the enemy at bay. We beat a rapid retreat together. Nobody but Cherny spoke for the rest of the journey. He told me to keep silent about the whole affair. Inevitably the story of what happened went the rounds of the embassy. I went there two days later and was slapped on the back and given enough vodka to render me incapable of further forward movement. Of course the Russians were keeping a file on all this, something I did not know at the time.

But there was another file that was being kept up to date. This one was maintained by the mystery men from British intelligence. They would contact me without warning. One of them might appear when I was polishing the car. The questions they asked didn't vary much: Anyone new who might have business at the bank? Had I picked up at the airport or the docks? How was I getting along with my masters? Would I mind making a note of any addresses I drove to that seemed outside the normal business of the bank? It would be of great assistance.

I was given an address in Rathbone Place, where I could drop off more information.

'Don't post the reports, drop them in the letterbox, no need to enter the building.' I sensed trouble in the air.

I had been four months at the bank when I was called into the chairman's office.

'Victor, tomorrow you go out and buy Cadillac.'

I asked his secretary to ask him what he meant.

'He wants you to go out tomorrow and purchase a Cadillac.'

'If he expects me to cart him around London at the speed of light in a Cadillac, tell him to think again.'

This was the only way to carry on a conversation with Cherny: talk to him straight from the shoulder. I explained that if I took a corner at anything like the speed that he was accustomed to the car would turn over. Cadillacs were too big and heavy for London traffic. It turned out that what was getting to him was the fact that one of his compatriots, who was in charge of the Baltic Shipping Line, had recently acquired a Rolls Silver Dawn. Cherny wanted something bigger.

'Leave it to me and let's see what I can come up with.'

It turned out that the garage where I kept the Humber up in Highgate village had been trying to offload a Mark 7 Jaguar. That evening I approached Mr Silver, the owner of the garage.

'How much in my hand if I can get a sale?'

'Sixty pounds.'

'Not enough, make it a hundred.'

'Settle at eighty then.'

We struck the deal over a couple of pints in the pub next door, he was happy, I was happy and the chairman would get the ride of his life. So the next day I reports to Cherny that I have got just the car to suit him. He baulked a bit at the colour; he wanted black and this Jag was a really grotty sandy colour. But he settled down for the ride home, all the blue lights came on on the dashboard, the car surged forward and I knocked six minutes off the journey home.

'Good,' he says, which meant that he liked it. I also liked it and I liked it even better when I went to collect my eighty quid.

A new man appeared on the scene, one Georg Borovitch, a bright lad who had come to the bank via the Moscow Narodny in Washington, DC. I later learnt that Borovitch was KGB. He spoke perfect English with a slight American accent; he was tall, handsome, very polite and always willing to buy his round of drinks. He acted the part of a Russian who, by force of circumstances, worked for Moscow, but really deep down preferred the West and especially loved London. If there was ever a man to put anyone off their guard it was Georg Borovitch. I know, as I was able to observe his methods from close up.

I nicknamed him 'Georgie' and his arrival signalled a change in my duties. I would be sent to the National Provincial Bank with one of the bank messengers, and there we would fill a suitcase with money. Then I would cart Georgie and the money around on one of his trips. Sometimes I would take him to a factory, sometimes to private houses. At first I assumed that the private houses he was visiting were the homes of the people who owned the factories. Not so. I wasn't the bagman, I was the bagman's bagman.

Quite often the meeting would be in a large West End hotel or restaurant. This was done quite openly, always in broad daylight. Georgie would disappear into the Marble Arch Hotel or some other well-known venue.

'Drive around for half an hour, Viktor, and then pick me up.' He always pronounced my name like that, with what appeared to be a hard 'K'; made it sound Russian.

Georgie was paying his informants with money sitting in the legitimate accounts of the Moscow Narodny Bank, and held in the vaults of the National Provincial Bank at Moorgate. All of this I wrote down and left in Rathbone Place for the benefit of my sponsors. I never knew who they were but I made a few guesses. I often wondered what particular pigeon-hole my paltry donations to the nation's security were placed in. They're probably still there to this day, those by now dusty pages of information that I passed on.

One day there was an almighty row in the chairman's office. Cherny and Georgie were going at it hammer and tongs and Georgie was, by all accounts, winning. The next morning I'm again called into the office and told that I must purchase a car for Mr Borovitch. Georgie boy, the bank's new KGB rep, had won the day. GRU nil, KGB one. So off again to Mr Silver.

'Got anything else you're finding it hard to move?'

Mr Silver shows me a Standard Vanguard.

'I can only allow you forty pounds on this one.'

So Georgie collected his nice new Vanguard, and forty quid went into my pocket.

After the 20th Congress the *Daily Worker* published Khrushchev's anti-Stalin speech. That speech caused big changes in the embassy. Under Chernuzube there were six Russians, all heading different areas of activity. They all lived in the nearby area. To get home they either walked or caught a bus or tube, just like any ordinary worker.

The day they received the text of 'the Speech', the six bigwigs had a meeting in Chernuzube's office. The peace and quiet of the bank was shattered by the noise of the heated discussion. The old man was steaming, more hammer-and-tongs work. That evening, come the time for knocking off, they all seven of them climbed into the Jag. No more buses or tubes for them. According to Georgie, these changes were going on right through the system.

For the time being, Borovitch held the dominant position, although Chernuzube, being the chairman of the bank, wasted no time in trying to reassert his position as Big Chief. His crown had slipped a bit, but, like all the rest of the old-timers, Cherny knew how to work the system.

The next sensation to hit the Russian fraternity was the Soviet invasion of Hungary in November 1956. Cherny would be ordered to attend important meetings at the embassy in Kensington and it was my job to get him safely through the crowds of sometimes violent protesters milling around the gates. These demonstrators were mainly Poles, backed up by a few Ukrainians, along with the ever-present National Front. The police made only half-hearted attempts to keep these people at bay. Some of the more witless elements would end up on the bonnet of the Jag. I would just carry on until I got on to the forecourt of the embassy, where they would be manhandled by the heavies employed for such emergencies. At the time I had little sympathy for this ragtag army of demonstrators. I saw my job as bodyguard to Cherny and I never failed to get him through. Again, I didn't realise that my actions were being carefully monitored by Borovitch and his colleagues in the embassy.

About two months after the Hungarian affair had quietened down, I was told by Chernuzube to report to a Mr Pavlov at the embassy. Pavlov told me that one of the Russian drivers had been sent home and they needed a replacement. Borovitch had suggested my name.

'But I'm employed by the bank.'

Pavlov pointed out that this was not true. Anybody whose work brought him into contact with Russian nationals came under the jurisdiction of the embassy. He told me that I was not being forced or coerced into taking on this temporary assignment, but they did need somebody they felt they could trust. I said that perhaps it would be better if they trusted nobody. He liked that.

In future, although I would continue to drive Mr Chernuzube, I would also, from time to time, be seconded to the embassy or the trade delegation. I was told to stay away from the CP.

Around this time, Freda and I decided that it was about time we had a holiday. I bought an old relic of a Robin Reliant for the princely sum of £10. This three-wheel vehicle must have been at least twenty years old. The front wheel was attached to a pair of motorbike girder forks, the engine was an ancient Austin Seven Ruby and the body was made of sheet aluminium. But it went. Stopping it, though, was a matter of luck.

Chernuzube gave me a fortnight off. Off we went, our old army tent in the back along with all the other gear, the three kids sprawled out on top, and everybody very excited. We made it up Archway Hill and then Barnet Hill, the kids singing their hearts out, and I thought we had a chance of making it to our planned destination, Criccieth in North Wales. We travelled all night and by morning reached Bala Lake. Time for a stop.

Get the tent up, in between the road and a railway line, then we all lay down to get a few hours' kip. The stop lasted two days. Alan discovered a small lake complete with waterfall. This is where Judith, aged three, learnt to swim. I jumped off a rock, about twenty feet above the water, with Judith in my arms. All the kids loved it. Freda was worried about the safety of her brood and well and truly gave me some stick. We made it to a place called Blackrock, and this time put the tent up on the beach.

That was a gem of a holiday. It got so hot that I cut the sides of the old crate open with a tin opener. When we finally made it back home to the Bourne, the Reliant gave up the ghost. I sold it to a lad for £20, so nothing was lost.

43

An Enemy of the State

I didn't hear from the embassy for a while and I thought maybe they had replaced the driver and didn't need me. My shadowy British security friends continued to appear out of the blue and I would hand over whatever information I had in return for a payment. These payments never amounted to much and I regarded them as a perk of the job.

Nevertheless I was worried that the Russians might twig what I was up to. I devised a ruse, a smoke screen, to cover my tracks. It became a habit for Borovitch and myself to have our lunch together when he was at the bank. I innocently used to tell him about the visits and my worries that the gentlemen concerned might be from British security. He just used to grin and say:

'Don't worry, I know the names of all these gentlemen, take no notice of them.'

One lunchtime he asked me how my interview had gone at the embassy. I told him that I hadn't heard anything and had pretty much forgotten about it. Then he gave me a warning. He said that if they did call on me to do a job at the trade delegation I was to keep my eyes on the rear-view mirror. If I thought I had a car following me, I was to turn round and go straight back to the delegation. 'If anybody tells you to do otherwise then refer them to me or Mr Popov at the embassy.'

He was telling me to watch my back.

Borovitch was a handsome brute, and he was by now having it off with Cherny's young secretary. One day we were chatting quite normally when he asks me if I could help him get an apartment in the area. I found a flat in Whitchurch Street, just off the Barbican. Because Georgie worked for the Russian embassy he wasn't able to sign anything, so the upshot was that Georgie's little love nest was rented in my name. Good luck to him, I thinks; good on you, mate.

Borovitch spoke perfect English and he also had a good command of French. I never quite knew what he was up to, but I think he knew every trick in the book. I know he carried a French passport when he travelled outside London. I once asked him why he did this dirty work for those bastards in Moscow. He didn't take offence and told me he had two children back home and added: 'We study at university, get a job with a state department, and then one thing leads to another. I just follow instructions and keep my nose clean as far as I'm able.'

Yes, he missed his children, but nobody but an idiot would want to go back home. He was a dedicated communist and would sit and rage at the shortcomings of 'the capitalist evil'. Yet he admitted, quite readily, that the biggest evil of the lot was the incumbent of the Kremlin. He hated the people he was working for but he hated the capitalist politics of the West even more. How he kept sane was a mystery.

44

A Minor Role in the Great Game

Britvic was by now the big chief of internal security at the trade delegation, and one day he called me in, welcoming me with a cheery grin and a slap on the back that nearly sent me to kingdom come. He started by asking me whether I still wanted to work for him and said that if I did I would have to keep myself to myself and never reveal anything about what I was doing. If I couldn't accept this condition I could go straight back to the bank and nothing more would be said. I was bored with the humdrum, day-to-day routine and this sounded like a welcome change.

'Tell me what you want.'

With those few words I propelled myself into a new life of intrigue. I was now deep in the double game, working for the Russians and the clowns in the British security services.

On one trip I went to Fraserburgh, right up on the far north-east coast of Scotland. There I picked up a woman, dropping her near Rosyth, one of Britain's naval repair yards just north of Edinburgh. If I ever needed confirmation that I was engaged in work of a dubious nature, that trip was it. I have to admit that I was revelling in all the excitement. I was back in the groove of living on the edge.

I was on what could be described as an ego trip. I was worried that the Russians might have a mole inside the British security service. If I was right, and they cottoned on that I was double-crossing them, I could be in very big trouble indeed.

Once, when I was in the Jag on the A3 to Portland, I noticed a black Humber behind me. It followed me along the Portsmouth Road and was still there when we went through Esher. I remembered Borovitch's warning about turning back if I ever thought I was being followed. At Bagshot I pulled into a transport café.

'Nothing doing,' I said to the passenger. 'I'm turning back.'

'What on earth for?'

I pointed out of the window of the café, and there, sure enough, was the Humber. My passenger went as pale as a ghost. I scrubbed the job and went back to London, no doubt much to the annoyance of the lads who had been tagging us. The Jag was never again used on that route. I believe that whoever was giving the information in Portland was arrested. Soon after I read that two people, a man and his girlfriend, had been pulled in.

I don't think Chernuzube knew what was going on. All he wanted to know was that I was keeping the embassy happy. I should say they were very happy. Foolhardy, well-dressed, cultured Englishmen and women were being driven all over the country to deliver and collect I don't know what sort of information by an equally foolhardy English ex-Rifleman.

The next time I was called to Kensington Palace Gate, I said to Popov that, in future, if I had passengers I wanted one of his people with me. The way I saw it was that if something happened and we were pulled in, I could claim that I was innocently carrying out my job as a civilian driver for the embassy. Popov didn't take too kindly to me attempting to lay down the rules but admitted that he could see my point of view. I wasn't called on for another six weeks.

I went on reporting to my sponsors (I may have been wrong, but I reckoned that they were MI6). One day a gentleman appeared at Finsbury Circus to summon me to the office in Rathbone Place. He gave me a handwritten note which he told me to 'hand to the girl on the first floor'. When I arrived they told me to carry on and to do nothing that might give the Russians cause to suspect the double game I was playing. They also hinted that when I was inside the embassy I was outside their protection. I was handed the sum of £200, the equivalent of £2,000 today, 'to be going on with'. It was a lot of money and I accepted gladly.

We settled into a routine. I would pick up Chernuzube in the morning with two or three of his staff. By the time I had reached Kentish Town I would have a tail, all the way to the bank. One morning, as we were going down York Way, towards King's Cross, Cherny saw that the now familiar Humber was behind us. He told me to pull up, then he jumped out and started a slanging match with the crew who had been following us. I don't know what he said, but they turned around there and then. The tail was seen no more.

A new man had appeared at the embassy and I was to take him to a reception at the Bulgarian embassy. As we were talking, in walks Borovitch, looking like he's been up for a week. He must have been getting his money's worth out of the secretary. He announced:

'Viktor, at the Bulgarian embassy I am going to introduce you to some people who may have need of your services.'

The old alarm bells began to ring, but, the way I looked at it, 'in for a penny, in for a pound'. At the reception Georgie would beckon me over and introduce me.

'I would like you to meet Viktor.'

Then, introductions done, I would go back to a seat near the bar and wait for the next one. I was introduced, separately, to three men and a woman, all Establishment types.

It was my policy never to get too familiar with these people. I kept my talk to practical details: where we were going, what time, etc. In the Western Desert, Major Peniakoff had once given me a short lecture on how to keep alive while carrying out covert operations:

'Keep in the background, never bring attention to yourself, never wear clothes, or do anything, which may bring you to the attention of anybody. If possible, never let your right hand know what your left hand is about to do.'

Good advice, which I was now putting into practice.

Over the next few months I made a lot of assignations with these people. My job was to pass envelopes to them and they would pass similar envelopes to me. The ones I gave them always seemed to be thicker than the ones they gave me. Perhaps pound notes take up more room than a closely typed script or microfilm?

Georgie asked me to identify some places where I could make contact with his people without drawing attention to myself. I had three ideas: the old Tatler News Theatre in Charing Cross Road, a café close to South Kensington tube station and the old reliable Lyons Corner House in Leicester Square.

Borovitch, or one of his henchmen, would set up the meeting; I would make the contact, collect whatever was necessary, go home and give the envelope or package to Georgie the next morning. I never received payment for this, nor did I ask for any. I was getting a big kick out of the new life I was leading. This cat and mouse game was one I had been playing all my life. I was allowed to act in any way I saw fit to preserve security. If I thought somebody was being tailed I assumed it was a trap. I stopped using the café at South Ken after two rendezvous; it just didn't feel right. The Tatler didn't work either because I was unable to see if the contact had a tail.

I had another idea for a meeting place and suggested to Borovitch that we go and have a meal in the cafeteria in Swan and Edgar at Piccadilly Circus. He'd be paying the bill, naturally.

The cafeteria at Swan's was raised above the ground floor, with an unobstructed view of the main entrance. There was also a quick escape route down the backstairs and through the fire exit.

'Perfect,' said Georgie boy.

It was a very good location. When I had a contact, I would get in position at least an hour beforehand. I would make myself known only when I was satisfied that my contact, he or she, wasn't being followed. I gave my friends at MI6 advance notice of these assignations but made it clear that if they wished to follow any of the couriers they had better be very discreet. If I spotted them, the meeting would be aborted. To my surprise they agreed to this. 'Carry on the way you are, Victor, you're doing well.'

By now I was hardly ever available to drive Chernuzube. I was being used almost exclusively by the embassy and the trade delegation.

I knew that I was being watched by British security. I did not mind this, but I was very worried about what the embassy would do if they tailed me and discovered what I was up to. I was ready to extricate myself from the whole business. The only person I felt I could trust was Borovitch. Unfortunately, his wife had appeared from Moscow and she had sussed what he was up to with Chernie's secretary. So now Georgie was in disgrace and shoved to the sidelines. I had nobody to turn to.

One evening word came that I was to meet a gentleman in the Strand Palace Hotel. My knowledge of the venue was non-existent and I had not met the contact previously. Against my better judgement I agreed to the assignation.

I had been told that the man I was to meet was short and somewhat stout and would come through the door precisely at 7 p.m. That afternoon I did a recce. I didn't like what I saw, especially as there was nowhere to make an emergency exit if things went wrong.

I turned up to take position at six o'clock and by 6.30 two couples had taken tables just inside the door. I recognised one of the men. At 6.45 another two gentlemen arrived. I recognised both of them and it was obvious that they were aware of my presence. I paid the waiter for the coffee and left. I walked up the Aldwych and along Kingsway with the hairs on the back of my neck standing on end, but nobody tried to stop me. Within half an hour I was home. I sat down for a think, shaking like a leaf.

The following day I went straight to Borovitch. I told him what had happened. I wondered if I was being used as bait to get at the real villains of the piece. Georgie said it would be better if I went back to the bank and got on with my normal work until things quietened down a bit. I couldn't have agreed more.

My break didn't last long. I was sitting in a café in London Wall having a nice cup of coffee and getting used to having nobody breathing down my neck when one of the bank's messengers burst in.

'You're wanted in the office straight away, Vic.'

I went back to find Borovitch with a couple of Russians I had never met before.

'Go straight home, Viktor, report to the delegation in the morning and tell your wife that you may be away for a few days.'

No other explanation was given. When I broke the news, Freda was very upset.

'We never see you these days. Do you mean to tell me that you're going away, and you can't even say for how long? I don't believe it.'

She was in tears and God knows what she thought I was up to. Perhaps I felt some pity, but if I did it was soon brushed aside by the thought of the operation. I had guessed that this was going to be no ordinary pickup. My existence was controlled by my vanity. I was living on the edge again, I had placed the bet, and I had not even seen the hand that was being dealt. And so I drove the last few nails into the coffin that was going to hold the remains of our marriage.

The next day at the delegation I found a group of six individuals. Three of them I knew – Borovitch, Britvic and the chairman of the delegation; the other three, the new lads, were eyeing me up as if I had come down from outer space. Borovitch opened up the conversation.

'First of all, Viktor, I must tell you that you will be operating on your own for a large part of this trip. If you agree to take it on you will have to exercise extreme caution. You should know that if you are picked up you will be in a very awkward position. If you wish to go ahead we will be in your debt. If you do not wish to you can leave now and, speaking personally, I will not fault you for your decision. If you stay in the room, you will be committed. We will have coffee while you give the matter some thought.'

Over the coffee there was a heated discussion among the six. At one stage Britvic nearly came to blows with one of them. Apparently the comrade had voiced some doubts as to my integrity. I didn't need to give it much thought at all.

'Count me in,' I said.

Then Borovitch filled me in. I was to take him and Chernuzube up to St Andrews in Scotland where Cherny was to give a speech. From St Andrews I was to go to Montrose with Borovitch where we were to pick up four individuals. Two were to be dropped in Manchester; the other two would come on to London, to the delegation.

Silence reigned in the room while I digested this information.

'What car do you propose I use?'

'The Jaguar, of course.'

I couldn't credit this. These six men were all experienced in clandestine operations and yet they wanted me to operate in a vehicle that was already under the scrutiny of British security.

'No go,' I said. 'I want another vehicle, preferably hired, and, furthermore, no timetable. If you want me to carry on then you must allow me to get them to the destination in the way I think fit. After all, it's my neck.'

Borovitch translated. More muttering, then they burst out laughing.

'What's the joke?'

Georgie boy told me that they'd said that if anything went wrong I could go to Moscow where I would be well looked after.

'You know my answer to that one,' I replied. 'Tell them that I would rather take my chances in Dartmoor than end up in some Soviet slave camp.'

Britvic wanted to know how I planned to carry out the mission. I said that I would think about it and talk to Borovitch at the bank in the morning. At that, Britvic rang the bell, in came one of their do-it-alls with a trayload of glasses, three bottles of vodka and the usual sandwiches, and the meeting closed with much slapping of backs and handshakes all round. I went straight home to tell Freda that I wasn't going away just yet. Peace settled on the Gregg family.

That evening I sat down to do some serious thinking. First I had to make contact with my MI6 sponsors, the difficulty being that, except for the address in Rathbone Place, I had no phone number, and no other method of contact. I even considered letting Borovitch in on the scam I had been perpetrating with British security, but decided against it.

I reckoned that if the four operatives were going to be on the loose on their own they would have a fair grasp of the English language. I decided that it would be too risky to have the four of them in the same car. I would drive to Inverness with the two who were destined for Manchester. From there they could get a train south with a minimum of risk. I would then go back to Montrose, pick up the other two, take them up to Aberdeen and put them on the train to York, where I would pick them up the following day. I would have to convince Borovitch that his presence was unnecessary; the way I saw it, if this enterprise was as risky as they thought it might be, the less time I was in contact with the nation's enemies the better. And I wouldn't use the Jag. I wrote out everything I knew about the coming operation. Freda wanted to know what I was writing. I told her that I was just setting out a possible route for the conference in Scotland.

Georgie boy and I had a lengthy discussion. He wasn't too keen on being left out of it and doubted if his superiors would agree, though he admitted that my proposals made sense. The next thing was to find a suitable vehicle for the trip. Back to Highgate and Mr Silver.

'I may wish to arrange the hire of a good-sized vehicle for up to a week.'

'No problem, what about the Princess?'

The Princess was a large coach-built job, one of the last of the big Austins to be made. It would have to do. I added thirty quid to the charge as my bonus. Two days later I'm called into Chernuzube's office.

'Take tomorrow off, Viktor, get the car ready for a trip to St Andrews in Scotland. We shall be leaving on Monday. Can we do it in a day?'

The Princess would never do it in a day, so I said no. This didn't please him one bit. I suggested that if we left not later than four in the morning, we might be able to do it. This settled the matter. It was obvious to me that the chairman was completely in the dark as to what had been discussed at the trade delegation. When I came out of his office Borovitch was waiting for me.

'Let's go.'

Out of the bank and into a café in Moorgate. I opened up:

'Chernuzube thinks we're going in the Jag.'

'Don't worry about it,' says Georgie.

He then explained that I had been overruled on going it alone. He would be coming up to Montrose with me. I left him sitting in the café with a worried look. I had the feeling that his usual self-assurance was slipping. I went to Highgate, picked up the Princess and went home for the weekend.

On the Sunday I walked to Rathbone Place to drop the letter in to MI6. When I got there, I found that the door had been changed and with it the letterbox arrangements. I didn't have a clue which was the right box. I came home with the letter still in my hand. I was going into this operation without backup. That could be a problem.

Monday morning, sharp at four, the Princess is purring outside

Chernie's house on West Hill. Out they all troop, Chernuzube leading the way, followed by the secretary, another Russian who was new to me, and, bringing up the rear, my mate Borovitch.

'Where's the Jaguar, Viktor?'

'Not fit for the journey, guv, the brakes are dodgy.'

The fact that the Princess was a nice gleaming black vehicle seemed to pacify him. In they all piled. The secretary, reeking of cheap perfume, sat in the front seat. Cherny immediately lights up one of his favourite fags and off we shoot, northwards. We rolled to a halt at St Andrews at nine in the evening. After attending to the luggage, off I staggers to my room for a good night's kip.

Montrose is typical of the many small fishing ports dotted around the British coastline, able to handle coastal traffic and the occasional medium freighters. The port was small enough for the local customs officers to lead a fairly cushy life.

Borovitch and I left St Andrews very early in the morning and midday found us cruising Montrose looking for a suitable hotel, just like a couple of visitors. I had concluded that, because we would be leaving before dawn, we would be long gone by the time any surveillance team started to look for us. Georgie went off and left me to my own devices. I was to pick him up in the fish market at four in the afternoon. I felt very tense during the wait. I was in a strange environment and I had no doubts that what we were doing was highly illegal. The tension drove me on. I don't think Georgie boy was feeling too comfortable either.

Right on the dot he turns up at the rendezvous with two scruffy looking individuals, one of whom was French.

'Carry on with your original plan, Viktor, these two men are for Manchester. I'm picking the other two up the day after tomorrow.'

The Russian could speak really good English, but the Frenchman could only mutter a few words. After Georgie had briefed them, we shot across the wilds of northern Scotland to Inverness where, after sorting out their tickets to Manchester, I left them at the

railway station. I couldn't get away quick enough. So far so good.
I had already decided on my next plan of action.

Instead of returning to Montrose I stayed the night in Aberdeen.
Then, leaving the car in the hotel car park, I took a bus down to
Montrose. Georgie boy would have to sweat it out for a few hours
– I was playing safe. When I finally got back late that afternoon
Borovitch was having a severe attack of nerves. I explained that I
was going to get a coach back to Aberdeen at six that night. He
should go and get the other two from the docks. I would be back
by eleven.

'You can go back to the hotel, have some sweet dreams and
leave the rest to me.'

And that's what happened. I didn't drop the two Russians at
Aberdeen or York, as I intended. Instead I drove them directly
down to London and left them in a seedy hotel in King's Cross
with instructions not to move until I came to pick them up the
next day. Which is what I did. And that was my part in the operation finished. It had been all too easy. I wondered whether it would
be as easy to infiltrate the Soviet Union. I doubted it.

Borovitch later congratulated me on the way I had used such
clever subterfuge. He didn't realise that I had deliberately over-
elaborated everything. It was essential that I appeared utterly
loyal to the Soviet cause and I think the plans helped to create a
smokescreen to hide what I was up to.

All that remained was for me to get down to Rathbone Place
and make a report to my minders. I got there to find that the
department I wanted had moved to Chenies Street. The new office
was in an attic above a perfume manufacturer. The only soul about
was a weary lady hammering away at a typewriter – Sod's Law
again. I told her that whoever was working on my case should
contact me as soon as possible.

By now I had served the bank for five years. Chernuzube left for
Russia and another man arrived. This new man demanded that I
open the door for him to get out of the car, 'like other chauffeurs

do'. By this time I was looking for an excuse to get out. This was as good as any.

'You want a lackey, then employ one,' I said.

I thought this was bound to get me my cards. The next thing I hear is that the new man has been told to apologise to me. But I had seen too much. I wanted to get out while the going was good. So my employment with the nation's enemies ended. Freda was glad: she was fed up with the late nights and never knowing what I was up to.

Before I left, there was one final episode. Borovitch had asked me to go to Oxford to pick up a friend of his. He would meet the car outside Notting Hill tube station at 7 p.m. I recognised the man I was to pick up; he was a well-known Member of Parliament. Back in London I collected Georgie at Notting Hill and he told me to go to West Hill. At Marble Arch I noticed that we were being followed. Georgie told me to lose the tail and then drop the two of them off somewhere. I drove on, down Oxford Street, across Oxford Circus until I got level with Wardour Street, then I jumped the lights, a quick right turn, and shot down to Shaftesbury Avenue, straight across into Whitcomb Street, left into Lisle Street, where I dropped them, and they disappeared into Leicester Square tube. The vehicle behind us just didn't stand a chance. After that it was dump the Jag in the garage and home on the bike as if nothing had happened.

During that last week of my employment, two of the well-dressed men who had been my shadows for the last couple of years appeared. They wanted to see me at Chenies Street. It turned out they had only just twigged what had been going on in the Scottish operation. I gave them a full description of the individuals, the times and dates. They asked if it was my impression that these men were important.

'Not to my way of thinking, just foot soldiers.'

'What gives you that impression, Mr Gregg?'

I was very tempted to reply that they seemed to me to be

just as stupid as their opposite numbers, but discretion ruled the day.

'Nothing obvious. It's a feeling,' I replied, which seemed to satisfy them. Then I dropped the bombshell.

'I'm leaving next week. I've decided that enough is enough.'

There's no doubt that I had been of considerable use to them, right inside the enemy fortress, trusted by the embassy. A difficult act to replace. In spite of the pleading and offers of more money, I remained adamant. I was through.

'What about that song and dance you led us the other night?'

I realised they were talking about the way I had given them the slip on the way to Leicester Square tube. I just grinned at them. They realised they were on a hiding to nothing and that they couldn't change my mind. So they wished me godspeed.

I left in the knowledge that, partly because of information provided by me, at least four spies had been arrested.

Before he left, Chernuzube had asked me if I would like to have a holiday in Moscow or Leningrad. I said that if I were ever stupid enough to set foot inside the borders of the Soviet Union I would probably find myself inside the Lubyanka. He agreed, saying he thought that my anarchistic leanings might be looked on with some disfavour.

45

The Final Cut

I left the Moscow Narodny Bank in early 1962. Freda and I had the offer of a new flat on an estate in Roehampton. By now our marriage was battling to survive; perhaps we could make a fresh start. I started back on the road for a few years, then I had five years at Putney Bus Garage, driving No. 14 buses backwards and forwards from Putney to Hornsey Rise. I was less and less involved with the Party, and, to be truthful, I was fed up with the airy-fairy ideas of some of the comrades. It wasn't that I had renounced my beliefs and suddenly seen the light; I had realised by now that there was no way of getting rid of the British Establishment unless one was willing to put them all up against the wall, and that just wasn't going to happen. I would do my best to earn a living and, if possible, repair my marriage.

The birth of Judith should have done the trick, but it didn't. I tried to kid myself that I was doing all I could to keep the marriage together, but in my heart I recognised that this was a lie. In the war I had spent six years on the edge, killing and keeping one step ahead of the opposition. That motor inside me was still running. My lust for new adventures and the desire to prove myself against the strength of others was as fierce as ever, if not more so. I was heading for disaster at breakneck speed and there was nothing I could do about it.

Eventually, entirely due to my own self-centred ways, my marriage crashed in a Magistrates' Court in the Strand, a noble thoroughfare but, to me, a scene of utter desolation. We had a cup of tea together after it was all over and I finished up with tears streaming down my face.

The enormity of the damage I had done hit me. My world had come crashing down about me. Life seemed to have no meaning. Everything I had loved had been lost and I only had myself to blame. The memory that really haunts me, even to this day, is the picture of my little Judith crying and holding my hand, imploring me not to leave her. What kind of an animal had I been?

Freda, able now to fulfil her true potential, climbed like a rocket in the profession she had chosen. Within a year she became a senior administrator on the staff of the area childcare system. I, on the other hand, was still pushing No. 14 buses from Putney to Hornsey Rise, as boring a job as anyone could wish to find. It was through the job at Putney Garage that I met Bett. I approached her one day during a meal break and asked her if she would be interested in being my conductor, and that's how it all started. After a while we began to live with each other but it still took me more than two years to pluck up the courage to ask her if she would consider marrying me. When eventually I did propose to her she accepted, and together we started a new life at the Hampstead Registry Office. In all the forty-plus years that we have now been together there has never been a harsh word between us. I have learnt my lesson. The divorce had supplied the catalyst that was needed to finally drag me out of the old world. The memories of death and destruction, the callous disregard I had held for everything not connected to my survival had gone. I vowed that I would never put my new marriage in danger.

After Betty and I married, we moved to Taunton in the West Country where we found employment with the local bus service. I couldn't stick it, so I set up in business as an industrial decorator, and things went well.

Some time around 1972, I started to go on motorcycle trips all over Europe with a group of friends. We followed the annual European rallies, or Treffs as they are called. One of these was in

Sweden at a town called Jönköping. I decided to travel via the DDR. During my days at the bank I had made some good contacts with the East German company Berolina Travel, so I visited them to see if they could arrange a visa. They still remembered me and I was given the visa without the usual formalities. On my way back I thought I would spend a couple of days in Dresden, perhaps lay a wreath if I could get one, then carry on to Prague and home.

I went to the Swedish festival and had enjoyed a comfortable and uneventful trip down from the north, bypassing Berlin. Then, in the middle of the Harz Forest, I saw a sign: *Campingplatz, 2 km.* I followed the sign and found myself by a lake, no tents, instead a collection of huts. By now it was quite late in the evening. No sooner had I stopped than I was surrounded by a crowd of people all standing and gawping at my brand new BMW.

I could hear the mutterings of *'Engländer, Engländer'*. I think I was the first English person some of them had seen. Then I was approached by a young lady who explained to me in English that she was the local schoolteacher and that I had arrived not at a general campsite but at a holiday site for German workers. Would I like to sit down at the communal table and join in the evening meal? Of course I would. I was delighted. She told me not to bother about the tent and my gear as the older boys and girls would fix everything up for me. That was the start of a very noisy night. The teacher sat with me all night, translating and answering questions.

There were lots of holiday camps like this in East Germany. Workers could enjoy a break at no cost except for the price of the food, which was minimal. There were about eighty families on this site. The facilities were simple, even primitive, but they worked well.

It must have been nearly dawn before I staggered back to my tent. I woke up to find a bunch of giggling children staring at me. I imagined that their parents were sleeping off the previous night.

I couldn't understand a word they were saying but I smiled and nodded and made my way down to the lake where I swam out to a raft. I spent the rest of the morning in heavenly isolation.

Back at the tent I decided to wash my clothes. This was something the men in East Germany never did. The clothing was abruptly taken from me and when I finally got it all back everything was washed far cleaner than I would have achieved, and neatly ironed for good measure. I spent four days on the campsite. On the last evening we were exchanging names and addresses when a couple mentioned the name Jünger.

The name seemed familiar; it rang a bell, but I couldn't place it. I went to bed that evening with the name still bothering me. Jünger? I awoke in the middle of the night in a cold sweat. It had clicked: Jünger! Arnhem! Old Silverhair with his gammy leg! Surely they could not be related. Then I remembered how Silverhair had boasted of his Saxony ancestry.

In the morning I found the couple and got the schoolteacher to translate. I asked if they knew an Albert Jünger. Silence: then I told them the story of my brief association with Silverhair. Then Marcus, the husband, spoke up. Yes, they did have an Uncle Albert, and, yes, he had been an officer and, yes, he still had all his hair, although no longer silver but white. Marcus said that they were at the camp for another four days and, if I wished to come to their flat at Schneeberg, he would arrange for me to meet him. I was very sorry that I couldn't. I had to be in Prague by the end of the week and then I had to get home, but I would write as soon as possible. It was to be several years before I finally met up with Uncle Albert.

46

I Get My Comeuppance

They made contact three months after my return from the DDR.

It hadn't been a good day, coating up two huge metal containers with two-pack epoxy resin. I had earned £300 but it had left me knackered, and then some.

As I signed off at the gates of the nuclear power station at Hinkley Point, the security man told me there were a couple of gents outside who wanted to see me.

'They look like the law to me.'

There they were, two well-dressed individuals, one tall and one short. The tallest of the two spoke up:

'Mr Victor Gregg?'

'That's me.'

'A couple of miles down the road there's a pub.'

'The Cottage,' I answered.

'I would like to suggest that the three of us have a quick drink and a chat.'

'Is there some sort of trouble? Are you the law?'

'Nothing like that,' says Shorty. 'We're hoping you can be of some assistance to us.'

'Follow me then.'

By the time they arrived I was well into my first pint of the day.

Lofty produced an official looking card. It had his photograph on it with the words 'Ministry of Information', and was stamped with a crown.

'Tell us in your own words what you have been up to since you left the Moscow Narodny.'

'You're joking. That was more than ten years ago.'

'Not joking,' says Shorty. 'But I will tell you that you're not in trouble – yet.' I wondered about that 'yet'.

I signalled to Ted to bring over another pint.

Shorty produced a ring file from his briefcase. The last time somebody had produced a file on me was at Telekabir in Cairo. That had consisted of no more than about ten pages; the bundle that now lay on the table looked more like a telephone directory. As well as the pages held in place by the rings, the file contained other pages stuffed in, some stapled together. About a dozen pages fell on the floor.

'That's not a dossier on me, I hope.'

'This is only a copy of what we're interested in at the moment,' says Shorty.

Then the skyscraper says: 'Now, tell us about your trip to East Germany, to the DDR, last August.'

By now I was a bit knocked back. 'Keep to the truth, Vic,' I says to myself.

I told them about the rally in Sweden, about the trip to Dresden, about laying a few flowers by the burnt-out cathedral and the trip home. I left out the details concerning the campsite and Marcus.

'That was all there was to it,' I said.

'How did you get your visa?'

'Through Berolina Travel in Conduit Street.'

'And you experienced no trouble getting in or out.'

'None whatsoever, easy as falling off a bike.'

'Before we go,' says the short one, 'are you planning to go over again, perhaps next year?'

'Shouldn't think so. Once is enough.'

That was all. I left them sipping their lagers. But, as I went, the tall one said, almost as an aside, that it had been nice meeting me and that I might hear from them again. I drove home deep in thought. It wasn't the fact that they knew about the DDR trip that worried me. What bothered me was that not only did they know where I was working, they knew where I would be on a particular day. The work took me all over the South West; even I was never certain from one day to the next where exactly I was going to be. I was certain I would hear from them again. They obviously wanted something, but what? In the end, I thought, 'Stop worrying, Vic. Take things as they come, it'll all come out in the wash.'

I got the news that the next motorbike rally to be held by FIM (the international federation of motorcycling) would take place in Budapest, Hungary. Visas for Hungary could be obtained from the Hungarian consul in Eaton Place in London. It was now early May. The rally was due to start in the last week of July.

Three weeks after my application for my visa I got a message on the answer phone: would I ring a number in London and ask for a Mrs Fairbrother? This made me very, very nervous. I left it until the last minute before I made the call.

'Yes, Mr Gregg, hold on while I put you through to Mr Leftbury.'

'Mr Gregg? We would be obliged if you could suggest a meeting place. We wish to send one of our officers down for a chat. We believe you may be travelling east in the near future. Perhaps you could meet him somewhere near Taunton?'

Taunton was far too close to home.

'You presume wrong, Leftbury. Bridgwater, at the railway station, would be a better choice.'

The train pulled into the station almost dead on time at 12.25 p.m. I was sitting in the waiting room, with a clear view of the platform. I had been there for half an hour. My contact had arrived and I could see him on the platform, standing on his lonesome, looking not too sure of himself. I slipped out of the back door of the room and sat in the van waiting for him to appear. When he finally came into view I flashed the lights. I could almost feel the relief that swept over him.

'Thought for a time I was on a wasted journey.'

'I've had you in sight for the last twenty minutes.'

'That figures,' says the man. 'I've read your dossier, including the stuff omitted from your army discharge papers.'

I wondered what he meant by that. Perhaps he meant my time with Popski or the work with the Long Range Desert Group. I asked him to come to the point. What did he want?

'We want you to go back into East Germany, pick up some papers and deliver them to a source in West Germany.'

This bald statement stopped me in my tracks.

'Let's get out of here. I know a nice pub. A nice pint and a snack with you paying might just put my wits in place again.'

'Agreed.'

The first pint of the day began to clear my brain.

'Well? Will you do it?' he asked.

'What's in it for me?'

'Nothing except your expenses. What about five hundred?'

That would pay for the whole of the three weeks' holiday.

'Make it six hundred and we've got a discussion. Three hundred before I leave, the rest on delivery.'

He nodded, then said:

'Pickup in Dresden, Leipzig or Karl-Marx-Stadt.'

'A maximum of four days from pickup to delivery and out of the three suggested points I favour Dresden as I have a good reason for my presence in the city.'

I named a restaurant at the main crossroads in Dresden centre as a pick-up point and anywhere between Hof and Nuremberg for the drop. I was familiar with these places and they made me feel safe.

He began to relax. He told me his name was Peter Jones and that the DDR had become a difficult place to operate in. He wanted to know how I could be so certain that I could carry out the work. I told him it was not my intention to put myself at risk.

'I won't make any move until I am satisfied that the location is clean. If I have suspicions to the contrary I just move on, operation over, nothing gained, nothing lost, nothing that is except your initial three hundred.'

We parted company like a couple of old friends.

Three weeks later I got another message. Peter Jones would be in Bridgwater on the following Tuesday: same place, same time. If I didn't answer the meeting would be taken as on.

By now I was beginning to have serious doubts about the wisdom of what I was doing. Common sense was telling me to tell them to stuff it, find another stooge. I didn't want to risk ending up in some grotty East German prison. But then the thought of the easy six hundred and the old feeling of anticipation made my mind up; doubts were swept aside, even though I knew that if things went wrong I wouldn't get any help from Whitehall. I was confident that I would be able to get myself out of any mess and I knew full well that if things did go wrong I would be abandoned. Nobody would know anything about me.

Peter Jones turned up as arranged. The six hundred had been authorised, Dresden had been accepted, the delivery would be Nuremberg.

'I still can't for the life of me understand how you people picked an old man like me to do a simple job like this. Surely there are government departments full of people who could do it just as well.'

'Lesson number one, Victor, never mention the government. Lesson number two, there are never enough people to satisfy our needs. Lesson number three, feel honoured.'

'Yes, and lesson number four, if I'm caught I'm in deep shit.'

He grinned. 'Lesson number five, you're dead right.'

He became serious for a moment.

'You can still refuse if you so wish, Victor. I can assure you that if you do you will not be approached by the department any further, but I must have the answer now.'

'When do you want me in Dresden?'

The three hundred was handed over. I didn't even have to sign for it.

I set off for Dresden in the last week of July. By the Wednesday I was setting up camp on a tourist site on the outskirts of that still burnt-out and shattered city. The rendezvous was to be just after three in the afternoon at the restaurant I had chosen.

A nice cooling shower in the camp washrooms, a change of underwear and a clean shirt under my bike gear, and I set off, nerves tingling. Any sign that there was something amiss and I would be on my way, hotfooting it for freedom. Keep your eyes skinned, Vic; the Stasi, so I had been informed, played for real. I remembered what Popski had said: 'Always keep a three hundred and sixty-degree surveillance, Gregg. If you ever have to look for a bolt hole it's invariably too late.' Too true, Major!

I parked the bike, and made my way to the restaurant which had two floors, a downstairs bar and coffee counter, and the first-floor restaurant itself. From the seats on the balcony one could sit at a table and observe the world sorting itself out on the pave-ments below. I sat drinking beer and eating a huge cheese roll. I had been given no description of the person I was here to meet. 'Just sit and wait. The contact is very experienced, he will contact you.' I waited more than half an hour, one beer gone and another one untouched on the table. The restaurant was half full, plenty of empty tables, occasional glances in my direction. I stood out like a beacon in my leathers. The Union Jack sewn on the chest left no doubt that I was an *Engländer*.

A party of young students trooped in, kitted out in walking gear. In no time at all they had commandeered a corner of the floor, dumping their rucksacks like students everywhere. They kept glancing at me and whispering '*Engländer . . . Engländer*' in hushed tones, as if an Englishman was some evil ogre ready to eat their children.

One of the girls came over.

'*Entschuldigen Sie, bitte, Sie ist Engländer?*'
'*Ja, ich bin Engländer.*'

I was invited to come over and join them, whereupon they all started to practise their English. Then the teacher spoke up. He explained that he taught English, French and the minor classics at the local high school.

'Everyone calls me Bob, otherwise it's Robert Halsey. And what do we call you?'

'Victor will do. I'm waiting for a friend, but there appears to have been some misunderstanding on his part, so I really must be on my way.'

By now, another beer had been shoved under my nose. The teacher asked whether I knew the local countryside. I said no. I was now on my guard. He was being too familiar, too open. People in the DDR just didn't behave like this. If this was the contact he was sailing very close to the wind.

He asked one of the girls to get a map from his rucksack and then spread it out on the table, pointing out, with the help of his chattering pupils, the various beauty spots I might wish to visit. By now almost the whole restaurant, including some of the waiters, was extolling the merits of their own favourite pieces of Saxony acreage.

'You can keep the map, Victor, but try not to lose it. They are not easy to come by. Good luck. Perhaps we will meet again.'

I realised he was telling me to get on my way. I said my goodbyes and left this oasis of goodwill, the map sticking out of my jacket pocket for all to see.

Back at the camp I sat down in the tent and opened the map. Out fell a slip of paper. It told me not to go to Nuremberg, but just to follow the route marked on the map from Hof to Münchberg. I studied the map but I couldn't for the life of me see anything but an ordinary well-used, large-scale map, the type used by walkers the world over. But, then, I had never heard of microdots.

47

The Handover

The next morning saw me on my way to the crossing at Hof. Although this was not a well-used route into and out of the then DDR, it was imposing and even frightening. With its watchtowers and machine-gun emplacements it carried a message of dark menace. Although I was sweating, everything went smoothly and I was waved out and was soon heading for Münchberg.

By midday I was in the Gasthof Reitsch, supping the watery liquid that passed for beer in the Fatherland.

'*Engländer?*' says mine host.

'*Ja, ich bin Engländer.*'

'Victor?'

'*Ja, ich heisse Victor,*' I replied, giving the Kraut the benefit of my lowly knowledge of the lingo.

He pointed to a man sitting at a table by the window.

'Sit down, Victor,' says the man at the table. 'Lunch is ordered. I dare say you could do with a bite of decent food.'

I rolled myself a cigarette. For the first time in the last thirty-odd hours I felt safe. The relief swept through my whole being.

'Let's see what you've got for me. And you can call me Charles.'

I handed over the map.

'That's all I've got.'

'Ah, he's a good man, our Duggie.'

'Duggie? He told me his name was Robert, Robert Halsey.'

'You hear a thousand names in this business,' he replied. 'So you're the new courier then?'

'You're joking,' I replied. 'This is strictly a one-off job, never to be repeated.'

'Time will tell.'

With the formalities over, we both got stuck into our lunch.

Feeling comfortable and once again quite sure of myself, I thought it was time to bring up the small matter of payment.

'This is news to me. I've never had to pass over money before.'

'I want you to get on to them in London, ask them to get in touch with me a month from now. All I want to do now is to get on to Budapest.'

'What, no more skullduggery!' says Charles. 'You certainly get around for your age. Don't worry about the cash, Victor. I'll get on to London and sort everything out.'

After the meeting I headed south to meet my friends.

That night in a campsite I thought long and hard about what I'd done and the unpleasant things that might have happened to me if I'd been caught. I made up my mind not to get into any more scrapes with British intelligence and fell into a troubled sleep.

About a month after I got home I received what I thought would be my last visit from Shorty and Lofty, the men from Whitehall. They wanted to know about any problems I had encountered and what my overall impression was. I told them that I wasn't impressed by the manner in which the young students had been used, and, while the exercise had gone quite smoothly, there had been too much reliance on luck.

'They have it all under control over there' was all they said. I kept my own counsel. My three hundred was handed over, still no signature, and that, I thought, was that.

The following year a bunch of us decided to go to the Pannonia International Motorcycle Rally in Hungary. Motorcyclists from all over Europe and Scandinavia would be present at this vast five-day event, new friendships would emerge, souvenirs would be bought and goodwill would pervade the whole area.

By the end of May we had our visas and everything was sorted. We were ready to leave at the end of June. Everything in the household was on an even keel.

The message on the answer phone was terse and to the point: would I be at the Cottage on the date and time mentioned? 'It would be appreciated.'

This time there were three of them. I met them at the Cottage. Lofty opened the batting:

'You've applied for another visa for Hungary.'

'No need to look surprised. We get to know these things, and, of course, taking a trip to the East isn't a crime. We want you to do another trip to the DDR, to Leipzig this time. You've just about time to get down to Berolina and arrange your visa. What about it?'

Well, I thought, talk about getting to the point.

By this time the third man, who was new to me, was a bit the worse for wear. He had been knocking back the local cider. He suddenly blurted out:

'I can't see what you're worried about. You must be better than the last man. He managed to get himself picked up.'

The other two looked as though they could have shot him on the spot.

'How exactly did the man manage to get picked up?'

It turned out that the idiot had attempted to carry a handgun through the metal detectors at the border crossing. I said that my limited experience had taught me that a bit of blarney can get you out of many a tight corner. A gun generally gets you into one.

'You've got it dead right, Victor. It's not that dangerous, as long as you play by the rules.'

Looking across the table at these three men, it occurred to me that those writers like Le Carré could never have invented these three clowns. It also occurred to me that possibly they had lost more than one poor sod and were scraping the barrel to see what else they could find. Raking around their dusty files, some bright spark had discovered me and my evil past. In the end I did the stupid thing and agreed to another run.

I was handed an envelope with instructions and, even better, another one containing £300 in cash and the promise of a further £300 when I reported back. Six hundred was now the going rate. I could live with that.

I left on 21 June, and five days later I was in Leipzig, staying at the tourist *Campingplatz*. The pickup was to take place in a music shop on the main *Bahnhofstrasse*. The contact was a German national by the name of Thomas Axster. I could feel the adrenalin pumping.

The dusty shop window of Musick Axster held a couple of cheap-looking violins and a baby grand piano complete with peeling veneer. I went in and as the door opened a huge brass bell rang, its melancholy chimes echoing round the dusty, worn-out interior. At the back of the shop a pair of velvet curtains parted and, slowly, out came an old crone who looked about ninety. She opened up with a stream of German.

'*Madam, ich bin Engländer, ich nicht verstehen Deutsch.*'

'Ah, so you are English.'

She spoke like an upper-class Englishwoman.

'And what brings you here?'

'I am Victor and I would like to meet with Thomas if he is here.' At this point the old velvet curtains opened again and Thomas made his appearance like a character in a Victorian melodrama.

When our meeting had ended, I left the shop with a small bundle of music, some song sheets and a second-hand harmonica.

'The harmonica is yours, Victor, gives you an excuse for coming here.' Thomas turned out to be of Jewish extraction, younger than myself, but looked ten years older. I wanted to get away as fast as possible.

The next morning I was back at the Gasthof Reitsch, where I

had to stay the night. That evening the same lad I had met the
year before turned up.

'Victor! I thought you weren't going to do any more.'

We had supper and afterwards we settled down to sup the local
brew.

'Well, Victor, that's another good piece of work, but surely you
don't do these pickups dressed up like you are now?'

I was wearing brightly coloured leathers.

'Who's going to suspect me of doing anything underhand
dressed up like a lighthouse?' I answered.

'Rather you than me.'

I changed the subject.

'Just how extensive is this Saxony cell?'

'Not allowed to divulge information of that nature, but it's not
as important as in the north of the country.'

I persisted.

'How many have been picked up to your knowledge?'

'Ask me another, Victor. I've been here for a year and a half and
there's been no trouble as yet.'

'You surprise me,' I answered, 'considering the amateurish way
it's all organised.'

It must have been some time early in the winter of 1982 that I
received a letter with the logo of the Ministry of Information on
the envelope. They were asking me to come to London. The
address was a room in a big office block in Hart Street, opposite
Bloomsbury Square (I knew this building of old. I had worked on
it when it was being built in the sixties). This was a bit of a joke.
I had just celebrated my sixty-fifth birthday. Always ready for a
laugh and an excuse to have a day in the Smoke, I telephoned to
say I would be there.

I presented myself the following week, and was shown into a
bleak room, austerely furnished with a couple of standard-issue
metal filing cabinets, a six-foot wooden table and half a dozen

chairs. Not even a telephone. A woman appeared and told me, 'Major Gardiner will be in directly. Would you like a coffee?'

That 'directly' turned out to be about half an hour, long enough to put me on tenterhooks.

Major Gardiner entered the room and apologised for keeping me waiting. He had the bearing of a senior army officer and the accent to go with it. At last I had come face to face with someone in authority. He was very polite.

I asked him if he wasn't surprised that his men had chosen such an elderly and unknown individual to carry out this tricky work.

'Not in your case, Mr Gregg. I've been through your files from the day you signed on all those years ago. You have fully justified our decision to use you. You haven't put a foot wrong.'

He handed me a sheet of headed paper.

'If, for some reason, you wish to contact me, you may do so by letter, using the address on that writing paper. I would be grateful if you'd refrain from using the telephone number unless you are in a dire emergency. Understood?'

I thought he was softening me up for a new mission. I was never more wrong in my life. He asked about the various campaigns I had been in, why I had transferred to the Parachute Regiment and what I considered to be the hardest of the battles. The interview ended on good terms. I think he just wanted to see at first hand what sort of an idiot I was. For my own part I had decided that I had had enough of these adventures. The risks and dangers were too great.

On the way out I was handed an envelope by the secretary. It contained £300 and a letter of thanks from the major. This time I had to sign for it. That was the first and last time I came face to face with any person of importance in the ministry, which, from the address I had been given, seemed to be the Foreign Office. But now it was all over: time to retire from the James Bond stuff. And so back to Taunton and the mind-numbing dreariness of the daily grind – how I hated it.

The following May I received a brown envelope that quite clearly stated it was from the Ministry of Information. Bett saw the letter in my hand and sensed that something was up.

'What do they want with you, Vic?'

'Oh, it's not important, Bett, something to do with some more work at the Point.'

I was really upset that they had contacted me at home. Up to now I had kept everything secret from Bett. She thought I used to go on trips with my motorbike friends. The letter said 'it was with regret' that they were again asking me if I could get into the DDR for one more pickup. As this was urgent, could I make the necessary arrangements in order to be at Magdeburg during the last week in June?

I could feel the adrenalin rising again. I knew I should refuse, but I was curious. The problem would be explaining to Bett why I wanted to go to East Germany so early in the year. I couldn't let on about the true nature of the trip; she would have put her foot down with the same firmness as her ancestors at Bannockburn. For the first time I would have to lie to her. This caused me some pain, but lie I did. I told her that one of the gang, Henry, was returning from Poland and I wanted to meet him on the border near Dresden.

My vanity and ego had got the better of me again.

I met Shorty and Lofty at what I now considered to be our office, the Cottage. I opened up by venting my wrath at the lot of them for sending the letter to my home. Then we got down to business.

They gave me a map of Magdeburg and told me that in a few days I would be given the time, date and location of the pickup. Later, I thought I had better have a word with my friend Henry, who knew a lot about East Germany. He was very clear:

'What do you want to go to that hole for, Vic? It's the biggest industrial shithouse in the whole of the DDR, and, what's more, the place is crawling with police and the bastard Stasi. They run you in just for blinking at them.'

That settled it. The next day I was on the phone to the major. He wasn't there so I left the message that I was to be contacted within the next twenty-four hours. Some underling rang back. I gave him the reference number the major had given me and in no time at all he was tuned in.

'Right then, Mr Gregg, tell me the problem. I'm assuming by the nature of your tone that you've got one.'

'Too true,' I replied. 'Tell your chief that I have information concerning the situation in Magdeburg and there is no way that I am going to meet with anyone in or near the town.'

I proposed a new rendezvous, the railway station at Schönebeck, thirty miles south of Magdeburg.

'Leave it with me, Mr Gregg. Someone will get back to you.'

The instructions arrived by letter with just over a week to go to the deadline. I phoned Berolina Travel and managed to get the visa on the basis that I was doing research into the Dresden bombing.

I made my way down to Würzburg to the local *Campingplatz* where I knew the old lady who owned the site. From Würzburg I aimed the bike east towards the small township of Meiningen, where I stopped for the night at a small tourist *Campingplatz* outside Erfurt. It was here that a policeman and two men in civilian clothes approached me and asked me to produce my documents. They told me to unload all my gear from the bike. I had two bottles of whisky which I had brought as a gift for Marcus, who I planned to visit on my way home. I also had two hundred English cigarettes. I laid all this out by the side of the road in a neat and regimental manner. I knew all about kit inspections. Marcus's fags vanished and inside half an hour all four of us were getting on just fine and one of the bottles was half empty. They told me that the authorities had been alerted by the unusually large number of visa entries in my passport.

'Why would a tourist wish to travel to the East when everyone in the East wants to travel west?'

I explained about my interest in Dresden and the reason for that interest. In broken English and German we all agreed that war was evil and that in future we should all be friends. With much slapping of backs, the four of us went our separate ways. Had I got away with it or had this been a warning shot across my bows?

The next day, after a sleepless night in a field, I got to the rendezvous thirty minutes early. It was market day, a drab affair with people aimlessly milling around. There was none of the hustle and bustle normally associated with these events. Everything on offer, except the fruit and veg, looked old and worn. One old woman was selling bundles of rusty nails obviously straightened and used many times.

Here was I, dressed up to the nines in my expensive suit of leathers, with the latest bike on offer from the BMW factory in the West. I stood out like a sore thumb, a blaze of colour and, more importantly, a symbol of what these people were missing. Me and the bike soon became the centre of attraction. This was turning into a disaster. I had to do something.

At the entrance to the station was a small police kiosk, three lads on duty. I wheeled the bike over and with the usual arm waving and my limited lingo persuaded them to keep an eye on it while I went walkabout. I handed them the half-empty bottle of Scotch.

The meeting time had long gone. I purchased a couple of what appeared to be the remnants of last year's apple crop and sat down on a bench to have a munch and a quiet smoke. I was certain that somewhere, hidden in the general throng, was a person who must be trying to make eye contact with me. I waited an hour in that market, then thought enough was enough. I went over to the lads who were looking after the bike, one of whom was sitting astride the machine pretending to drive it. I thanked them with some profusion, indicating that they could keep the rest of the bottle, and gave them the remains of the fags. With good-natured farewells to the police and a wave to the admiring throng, I gave the township the benefit of seeing my rear wheel diminishing in size. If those clowns in London thought for one moment that I was going to put myself at risk, hanging about for some Kraut to appear whenever he wanted, they had another think coming. They had wasted their money.

And that was almost the end of my involvement with the nation's intelligence services. The two gents who came down to Bridgwater a couple of weeks after I got back agreed that I had done the right thing. Apparently contact had been broken with the Magdeburg cell which had either found it too difficult to operate or, worse, had been arrested. I was given the usual thanks and never contacted again.

48

The Magyar Experience

For a small group of us, Mark, Alec, Tom and me, the trips to the motorcycle festival at Pannonia in Hungary became an annual event. At the festival we had encountered a woman called Marlais who spoke good English and who was part of a political organisation called the Hungarian Democratic Forum. We would all spend hours talking about the political situation in Eastern Europe and updating them on news we had heard in the West. Each year, after the festival, I would try to make a visit to Marcus at Schneeberg.

It was on one of these visits in 1984 that Marcus said he had arranged for me to meet his Uncle Albert. When we met I recognised him at once. He was older and frailer but definitely old Silverhair. At first he couldn't place me. I told him how I had escaped execution and the penny dropped: 'I never expected to see you alive again.'

In my now improving German I explained how I had managed to extricate myself from the fate that had been awaiting me after being locked up in the *Straflager* in Dresden. Albert revealed that the officer in charge of the camp at Niedersedlitz had received a report stating that both myself and Harry had been executed the night we arrived. We talked about Arnhem and he told me his impressions of us paratroopers.

'Do you know,' he said, 'when we were finally rounding you all up, we had to reach you through a hail of stones. It was amazing; you were throwing stones at us because you had run out of ammunition. At the time I thought you should have been kept together and out of contact with any other prisoners, in a compound surrounded by double barbed wire and starving dogs. Only under those conditions would I expect to keep you under control.'

We both laughed. That was quite a memory, I thought, and quite a tribute to the spirit of the Paras.

Later that first evening the three of us walked to the village where I was introduced to a number of Albert's ex-army comrades, another drunken evening during which I told them about the Democratic Forum and about unrest that was brewing in Hungary. This was all news to them.

Then Albert said something that was to have far-reaching consequences.

'Tell your friends in Hungary that never again will the German Democratic Army support any more adventures like Prague.' He meant, of course, the way the Soviets used the East German army to keep order. He was serious. In Saxony, at least, people were sick of the way the Russians blighted their lives.

A year later I was able to tell Marlais and her friends what Albert had said. They were amazed; they had no idea that they had support outside Hungary and were excited that some of it came from a group of veteran German army officers. This was particularly encouraging because the Democratic Forum was gaining strength; it had nearly doubled in size since the year before. I was asked if I could arrange a meeting between some representatives of the Forum and Albert and his friends. I said that they would have to go to Albert because he was now too frail to travel.

'No problem, Victor. You fix up a meeting and we'll be there.'

Later, Tom, one of the four of us, said:

'Surely you're not going to get involved with this, Vic. They shoot people over here for messing about with politics.' I didn't tell him of my previous escapades. The gang would have dropped me like a ton of bricks.

After the rally, instead of heading back to Blighty I made a detour to see Albert and told him about the proposed meeting. He agreed to discuss the problem with his old cronies but warned me not to expect too much. We agreed that we would put as little as possible in writing. I said that, apart from Christmas cards and the like, I would minimise contact with Marcus and his family. These were murky waters.

All of this news I put in a carefully worded letter to Marlais. Two weeks had barely gone by when a letter arrived from her. My news had generated some excitement. They were very keen to make the meeting with Albert and his friends. I promised to try to arrange a meeting for the following May. I was aware that yet again I was in danger of taking on the role of a bagman again and I had no idea of the scale of what I was getting involved in.

Hungary was by far the most easy-going of the 'Eastern Democracies'. It was far tougher in countries like Czechoslovakia, Bulgaria and, of course, the DDR itself. I think Czechoslovakia was the worst. The fear the people felt as they went about their daily routines was palpable, and the unhappiness of those in the streets said it all. It wasn't a good place to take a holiday.

Safe back at home and Christmas was coming. Bett and I went round Taunton and made up parcels of clothing and small luxuries that our friends behind the Iron Curtain in Schneeberg were always short of. Even bars of soap and toilet rolls were much appreciated. Marcus would send letters of thanks and he and his wife were ecstatic when we sent the two girls sets of American-style jogging suits.

Freda had by now remarried. The chap who had taken my place gave her all the encouragement and love that I, to my everlasting shame, had failed to supply. His devotion had enabled her to get through college, with the result that she became a government social worker and a respected person of consequence in her chosen profession. My son David said that, in his opinion, the parting of the ways enabled both me and Freda to find our true worth in life. 'Would she have gone through college if you had still been together?'

He had a point and was trying his best to help me forget the past. But it only made me feel worse. Had I really been that much of a swine? To my way of thinking the answer was yes.

It was around Christmas that I received a letter from Marlais asking me to write to Albert. Four of them would be in Karl-Marx-Stadt on 1 June: could I get things organised? I didn't want to put this information in the post to Albert. Exactly what might have been his fate and that of his friends if the letter was intercepted is anyone's guess. I decided that I would have to collect and deliver the letters myself, just like in the old days. Once again I was the bagman, working inside a regime that had made an art form of surveillance.

My passport had run out and on my application for a new one I put my occupation as 'Historian'. If questioned, I would say that my special interest was Dresden. The new passport arrived; its pages were clean, freed from all the old visa stamps. Of course, every future visit to the DDR would be stamped in my passport; too many visits and the authorities would again be alerted, as in the past.

As I made more trips I became aware that Marcus and his wife were becoming uneasy about my liaison with Albert. They sensed that something was afoot but they didn't know what. As for Albert himself, he seemed more concerned about the possibility of me getting picked up. He once asked me if I thought it was time to settle down and stop living on the edge.

'You've got away with it so far, but you might not go on being so lucky.'

I decided that it was in the best interests of Marcus and his family that, for the time being, I cut off contact with them completely. I knew that Albert and his cronies were sailing close to the wind, as well as which I suspected that these former Wehrmacht officers had far more power than it seemed on the surface.

In all, there were seven uneventful trips to the DDR, three in the Dresden area and four in Leipzig, which appeared to be the main centre of the opposition to the Soviet regime. As bagman I would get a letter from Budapest. I would take the letter to Albert or whoever, then take the answer home to England from where it would be safe to post it to Hungary. I never knew the contents or whether the DDR ever got wise to what was going on.

Entry into the DDR under these conditions was like a game of Russian roulette. Would there be a reception committee? What would happen if I got picked up? Not a prescription for a good night's sleep.

The game had very serious implications: one false move would place not only myself but possibly Albert and all his companions in extreme danger. Just as I had been taught in my early years, I made every move in broad daylight and in the open. Not for me the time-honoured methods written about in spy novels, the skulking in dark alleyways under dimly lit lamps. Victor was there for all to see, cracking a joke with the police and the Stasi if by chance they showed more than normal interest. In this manner I survived time and time again.

49

1988: Free at Last

The year that Freda died finally killed off whatever bits of my old egotistical self that remained. She at last succumbed to the dreaded cancer she had been fighting for seven years. The night before her passing I sat by her bedside. It was evening and in the rooms below we could hear the children (as we still called them) chatting and talking. We both knew that these would probably be our last moments together. Freda said to me, 'Where did it all go wrong, Vic?' I think that we were both, in those last few hours, trying to resurrect the past, as if by admitting our mistakes we could reignite the life of love and caring we had both dreamed about. Everything we had done at the start we had done together. The early years with our two young sons, Alan and David, had been a sort of reward for the years of trauma that we had both experienced in the war.

It felt as though I was holding her hand for hours in that bedroom. We were both clinging to each other as if daring the moments to stay and in those moments I know that we both experienced the love we had once enjoyed flowing back. The truth is that what had gone wrong had been caused by my complete lack of understanding of what was required of me, my lack of compassion and responsibility, and my being utterly incapable of seeing the world from anybody's side but my own. I knew nothing about the rules of ordinary society, a society not governed by the soldier's constant awareness of the need for survival. There must have been any number of similar casualties among the men who had served

their time in front-line units – men whose minds had been brutal-
ised by the killing and the terror of modern war. And it is no
different for soldiers today.

I returned that night to South Wales and the understanding of
Betty. It was entirely due to her love that I eventually returned to
sanity and became a responsible, caring man. I have had two wives
in my life. The first, Freda, gave me encouragement during the
years of war, a time when I, like all men, most needed it. She gave
me three lovely children. Freda had the worst of the deal, she had
to suffer as my mind reverted to the front line and I lived as
though I was still dominated by the brutalities of the battle field.
Our marriage died because of my inability to control my own
actions. My second wife, Betty, without being aware of what she
was achieving, nursed me back to normality. I owe what I am
today to both of them.

The next time I saw Albert was in early 1989 and I was much
better at speaking German. I was now a pensioner and had been
able to attend a two-year language course at the local college,
courtesy of the state. I was able to give Albert and his companions
news of the changes that were taking place in Eastern Europe. It
was clear to me that they were in the dark about a lot of what was
going on. I felt that, for their part, the Hungarians were playing
their cards close to the chest. They had made contact with the
DDR but were not sharing their plans. I sensed a distinct lack of
trust between the two, but I was certain that the next few months
would see some very big changes.

On my last visit to Dresden I was sitting in the usual café, on
the first-floor balcony, drinking my coffee. I had arranged to meet
Albert the next day. Suddenly, two smartly dressed individuals
plonk themselves down in two of the three vacant chairs.

'*Wie heissen Sie, bitte?*'

I told them my name and produced my passport.

'*Ach so, Engländer. Sprechen Sie Deutsch?*'

'No, can't speak a word, mate.'

I was nervous and hoped they wouldn't notice my sweaty palms. They asked about my reason for being in the DDR and then talked non-committally about the weather. Then they got up and, as suddenly as they had appeared, they were gone. I started breathing normally again. Things were hotting up. 'Be careful, Vic,' I muttered to myself.

Around the end of March I received a letter from Marlais asking me if I could set up a meeting in Dresden with Albert. They had more questions for him. I told them that I thought it was very inadvisable for them to go and visit him in person. I said that I would be willing to visit him one last time on their behalf, possibly the first week in June. I said they should send me their questions and I would do my best to get the answers for them. With so much going on in Dresden that I didn't really know about, I was nervous about putting my neck on the line and said that I would only meet Albert if I was satisfied that it was safe to do so. Within ten days I had their reply with a bundle of questions, all in German.

I wouldn't blame Bett for thinking I had a bit on the side in Dresden. I managed to get her blessing for yet another trip, which I would make in May, as soon as I thought it was safe. I didn't tell anyone I was coming, especially not Albert. I arrived at the Dresden campsite to find that the situation had calmed down a bit, so I sent a letter to Albert suggesting we meet. Three days later a letter arrived saying that the meeting was on.

Albert told me there had been unrest in Leipzig and Karl-Marx-Stadt and that the security services of these two cities had been reinforced by drafts from the quieter areas of Saxony. Albert said the resistance was based mainly around church organisations. He thought blood would have to flow before anything was achieved and didn't believe church congregations were up to it. He also told me that he had had no recent communication with the Hungarian Democratic Forum.

Then I gave Albert the notes that had been sent to me from Budapest, saying: 'I haven't a clue what all this is about. They wanted to come to Dresden. I put them off. Whatever they are up to it's obvious to me that something's going to happen this year and it's also obvious to me that they want the support of people like yourself.'

'You've got it partly right, Victor, but I must tell you that they have asked us for information about troop movements and the state of play between the state and the army. If you ask my opinion, I think they're going to stage an uprising. We naturally encourage them but we don't think they stand a chance.'

He read some of the papers I had delivered. He scribbled things on them and then looked up.

'Your friends are asking about the possibility of the German army going through Czechoslovakia into Hungary. I've answered in two words: "Not possible".'

Albert was confirming that the East German army would not allow itself to be used as a tool of the Soviets to quell a possible uprising in Hungary.

He handed me back the papers. It was at that moment that we were joined by two individuals, one of whom I recognised from previous meetings, the other, better dressed, I did not. Albert introduced the stranger as an officer of the dreaded *Staatssicherheitsdienst*, better known as the Stasi. I nearly choked on my coffee.

The stranger smiled and offered his hand. He gave no indication of his name, but he knew mine.

'Victor, listen carefully. Tonight you will stay in your *Campingplatz*. Tomorrow you will leave the DDR by the border crossing at Hof. You must not go through until after 1.30 p.m. and not later than 4 p.m.'

To be on the safe side, Albert was translating all this and he didn't seem at all worried. Me, I was shitting bricks. I left for the campsite as per instructions. I wondered what would happen if Albert's trust in his Stasi friend was misplaced. My pockets were stuffed with the incriminating papers he had scribbled on.

I left the camp the next day and went through the border at Hof. I was shaking like a leaf but, to my amazement, I was waved through without any trouble. A couple of kilometres into the West, I pulled up the bike, sat down on the grass verge and puffed away at three fags on the trot. Back home, I sent the letters to Marlais with a note saying that there should be no further attempts to contact sources inside the DDR.

I also decided to do one more favour for the British Establishment. I phoned the number that had been given me by Major Gardiner in Hart Street and told them that if they sent a man down I would give them a written account of matters that might be of interest. I typed out a twelve-page report on everything I had recently seen and had been doing in Eastern Europe. I omitted the names of those I had been in contact with.

Two weeks later I handed it over. I did not know the man I was giving it to.

'You're a dark horse,' he said as he glanced through my report.

'Just doing my little bit to help a few friends.'

He asked me if I could vouch for the authenticity of what I had written down.

'Something is going to happen this year, that's all I know.'

I received no further communication from London, not even a word of thanks.

At the beginning of July the four of us in the motorbike group received a letter from Marlais pleading with us to make it to the Pannonia. A very important unofficial event was going to happen and we should make a special effort to attend.

That year the rally was to be held at Sopron, a Hungarian town right on the border with Austria, just south of Vienna. When we arrived on 16 July, Marlais and her husband were already there, along with some of our acquaintances from Poland and East Germany. There was a big contingent from Berlin.

On the 18th we were contacted by our Hungarian friends and told to look out for the notices that would soon appear all over the town. Sure enough, that evening small posters began to appear.

They were stuck on walls, lamp posts, mail boxes and the walls of houses. The posters advertised a 'Picnik' organised by the Magyar Party for Democracy and the Hungarian Democratic Forum. The event was to take place just outside the town. There was no sign of the police getting involved. The town continued to fill up with people from all over the East: Poles, Czechoslovakians, Bulgarians and, most obvious of all, the East Germans.

The 19th arrived, baking hot. Around midday we began to make our way to the designated site for the 'Picnik'. It seemed that the whole city was heading for the rendezvous. On arrival we found our friends who had a long table above which was a huge banner carrying the slogan 'PICNIK SOPRONBAN' and in smaller letters 'MAGYAR DEMOCRATIC FORUM'. There were other slogans in Hungarian, as well as lots of leaflets printed in Hungarian that we couldn't even begin to understand.

At the centre of everything was a huge pot of goulash, cooking over an open fire. In charge was no lesser a figure than the Mayor of Sopron, a jovial chap who was certainly as round as he was tall. The pot must have contained about forty gallons of the stew. The Mayor was dishing it out to anyone with a plate. Someone else was playing an accordion.

This was just the beginning.

There was a barbed-wire fence round the edges of the field and people started to cut it down. We were told that this wire was the first fence that made up the border. The main border wire was two kilometres away and would be cut at 3 p.m. They wanted us to get there as soon as possible. Alec had a heart problem and Tom was suffering from a slightly sprained ankle so it was left to me and Mark, another friend from the Isle of Wight, to walk across the fields to the scene of the action. Two of our friends from Berlin refused to go; they were frightened of possible reprisals if they were spotted by film cameras.

We were told that we were to be given the privilege of joining the group who were going to make the first cut in the main border wire. Why us? Surely we had had nothing to do with this historic event. We were told in no uncertain terms that without the evidence that the East German army would not be deployed to restore order it would have been difficult to get the support from the general public. We had supplied this evidence through our contact with Albert and his like. This had helped them to come to the final decision to go ahead, and they were grateful.

By this time the other three were beginning to look a wee bit mystified. They knew nothing about the goings on with Albert and his friends and I didn't let on. I felt very honoured. After all, what were we? Nothing more than a group of like-minded motor-cyclists of no standing. Yet they made us feel as if we had done a service to their cause. My three mates were mystified. To the end, I never did let on.

We went over the fields and along a muddy lane and then we were marching the last few hundred yards. I noticed two camera crews; one, I believe, was French. Mark and myself were handed a pair of wire cutters and there and then we made the first cut in the wire which formed part of the border between the East and the West. On the other side the Austrian border guards stood around trying to look official. Soon a human wave of happy, excited people flung themselves through the gap and across no-man's-land into the West. I think seven hundred people were involved. It was a wonderful moment and one that I will treasure all my life.

Later, Mark and myself trudged back to the main field thinking on the enormity of the event we had been privileged to have taken part in. A few weeks later, in November 1989, the Berlin Wall itself fell. A hated symbol of repression had at last been destroyed and I felt proud that I had played a small part in its destruction.

50

Time Expired

So, at the age of seventy, my years of adventure ended. Future journeys out of Britain were confined to more mundane camping trips to France and the occasional hated package tour (hated by me at any rate) to Spain, Corfu, Cyprus and the like. Betty loves these trips: get in a taxi, an hour to the airport, two or three hours in the plane and you're there, no hassle, just the job, she says, so I give in gracefully and make sure she enjoys herself.

My life has been very good. It is true there have been some down moments, such as the day my business failed. It was my sixty-sixth birthday and a main contractor had gone bankrupt owing me many thousands of pounds. But mainly my world has been full of ups. I am ninety-one, I have the love of my dear wife Bett and I have my health. My children are all married and I have a brood of lovely grandchildren.

Bett and I lived happily in South Wales, until we were offered a flat owned and run by the welfare office of my old regiment, the Rifle Brigade. Our neighbours include men who have served their country in every corner of the globe, men who, at some stage in their lives, have had to put their heads above the parapet and place their trust in the mates around them.

The battlefield is the devil's playground. My comrades and I saw violent action day in, day out for nearly seven years. When the smoke cleared many of us, close friends and comrades, had fallen, destroyed by the cannon, the machine gun or the bomb.

What did I think when it was all over? Lucky to be alive? I

suppose so, but I'm not sure. When I came back from the war I had no respect for authority and ignored all standards of good behaviour, and I think that it is because of what I experienced at Dresden that I behaved badly to those I should have loved.

I still occasionally suffer nightmares about those two nights of bombing and the firestorm, people burning in the street, flames reaching down from the heavens like huge claws, sucking up human life as if to satisfy some inexhaustible appetite. I wake up bathed in sweat with the sound of terrible screams ringing in my ears.

Several years ago in Wales I told my community doctor about the nightmares and feelings of guilt. He said, what did I expect after what I had been through, and added that I was not alone. I was not the only soldier to come to him with his head full of horrors. He thought that I would always have my demons.

After the trauma of my divorce, I never again knowingly did anything to cause hurt to another person. The divorce caused something to switch in my brain and it brought me to my senses. I became more reasonable in my dealings with others. I was helped in this by all the love and care bestowed upon me by Betty, and by the fact that my children did not desert me. All of this helped me back to normality, a normality that the war, with all its satanic evils, had almost destroyed.

The terrible dreams are, happily, now few and far between, though some images will never go away. I hope that in writing this account I will help to persuade people that killing and violence are not good ways of solving differences.

Looking back on my life, I know that I have been lucky. I have got out of endless scrapes because I am an incurable optimist, and that is one of my better characteristics. I believe that when things are getting rough, take a breather and brew up the tea – it'll all come out in the wash.

AFTERWORD

The name Oradour-sur-Glan probably doesn't mean much to most British people, which is sad. It is a place where a terrible massacre took place. On 10 June 1944 the First Battalion of the 4th Waffen SS Panzer Grenadier Regiment, commanded by Adolph Diekman, burnt the village and murdered its inhabitants. The men were shot in the legs, covered in petrol and set alight. The women and children were locked in the church and burnt alive. The village itself was looted before it was destroyed. There were few survivors. Six hundred and forty-two people died, of whom the youngest was a one-week-old baby and the oldest a ninety-year-old man. Today the village is preserved almost exactly as it was when Diekman and his men had finished their work. It is a silent, solemn place.

Every returning soldier abhors the thought of future conflict and knows that, while there may be victors, there are no winners in the wars between nations. But sometimes war is necessary. I believe it was necessary to stand up against the regime that allowed the massacre at Oradour-sur-Glan and other places, like Lidice, Babi Yar, Wola – the list is very long. I would urge anyone who doesn't believe me to visit the remains of Oradour-sur-Glan and to ask themselves whether they would submit to a power that allows such things, and to remember that there may be other regimes we will have to fight in the future. I hate war – I have seen what it does – but in my view we must keep our guard up, sometimes pacifism just isn't an option, sometimes we have to use force.

I believe it is right to remember those who gave their lives fighting against the Nazis in the Second World War. On Remembrance Day I prefer to remember my fallen comrades at a small ceremony held in Gloucester Place near Victoria in London, where our regimental memorial stands. I don't really like the big parades you see in Whitehall with all the leaders of the political parties present. The last time I visited Oradour-sur-Glan I saw an act of remembrance that gave me more hope for the future than all the prattling that comes from the mouths of our so called leaders.

I watched a small group of German motorcyclists who had arrived in the village – young men and their girlfriends whose attire and demeanour served only to accentuate their nationality – walk silently and with reverence through the whole village and then visit the museum. What was going through their minds is anybody's guess. In the end they quietly got back on their bikes and rode on. To me this was an act of courage comparable to any I have ever witnessed. I thought that these young people were doomed by history to carry the weight of the sins of their ancestors and that they accepted this.

The manner in which those young men and women behaved that day at Oradour-sur-Glan meant more to me than all the official remembrance parades in the world.

Victor Gregg
Winchester
November 2010

ACKNOWLEDGEMENTS

As a result of and because of the continued insistence of my grand-children I commenced the drafting of this manuscript some twenty years ago. Today, all these years later and after many revisions, this work is now being offered for general consumption.

There are many people to thank, not necessarily for their input but because of their encouragement. On the professional side, of those who have helped and assisted me in this compilation of the events that have made up my life, top of the list must be Rick Stroud who has been the main liaison with the publishers and whose job was editing the manuscript and making sense of my airy-fairy views, which must have tried him to the utmost. Next on the list is Bill Swainson of Bloomsbury Publishing and his dedicated team in Soho Square who, despite my reluctance to mention this or that, have pointed out that there is a moral behind the message I have tried to put forward: 'Include it, Vic, people have a right to know about these things.' I also thank my agent, Victoria Hobbs.

On the personal side, I am certain that, of all the people I have to thank, at the very top of the list is Elizabeth, my dear wife, who through the years has quietly understood my somewhat self-destructive way of living and guided me without rancour along the difficult path of righteousness. Without her support I would most probably have sunk into a mire of self-pity, with a chip on my shoulder bigger than a house. Bett was helped along the road by my children and grandchildren who, despite everything, gave both of us their love and understanding. I have indeed been a very lucky man.

And so this list of acknowledgements is small, but before I go I would above all else dedicate this book to the women of all levels of society who take back their husbands, sweethearts, sons and brothers, and give their love, understanding and devotion to the task of repairing the fractured bodies and minds that are, with some certainty, the lot of any soldier who has served his time in the front line of military combat. They will never be able to eradicate completely the horrors that lie buried in the dark recesses of the man's mind, but their devotion will certainly give him the ability to take his normal place in the world he has to return to.

INDEX